Using Functional Grammar

An Explorer's Guide

Second Edition

David Butt
Rhondda Fahey
Susan Feez
Sue Spinks
Colin Yallop

National Centre for English Language Teaching and Research
Macquarie University

Published and distributed by the
National Centre for English Language Teaching and Research
Macquarie University
Sydney NSW 2109

Using functional grammar: An explorer's guide.

2nd ed.
Bibliography.
Includes index.
ISBN 1 86408 550 9

1. English language – Grammar. 2. Functionalism (Linguistics). 3. Interpersonal relations. 4. Discourse analysis. I. Butt, David, 1950–. II. National Centre for English Language teaching and Research (Australia).

MACQUARIE
UNIVERSITY ~SYDNEY

First edition printed 1994
Reprinted with revisions 1996
Reprinted with corrections 1997
Reprinted, 1998, 1999

Second edition:
© Macquarie University 2000

The publisher would like to thank the following for permission to reproduce copyright material:

Board of Studies NSW for material on pp9, 11–13, 218–20, 222–3, 225–6, 234–5, 241, 243, adapted and reprinted from *English K-6 syllabus* © Board of Studies NSW, 1998 and *English K-6 modules* © Board of Studies NSW, 1998

Federation Press for the right to reproduce an extract on p174, from *Mabo: What the High Court said* (Butt, P J and R D Eagleson, 1993)

The Macquarie Dictionary Library Pty Ltd for the right to reproduce the following definitions: adjective, adverb, article, conjunction, noun, preposition, pronoun, verb on p27, from the *Macquarie dictionary: Second edition*, 1997

News Limited and the authors for the reprinting and adaptation on pp229–31, 294–6 of the article 'City battered by giant hailstones' (Georgina Safe and Matt Price) in *The Australian*, 15 April, 1999 © Georgina Safe and Matt Price

Phoenix Education for text adapted on p179, from *Creative writing skills: Literary and media text types* (H de Silva Joyce and S Feez 2000).

The National Centre for English Language Teaching and Research (NCELTR) is a Commonwealth Government Key Centre of Research and Teaching established at Macquarie University in 1988. The National Centre forms part of the Linguistics discipline at Macquarie University. NCELTR's Key Centre activities are funded by the Commonwealth Department of Immigration and Multicultural Affairs.

DTP 2nd edition: Helen Lavery
Printed by: Robert Burton Printers

Contents

Acknowledgments

The systemic functional grammar which is explored in this book originated with Michael Halliday. His ideas were gathered together in his *An introduction to functional grammar* (2nd edition, 1994. London: Edward Arnold), which remains the most important teaching document for this theory of grammar. Others such as Ruqaiya Hasan, Christian Matthiessen and James Robert Martin have explored Halliday's ideas and carried the theory further. This book has no such pretensions. Rather it is an introduction to the *Introduction*. We hope that it encourages people to read Halliday and Hasan, then Martin and Matthiessen. It necessarily simplifies and leaves out the harder parts of the grammar without dumbing down the parts it includes.

Michael Halliday has also underlined the links between learning language, learning through language and learning about language. This book now includes some reflections on these connections directed especially to those involved in language education and TESOL, but it is written for everyone who puzzles over the patterns of language and their place in the system as a whole.

The writing of this book has been very much a team effort – in fact the efforts of a community of linguists at Macquarie University over a considerable period of time. A significant debt goes back to those who set up the context for our work, in particular, our teachers and supervisors: Professors Arthur Delbridge, Michael Halliday, Ruqaiya Hasan and Jim Martin.

Also part of the community effort are the many colleagues who have offered advice and encouragement over the many years of development of this textbook. Special thanks must go to Professor Chris Candlin for his support and for writing such an enthusiastic preface to the book.

In addition to colleagues, we need to thank the several generations of linguistics students at Macquarie University who have offered constructive criticism along the way as each new edition (published initially as course notes and since 1995 in book form) was tested in our teaching program. We also want to express our thanks to the children (some of them now young adults) who have allowed us to use their texts; to our editor and designer; and to our families and friends.

And finally each one of us would like to thank the other four for the unfailing friendship, generosity and support which has meant that, at the end of a long and sometimes difficult process, we are still all friends as well as colleagues.

David Butt
Rhondda Fahey
Susan Feez
Sue Spinks
Colin Yallop
February 2000

Preface

This is a book which aims to defuse controversy and chart an exploration. Its subject matter, Grammar, is one on which pretty well everyone has strong views, even if they haven't had very much direct and thoughtful contact themselves with any of its various meanings. Grammar simply is a topic which incites an enormous amount of active and sharp debate. For a subject which hasn't been highlighted in schools, except in a few places, for a long time, it is curious that it's rarely absent from the newspapers. There are two main reasons for this: the first is that for many people (and not only those in authority), grammar is seen as a type of selection test – being good at it (whatever 'good' and 'it' mean) is regarded as a form of educational quality control exercise, serving to separate the linguistic sheep from the linguistic goats. The second is that it's a kind of mystery, full of arcane terms which hardly anyone understands, but the mastery of which is seen to be good for you, like cod liver oil, or part of growing up. You get inducted into it. On both counts, grammar is everyone's property; it is not directly linked with effective context-sensitive communication and everyone has a strongly-held view on what grammar is. In both cases its effect is pretty alienating.

So, if we want to turn that perception around, the first obvious place to begin is to unpack the metaphor of grammar and set out what these meanings might be. To do that, though, we need to place our study of grammar in a broader framework of language and understanding, and to reaffirm from the start that grammar as a means of explaining the significant and functional patterning of words in the making of meaning can't be wished away. After all, if language was just a random collection of words, you couldn't acquire it, you couldn't learn it and you'd be imprisoned in the here and now because you couldn't talk about what was, what might be and what will be. You couldn't express someone else's point of view any more than your own and you couldn't evaluate what someone else had said. You couldn't construct complete and coherent texts. You couldn't distinguish one type of writing or speaking from another. You'd be in a 'me Tarzan–you Jane' situation, swinging from the wordtrees, pointing at things with little labels on them to try to make your partner understand. Grammar frees you from the shackles of vocabulary in that sense, so we had better work out how these conventional patternings liberate rather than imprison us.

In a sense, I've already given the game away. I've introduced the idea of grammar as language patterning and by that implied some system that allows principled choices to be made. What we say or write is always a matter of exercising these choices, designing our texts with some purpose in mind. I've also implied, by using the metaphor of patterning, that the patterns don't have to have the same dimensions. You can talk about the grammar patterns of clauses and you can talk about the grammar patterns of whole texts. It's all a matter of perspective, but it's crucial to agree what the focus is. Make sure that whoever you're talking to about grammar, you're talking about the same view of grammar. Not doing that is most of the problem. So, there are two central points to make: grammar is a matter of meaningful, flexible but patterned choice and grammar is not just a matter of labelling classes of words – it's a purposeful, constructive and above all social enterprise.

Given this focus on patterns for meaning, a good way to start is with whole texts, not just words on a plate, to get a sense of how texts are structured, varied and how they are built up of clauses, themselves the product of careful, conditioned co-selections of vocabulary. If you start from texts, then you begin with the main point. Grammar is about communicative purposes, it is always contextualised to the particular social participants (writers/readers and speakers/hearers). It's about turning words into messages, and it's always negotiable (the meanings, that is). To see how flexible the patterns are take a look at the poems of Dylan Thomas, the plays of Shakespeare, the lyrics of the Rolling Stones or your favourite TV ad. The point is that grammar is not random and if you master the patterning potential, you can always say what you mean and write what you intend to get across, and anyone else who shares the code can get a handle on what you had in mind. The sky's the limit (almost).That is why in this book of explorations and maps of the wonderful world of grammar, you will keep on coming up against words like choice, function, system, context, (and even goings-on). That makes a refreshing change from breaking your head on some anonymous rules.

So, this isn't a revolutionary little red book and it isn't a set of rules for the blind following of. It isn't about knocking down 'traditional' grammar' (whatever that is) and it isn't about thrusting a new model down your throats. What it does is to explain what you can learn to mean if you have a bag of appropriately selected words, a set of patterns and a sense and a skill of just how you can weave from them a texture of messages which will be just what your audiences need and can understand. (Of course, it also helps to have something worth saying or writing, but then grammar can't do everything, though it can make it appear very effective). It will show you how factors outside a text (purposes, audiences, the nature of the subject-matter) all have an effect on the choices that you are ultimately going to make.

The people who have written this book know what they're talking about. They've been teaching functional grammar for years to all shapes and sizes of people (and not only school and university students – you'd be surprised how many teachers, lawyers, business people, writers are aching to get a handle on a functional, user-friendly model of grammar). Look no further! They know their readership.

What the book does is to start where you might be, by asking those questions which will allow you to build up your own metaphor of grammar. Whatever your starting point is, you're going to be engaged by questions and by tasks, so that by the time you've been at it a while, you'll be as much of an analyst of what the authors write as of what you yourself write subsequently. Sharpening up your self-editing skills is a bonus by-product of buying this book. Don't read every page, don't always read the pages in order. Learn to dodge around. Go for the parts that interest you or speak to the problems and issues that are on your mind. You'll find that the authors have packed the text with examples and that the argument is very clear. The book is very well designed and laid out, so it's not going to be a hard map to follow. You might well try walking the pages with a friend; it's a good way of realising quickly that if you want to talk to someone about language and its grammatical patterns, it gets pretty tricky if you don't have a language in which to talk about language. You'll need a code and this book offers you one that anyone can work with.

Above all, remember what I wrote at the beginning: grammar is a loaded weapon and you'd better handle it gingerly while you're getting the knack. It's there to solve problems, not create them. The authors don't make any apology for the power of the weapon. Grammar is the main means by which we can be creative, systematic and purposeful in our communication. It makes sense to take it seriously, to talk and write about it, to share our understandings of it around, and to become very conscious indeed of its power to shape what we want to mean. Seen like that, grammar isn't a selection device, it's not a debilitating and enslaving process, it's not a magical mystery tour – it's what it's always been – the only way we have of achieving, through effective use of language, what we can all be. This book is both a map and a guidebook that will help you chart your journey to permit your own consistent explorations of your language and your culture, and if you're a language educator, look no further: the basis for your language curriculum is hidden inside!

Professor Christopher N Candlin
Centre for English Language Education
and Communication Research
Department of English
City University of Hong Kong
and
Adjunct Professor of Linguistics
Macquarie University, Sydney

How to use this book

When we wrote the first edition of this book, we were writing for people just beginning to study functional grammar. In fact, the first edition was a published version of teaching materials developed over many years for students in our first year program. These students included budding teachers, lawyers, journalists, translators, editors and literary analysts. Their interests were reflected in the texts and exercises we chose.

This second edition of the book has an extra focus. At the end of each chapter there is a section titled 'Implications for language teaching', which is especially directed at language educators and their students. These sections re-examine the grammar from the perspective of first and second language education, offering focused reflections and exercises. The final chapter of the book is an 'applied' chapter specifically directed at language teachers.

In the first instance, not everyone will want to do all the exercises. Some readers may finish each chapter before the final 'implications' section; others will be most interested in this section. Finally, of course, we hope all readers will return to all sections of each chapter, seeing the grammar as both analysis and application.

The audience of this book, then, will be everyone who wants to explore language in general, and English in particular, from a functional perspective. All readers will be undertaking this exploration because they are interested in language and how it works in context. This book offers a beginner's guide to such exploration, but we hope that our readers will become excited enough about language study and the usefulness of this model to take the journey much further.

The second edition of *Using functional grammar* is the set text for distance-teaching units jointly developed for the Master of Applied Linguistics (Macquarie University, Sydney) and the TESOL module of the Master of Education (The Open University, UK).

For further information on these courses, contact:

The Call Centre, The Open University
Walton Hall, Milton Keynes
MK7 6AA, England
Telephone: +44 (0) 1908 653231
Website: http://soe.open.ac.uk

Linguistics Distance Learning Office
Deptartment of Linguistics
Macquarie University, Sydney 2109, Australia
Telephone: +61 2 9850 9243
Website: www.ling.mq.edu.au

Ideas and philosophy underpinning this book

Introducing ...

- The influence of context
- Texts in context
- Functions of language
- Levels of language
- Metalanguage
- Text types

Discussing ...

- Implications for language teaching

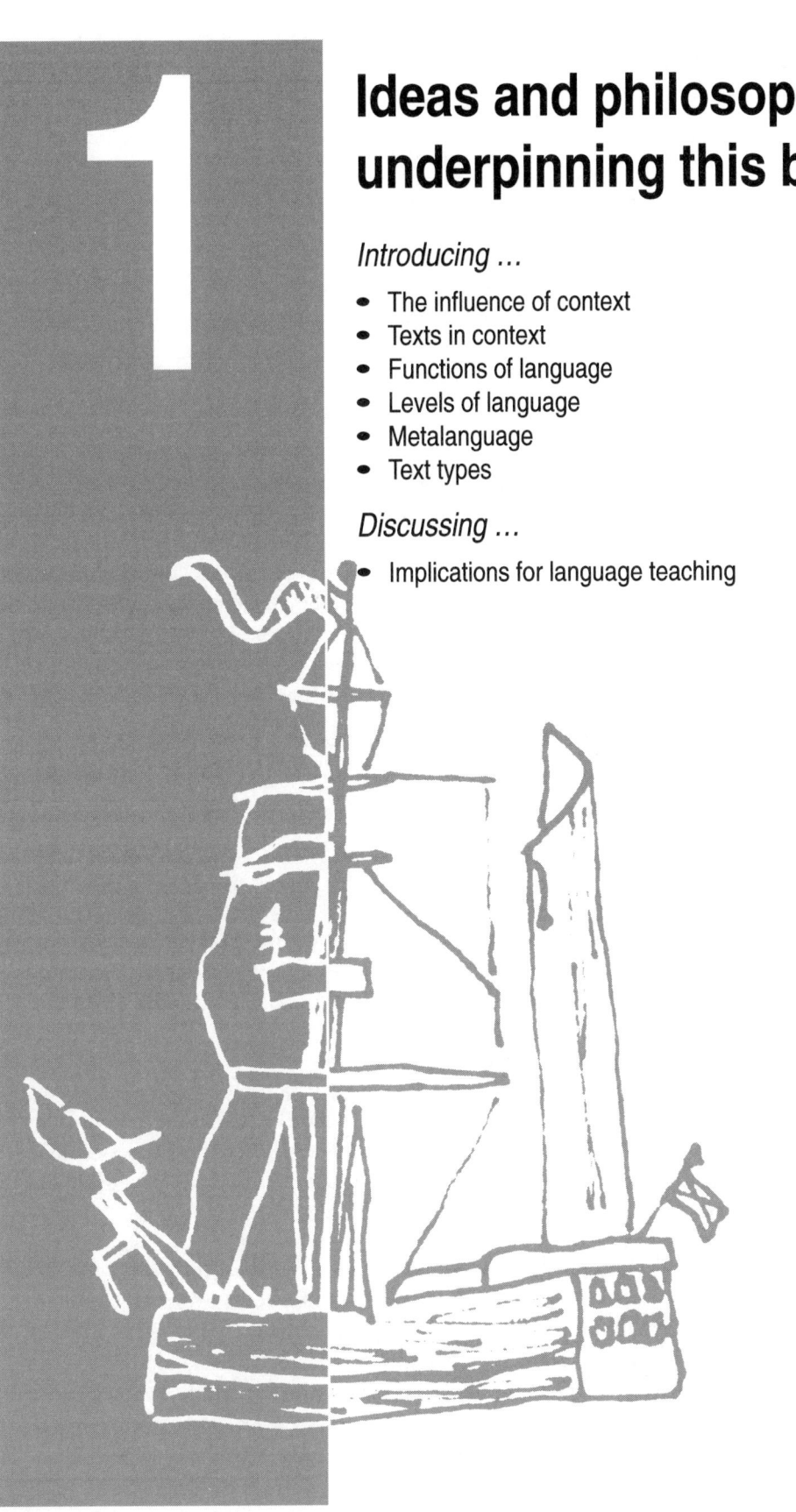

Welcome on board!

The influence of context

Quite early in life, perhaps as young as three years old, we become aware that the language that surrounds us is not always the same but that it changes according to different situations. As we hear people using language to talk about what is going on and to interact with one another we notice that their language changes along with what they are talking about and who they are talking to. As our experience widens, we may also realise that spoken language is subtly different from written language, and even that there are subsets within the larger spoken and written varieties. When we notice just how the changes occur and the reasons for the changes, we are taking a functional view of language and in this sense we *all* do functional linguistics.

As adult speakers and writers of English we have a finely tuned ability to use appropriate language at different times and for different purposes. We are aware, if only subconsciously, that language choice is influenced by certain aspects of the context in which it is used. We know that the English used in a sermon would not do for a love letter, and the English of a game of cards is not exactly the same as the English of a cat food advertisement. This discrimination has been built up from our accumulated experiences of different situations and the language choices made within them.

Using the same, often subconscious, knowledge, we are usually able to deduce the context of the language we hear or read, and can classify it quite finely; distinguishing, for instance, between a general warning, mild reprimand or serious chastisement. Our ability to discriminate and classify language experiences comes about because we have ourselves experienced how English works in different contexts and we recognise and reproduce appropriate language when the situation arises and contexts recur.

Most people don't think very much about the different 'Englishes' they use, probably because they've always kept them in separate context-specific compartments. However, those linguists who take a functional view of language are supremely interested in what makes one piece of language different from another. In this book we guide our readers from an intuitive knowledge of the functional basis of language to a fully aware appreciation of functional grammar by introducing techniques and appropriate vocabulary to explore English texts and to describe their contextual features.

This introductory chapter attempts to provide, in the most general way, a philosophical underpinning for the tools of grammatical analysis that *Using Functional Grammar* explores. Our grammatical analysis will be functional in the sense that we will account for each element in the language by describing how it functions. As readers you will bring your own language experiences to this book; some of you will have formal training in other grammars and some will never have studied grammar before; some will be teachers in a wide variety of subjects and schools, others will be students, mums or dads. We can't emphasise strongly enough that all your previous language experiences are valuable as you begin this exploration of functional grammar. As you work through the book, we hope you will come to share our view that functional grammar is not a set of rules but a set of resources for describing, interpreting and making meaning.

Being able to see the relationship between the often unconscious language choices each of us make all the time and the intricate social lives we lead is one of the most exciting language experiences for students and teachers.

Texts in contexts

A good place to start is to say more precisely what functional linguists mean by TEXT. A text is a piece of language in use; that is, 'language that is functional' (Halliday and Hasan 1985). A text's length is not important and it can be either spoken or written. What is important is that a text is a harmonious collection of meanings appropriate to its context. This unity of purpose gives a text both *texture* and *structure*. Texture comes from the way the meanings in the text fit coherently with each other – in much the same way as the threads of a piece of fabric or carpet are woven together to make a whole. Structure refers to the way that most pieces of language in use will contain certain obligatory structural elements appropriate to their purpose and context.

Actually, a text always occurs in two contexts, one within the other. This is represented visually in Figure 1.1. The outer context around a text is known as the CONTEXT OF CULTURE. When you think of the differences in forms of address, in ceremonies, in politeness and in significant activities between one culture and another, you get some idea of the importance of context of culture in shaping meanings. The context of culture is sometimes described as the sum of all the meanings it is possible to mean in that particular culture.

Within the context of culture, speakers and writers use language in many more specific contexts or situations. Each of these is an inner context, which functional linguists call the CONTEXT OF SITUATION. The combination of context of culture and context of situation results in the differences and similarities between one piece of language and another. The spoken texts accompanying vegetable shopping, for example, would be quite different in a North American supermarket from those in a Pacific island marketplace, and both context of culture and context of situation would be implicated in the differences. The barter and trading of the island market place simply don't occur within the context of culture of the supermarket conglomerate and this cultural difference will influence aspects of the buying context of situation.

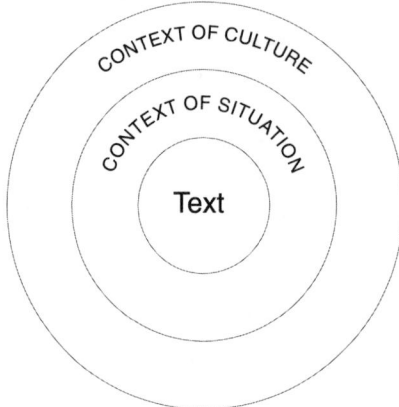

Figure 1.1: Text in context

Context of situation is a useful term to cover the things going on in the world outside the text that make the text what it is. These are the extralinguistic features of a text which are given substance in the words and grammatical patterns that speakers and writers use consciously or subconsciously to construct texts of different varieties, and that their audience uses to classify and interpret. Although at first it may seem astonishing, the situational differences between texts can, in fact, be accounted for by just three aspects of the context. Systemic functional linguists refer to these three aspects, or parameters, of the context of situation as FIELD, TENOR, and MODE OF DISCOURSE. We see this represented visually in Figure 1.2.

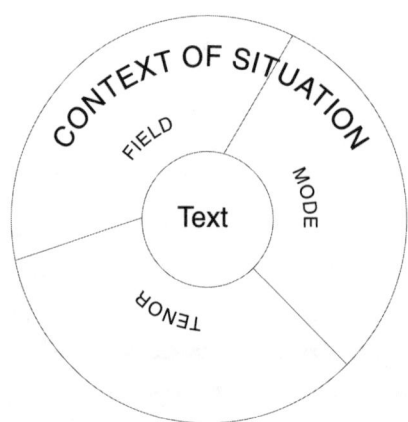

Figure 1.2: Parameters of context of situation

Field, Tenor and Mode

In very general terms, we can define field, tenor and mode as follows:

Field: what is to be talked or written about; the long and short term goals of the text;

Tenor: the relationship between the speaker and hearer (or, of course, writer and reader);

Mode: the kind of text that is being made.

When you think about these parameters of context of situation you will realise that only one of the three needs to be different to create a substantially different text. Imagine the differences between a job application letter and a letter to a friend about your hopes of getting the job, and then compare the letter to a friend with a conversation with the same friend on the same topic. All three texts are about a job application (field) and two of them are made in the form of a letter (mode). What particularly makes the two letters different is the difference in the relationships between writer and reader (tenor).

Functions of language

The three parameters of context of situation affect our language choices precisely because they reflect the three main functions of language. Language seems to have evolved for three major purposes. These are:

- to talk about what is happening, what will happen, and what has happened *field, ideation*
- to interact and/or to express a point of view *Tenor — interpersonal*   *texual*
- to turn the output of the previous two functions into a coherent whole. *mode, interpersonal*

Halliday, who originated and refined systemic functional grammar and who has written about it in *An introduction to functional grammar* (1994), calls these main functions the ideational (experiential and logical), interpersonal, and textual metafunctions. Each of these functions is defined in the following paragraphs. While these definitions are more formal ways of describing the metafunctions than the simple definitions above, they are basically describing the same thing.

The IDEATIONAL metafunction uses language to represent experience. There are two parts to this representation: experiential meanings encode the experiences and logical meanings show the relationships between them. Experiential meanings are discussed in Chapter 3. Logical meanings are not fully discussed in this book although you will find some mention of them in Chapter 2 and a simplified discussion of the connections between clauses in Chapter 7.

The INTERPERSONAL metafunction uses language to encode interaction, to show how defensible we find our propositions, to encode ideas about obligation and inclination and to express our attitudes. Chapters 4 and 5 explore the analysis and description of interpersonal meanings.

The TEXTUAL metafunction uses language to organise our experiential, logical and interpersonal meanings into a coherent and, in the case of written and spoken language, linear whole. Chapter 6 explores the analysis and description of textual meanings.

It is central to any study of language that the words we use and the way we organise them carry, or more technically *encode*, meanings. In the systemic functional approach to language study, each sentence encodes not just one but three meanings simultaneously, and these meanings are related to the three different and very basic functions of language. Throughout the book we will be looking first at one kind of meaning and then another, always remembering that after dissecting each different meaning separately we will combine them again. By Chapter 8, when we return to context of situation, we will have at our disposal the grammatical tools for a full contextual analysis and description.

Levels of language

When we take a recording of a spoken text or a similarly disembodied written text and make some accurate pronouncements about its context of situation, or when we ourselves fabricate a text which constructs recognisable relationships and purposes, we are demonstrating the fundamental relationship between context and language – that the extralinguistic levels of context are REALISED in the meanings of a text.

Linguists often think of language as a series of levels or strata and use the term REALISATION to describe the relationship between levels. Figure 1.3 is a diagrammatic representation of the way the levels are related by realisation. Reading from the top of the diagram downwards, the extralinguistic contexts are realised in the content level of our language, and the content is given form in the expression.

The content level of language

The content level of language is more accurately two levels, the second realising the first. We could think of the first level as systems of meanings that are realised in the second level – the systems of wordings. (In the case of signed languages, such as Auslan, ASL or BSL, meanings are realised in systems of signing.) More technically, we refer to systems of meanings as SEMANTICS and systems of wordings or signing as LEXICOGRAMMAR, which simply means words and the way they are arranged.

The notion of system is important because it refers to the whole potential of language at each level. Clearly, systems of meanings include experiential, interpersonal and textual systems and this book mainly focuses on the ways each of them is realised at the lexicogrammatical level.

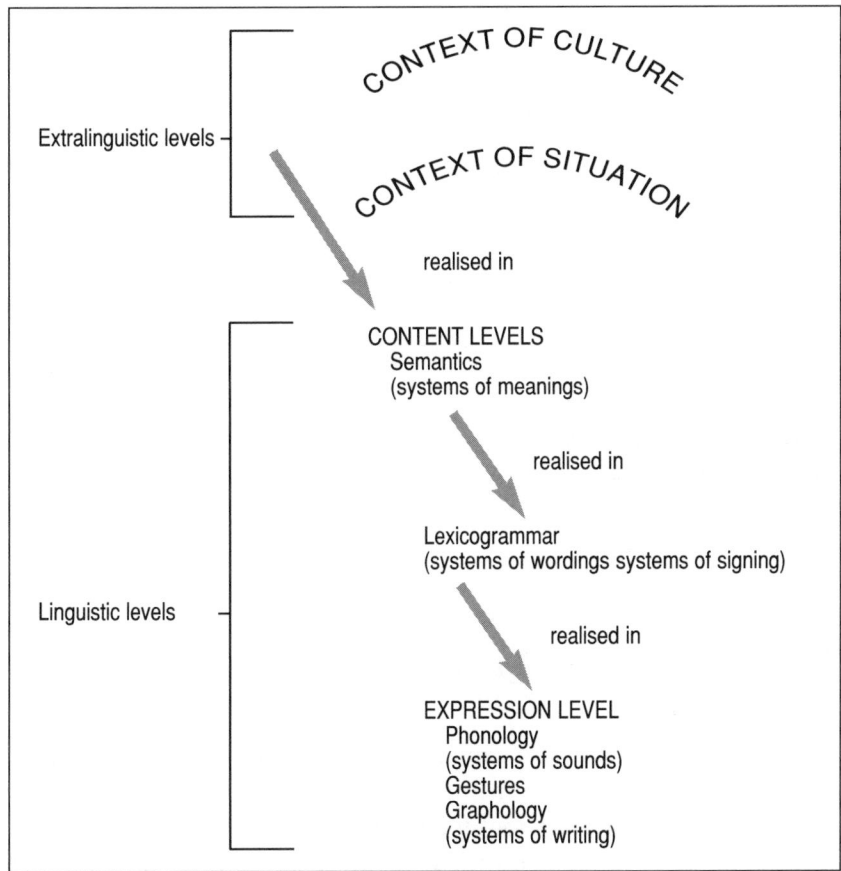

Figure 1.3: Levels of language

The expression level of language

Of course there are different ways of expressing the lexicogrammar which realises our meanings. At the expression level we make choices from systems of sounds (PHONOLOGY), systems of gesture (the phonology of signed languages) and systems of writing (GRAPHOLOGY).

Finding a metalanguage

Systemic functional grammar is a way of describing lexical and grammatical choices from the systems of wording so that we are always aware of how language is being used to realise meaning. Obviously we need some specialised vocabulary to describe and write about texts, just as musicians need a specialised vocabulary to describe and write about musical sounds or geographers need a specialised vocabulary to talk about how the earth's surface is differentiated. The problems that arise if we try to do without technical terms are amusingly illustrated in an excerpt from Lewis Carroll's poem 'The hunting of the snark' (next page).

The hunting of the snark

He had bought a large map representing the sea,
Without the least vestige of land:
And the crew were much pleased when they found it to be
A map they could all understand.

'What's the use of Mercator's North Poles and Equators,
Tropics, Zones, and Meridian Lines?'
So the Bellman would cry: and the crew would reply
'They are merely conventional signs!'

'Other maps are such shapes, with their islands and capes!
But we've got our brave Captain to thank'
(So the crew would protest) 'that he's brought us the best –
A perfect and absolute blank!'

Lewis Carroll

A specialised language allows us to explore texts by describing how different elements function to realise experiential, interpersonal and textual meanings. When our specialised language becomes our tool for analysing the lexicogrammar and meanings of texts, it opens up opportunities for comparing texts with each other. Indeed, intertextual comparison can not go very far without a specialised vocabulary to tease out the differences and similarities between texts. This specialised descriptive language is known as a METALANGUAGE and the investigation and comparison of texts is often known as STYLISTICS.

Stylistics is not just for literary texts. We can use our metalanguage to compare any texts we choose; for example, scientific or literary, written or spoken. We can investigate why one teacher seems to get the message across better than another, we can interpret advertisements as well as lyrics, we can compare newspaper stories, define the style of an individual barrister, or uncover similarities between authors of the same period.

Text types: Registers and genres

In general, texts which have the same sorts of meanings and/or the same structural elements are said to belong to the same TEXT TYPE. In particular, texts with meanings in common are said to belong to the same REGISTER and texts with obligatory structural elements in common are said to belong to the same GENRE.

Register

When texts share the same context of situation to a greater or lesser extent, they will share the same experiential, interpersonal and textual meanings and so they belong to the same register. We can talk about a register of cat food advertisements or a register of doctor-patient interviews because we know the same general meanings will be realised in texts produced in these contexts. We can even talk about a register of teacher talk because, although the lesson contents will be different, the texts will realise the same purposes and relationships. Because texts belonging to the same register have meanings in common, they also share patterns of lexicogrammar. This knowledge is very useful for creating our own texts; it is easier to produce a text of a certain type when you know the grammatical patterns to use.

Genre

When texts share the same general purpose in the culture, they will often share the same obligatory and optional structural elements and so they belong to the same genre or text type. Of course it's much easier to produce an appropriate text when you know its structure, and for this reason awareness of text types is now part of the curriculum in some schools.

One primary school syllabus document is based on a set of text types which fulfil specific social purposes. The text types are used to specify what students should be able to achieve with language if they are to meet the stated outcomes of the syllabus. The document begins in the extralinguistic context with a set of purposes for using language (see Figure 1.4).

	Purposes for using language	Text types
A	to tell what happened, to document a sequence of events and evaluate their significance in some way	RECOUNT
B	to construct a pattern of events with a problematic and/or unexpected outcome that entertains and instructs the reader or listener	NARRATIVE
C	to tell how to do something	PROCEDURE
D	to present information about something	INFORMATION REPORT
E	to tell how and why things occur	EXPLANATION
F	to argue a case	EXPOSITION
G	to look at more than one side of an issue; to explore various perspectives before coming to an informed decision	DISCUSSION

Figure 1.4: Adapted from *English K-6 syllabus*
© Board of Studies NSW, 1998

The social purposes for using language listed in this table are necessarily very general, and are certainly not exhaustive. Teachers working with this syllabus will select examples of text types to reflect the learning needs and goals of the particular students they are teaching.

Different social purposes will produce texts with distinct structural elements, each of which contributes to the achievement of the text's purpose. Some texts are a combination of several text types, but the following texts are fairly straightforward examples of each type. The structural elements are marked in the left-hand column. You will notice that certain structural elements are missing in some of these texts. This is because they are real texts written by fairly young children, some of whom speak English as a second language.

These particular texts have been selected for two reasons. The first is a very pragmatic one: texts produced by young learners are short and because we are concerned with whole texts rather than isolated fragments of language, it is important that we are able to explore grammar in the context of whole texts. Longer texts would be beyond the scope of a book of this size to explore in a comprehensive way. In addition, young learners use meanings and grammatical structures that are comparatively easy, for those of us exploring functional grammar for the first time, to manage.

The second reason for our selection is perhaps more significant for those of us who work in language education. In the early years of schooling young learners are building foundation knowledge about language and its use. This foundation knowledge becomes the basis for their future development in language and literacy. It is in texts such as these that language educators can see what underpins English language development at all levels.

Recount: **Caitlin's text**

Structural elements	Text
Orientation • information about *who*	There's this girl in my class …
Record of events • in the order in which they occurred	she tried to do a backward roll and she um like her neck clicked or something and um she was taken to hospital in an ambulance
Reorientation • rounding off the sequence of events	and I had to write down what happened because I was in her group
Coda • personal evaluation	I've done that before and it doesn't hurt that much. I think she's over-reacting just a bit

Narrative: Josephine's text

Structural elements	Text
Orientation • information about *who* and *where*	One day a monster came out of my hot water pipe.
Complication • events that constitute a problem or crisis • evaluation of the problem	I was very frightened. I called my mum and she came and saw the Floogleboogy and ran outside.
Resolution • information about how problem was resolved and normal events resumed	I wanted to make friends with it and give it a name so I called it a Floogleboogy and that night it came to bed with me.
Coda • personal evaluation	And I found that a Floogleboogy snores very loud indeed and mum was too frightened to come and kiss me goodnight.

Procedure: How to catch a wave

Structural elements	Text
Goal	**How to catch a wave** Here's some advice for kids who are just learning to surf.
Materials	Use a light, small, fibreglass board with a legrope and a wetsuit if it's cold.
Steps (in sequence)	Find a safe, uncrowded spot on the beach. The water should be not too choppy so that you will get a clean ride. Don't go out too far if you haven't surfed before. Wait until you see a small wave then lie on your surf board. When the wave is close, start paddling furiously. If you are more experienced, you could try kneeling on the board once you are on the wave. The most important thing is to keep your balance or else you will end up falling off the board!

'How to catch a wave': *English K-6 modules* 1998: 312 © Board of Studies NSW

Information report: **Pelicans**

Structural elements	Text
General Statement • identification and classification	**Pelicans** Pelicans are part of the Bird family.
Description • information organised in bundles (appearance, habitat, behaviour etc)	Pelicans have a big bill with a pouch. Most Pelicans have white body feathers. All Pelicans have short legs. Most Pelicans have webbed feet. Most Pelicans live around the coast. Pelicans eat crustaceans, crabs, fish and shrimps. Pelicans fly with their head back. Pelicans lay two, three or four white eggs. They take thirty-five days to hatch.

'Pelicans': *English K-6 modules* 1998: 135 © Board of Studies NSW

Explanation: **Susan's text**

Structural elements	Text
Identifying statement	**How hail is formed** Hail is rain or snow which has frozen into round pellets.
Explanation sequence • the phases of the process in the order in which they occur	Sometimes in storms strong air currents force raindrops upwards into clouds of freezing water. When the raindrops begin to freeze into round pellets they become heavier and start to fall. As they fall back into the air currents, they are forced upwards again into the freezing clouds. This coats the pellets in another layer of ice. The pellets continue to bounce up into the freezing cloud to be coated in more layers of ice and down into the air current until they become too heavy for the air current. They then fall to earth as hailstones.

Exposition: **Cars should be banned**

Structural elements	Text
Statement of position	**Cars should be banned in the city** Cars should be banned in the city. As we all know, cars create pollution, and cause a lot of road deaths and other accidents.
Preview of arguments	First, cars, as we all know, contribute to most of the pollution in the world.
Arguments (supported by evidence)	Cars emit a deadly gas that causes illnesses such as bronchitis, lung cancer, and 'triggers' off asthma. Some of these illnesses are so bad that people can die from them. Second, the city is very busy. Pedestrians wander everywhere and cars commonly hit pedestrians in the city, which causes them to die. Cars today are our roads biggest killers. And third, cars are very noisy. If you live in the city, you may find it hard to sleep at night, or concentrate on your homework, and especially talk to someone.
Reinforcement of statement of position	In conclusion, cars should be banned from the city for the reasons listed.

'Cars should be banned in the city': *English K-6 modules* 1998: 312 © Board of Studies NSW

Discussion: **Homework**

Structural elements	Text
Issue	**Homework** I think we should have homework because it helps us to learn and revise our work.
Arguments for	Homework helps people who aren't very smart to remember what they have learned. Homework is really good because it helps with our education.
Arguments against	I think we shouldn't have homework because I like to go out after school to a restaurant or the movies. Sometimes homework is boring and not important. I think homework is bad because I like to play and discuss things with my family.

'Homework': *English K-6 modules* 1998: 151 © Board of Studies NSW

Each of the texts featured on pages 10–13 has a general structure which it shares with other texts of the same type. In each case the writers have also made characteristic grammatical choices. As we will need grammatical metalanguage before we can explore these choices, we will return to this topic in Chapter 9.

To sum up

People sometimes think that 'learning a language' is a simple matter of learning vocabulary and grammar, but anyone who has visited a country where an unfamiliar language is spoken can tell you this is only part of the story. Our everyday lives are conducted in situations that are part of our context of culture and, to a large extent, these situations are familiar – which is partly how we recognise and understand other people's meanings – because we share the same cultural knowledge. Whenever we speak or write we make selections from the entire lexical and grammatical system of English to produce appropriate meanings for the field, tenor and mode of a context of situation. When we first operate in a second language we may know the words but not the appropriate contexts; we really only understand other speakers when we share, not only words and grammar but also *which* words and *which* grammatical choices are appropriate for a situation.

Exercises

1 Why do we need a metalanguage?

2 What differences and similarities can you find among
   a. a recipe
   b. a curriculum vitae
   c. a joke
   d. an essay written in the last year of secondary school
   e. the news on the radio

3 Find four examples of texts you have heard or read in the last week.
   What can you say about their context?

[handwritten notes:]
language is:
· a process of making meaning
· a text in context (Vs words or sentences)
  harmonious set of meaning
  appropriate to its context. Text
  emerges from context

Implications for language teaching

For language teachers the most important concept introduced in this chapter is that learning language is more than learning vocabulary and grammar. Learning a language involves learning how to **use** the language in a way that makes sense to other people who speak the language. In other words it is about making meaning with that language. Chapter 1 introduces us to a way of thinking about, and describing, how we use language to make meaning.

We are asked to think about language in terms of units called TEXTS. A text is not described in terms of language fragments such as sentences or words, but in terms of a whole, harmonious collection of meanings that has unity of purpose. The words and structures encode the meanings in a text. These meanings are given their harmony and unity through two design features – texture and structure.

The metaphor of a piece of woven fabric or carpet is used to describe texture because meanings are *woven* together in a text to create harmony and unity. At the same time, however, the meanings in a text are configured in such a way that the text has a structure – a kind of architecture with a unifying, structural shape – through which the text achieves its purpose.

Once we take a functional view of language, we begin to think about language as a process of making meanings, weaving these meanings together coherently, and shaping them into purposeful wholes, or texts. The task of language education thus becomes one of supporting language learners so they can participate in this process effectively.

What approach will be used by teachers who think about language as text?

Teachers who think about language as text are most likely to design activities in which students work with the language of whole authentic texts. They are less inclined to design classroom activities in which students work with unconnected language fragments, for instance activities with sets of unrelated sentences which they are asked to change into the past tense or make plural. Teachers with a background in functional grammar are also less likely to design activities in which students have to learn the dictionary definitions of sets of unrelated words separate from the texts in which these words are used. Instead they are more likely to design activities in which students work with the language of whole authentic texts.

Is it enough to teach language from the perspectives of whole texts alone?

In this chapter we discuss the concept of language as text and the relationship between texts and the contexts in which they are used. In a functional approach to language a text is seen as 'a harmonious set of meanings appropriate to its *context*'. In other words, a text emerges from a context.

In this chapter context is described from two perspectives: from the perspective of the general culture in which the text is being used, and from the perspective of the specific social situation in which the text is being used. The combination of these two contexts accounts for the differences and similarities between different pieces of language.

Teachers who accept that context and text depend on each other in this way will teach students how to investigate the context of the texts they encounter and how to use knowledge of context to work with texts more effectively.

What approach will be used by teachers who think about language as text in context?

If we accept that understanding the context is essential for understanding a text completely, then students must be able to explore the social and cultural world of the communities who use the language they are trying to control. In this way students will learn to use the target language in culturally and socially relevant, appropriate and purposeful ways. They will also learn how variation in context accounts for variation in language use.

How can teachers explore the complex relationship between text and context?

In this chapter we are given two tools to explore the relationship between text and context in a systematic way: the first allows us to describe how a context of situation is reflected in the variety of language used in that situation and the second allows us to explore the link between structure and social purpose.

The three aspects of the context of situation — field, tenor and mode — are configured in different ways from one context of situation to the next. These different configurations account for the differences between the language used in one context and the language used in another.

Teachers can use field, tenor and mode to describe the variety of language which is likely to occur in any context of situation in which their students need to use the target language. Using these descriptions, teachers can identify the meanings, words and structures which are possible, or even probable, in that context. More specifically:

- having explored the field of a situation, teachers can identify words and structures for making meanings about experience in that situation (experiential meanings)
- having explored the tenor of the situation, teachers can identify words and structures for building relationships and expressing points of view in that context (interpersonal meanings)

- having explored the mode of a situation, teachers can identify words and structures for organising these meanings into a text in that particular context (textual meanings).

As well as describing the varieties of language needed in different contexts of situation, teachers can also identify texts which share the same kinds of meanings; that is, the same *register*. These texts will become the basis for activities in which students transfer what they have already learned about language use from one text to other texts which share the same or a similar register.

Once teachers have explored the contexts of situation relevant to their students' learning needs and goals, they are able to describe the different varieties of language their students need to control in order to achieve these goals. Teachers can then design courses based on these language varieties.

Teachers can also help students build strategies for recognising and analysing varieties of language appropriate to different contexts, strategies that guarantee meaningful language learning will continue long after formal classes have ended. In addition, teachers can show students how to recognise texts which share the same kinds of meanings. In this way students can transfer knowledge about language use from one context to related contexts.

The second tool introduced in this chapter for managing the relationship between text and context allows us to explore the link between structure and social purpose. The structures of texts reflect the general purposes language is used for in the culture in which the target language is used. For example, different text structures are used in English to:

- tell stories
- persuade people to a point of view
- give instructions
- explain things.

Texts exemplifying these structures are found on pages 10–13.

Texts that share the same general social purpose in the culture share the same underlying structural pattern, or the same *genre*. When students are introduced to the structural patterns of different genres, they build a rich repertoire of text elements. This repertoire becomes the basis for constructing whole texts that are sensitive to the demands of the culture and, therefore, effective in the culture. As students gain confidence and expertise with different text patterns, they are able to adapt, combine and customise these patterns to meet individual and complex purposes. Knowledge of register makes it possible for learners to vary the language used within generic text patterns in order to meet the specific demands of immediate situations.

How can teachers find their way around this complex terrain?

This chapter presents us with a rich and detailed picture of language that offers teachers both opportunities and challenges. Language is described in terms of:

- whole texts
- the contexts of its use, both cultural contexts and immediate social situations
- the systematic links between text and context.

When we explore a new terrain, we are less likely to lose our way if we have a map. It is also useful to know the names and characteristics of the features of the landscape so we can recognise them and understand how they relate to other features of the landscape. In this chapter we have been given a complex 'map' of language and context that is designed in layers, or levels, not unlike the levels of many computer games. The most abstract and general layer of the map is the context of culture and the most concrete layer is the expression level of language (see Figure 1.3).

Functional linguists are able to describe systematically what it is possible to do with language at each level of this map. In other words, they can describe the **potential** of each layer of language. Language users tap this potential every time they choose to use a sound or a word, every time they structure words into grammatical patterns to make meaning, and every time they weave and shape meanings into a text in a context.

The more teachers know about the potential of each layer, the more they can draw students' attention to salient language features and patterns. The more students know about the potential of each layer, the more conscious, strategic and effective their language choices will be.

Functional linguists use a specialised language, or metalanguage, to describe the potential for making meaning of each layer of the language-in-context map. This specialised language makes it possible to:

- describe what language does
- analyse how language does what it does
- compare and contrast language use from text to text and from context to context.

This specialised language offers teachers an opportunity to build a rich and detailed body of knowledge about language and its use, a body of knowledge that can greatly enrich professional expertise. Teachers can use this metalanguage to bring to their own and their students' consciousness key features and patterns of language. In other words the metalanguage provides a common language which teachers and students can use to talk to each other about language and how it works.

A rich metalanguage, such as the one introduced in this book, also offers teachers the following challenges:

- It takes time and effort to learn this specialised language.
- It takes considerable professional judgement to decide how much of this specialised language to share with students in order to achieve optimum learning outcomes.

We will return to these challenges in the final chapter. In the meantime, the exploration continues.

Further reading

In *The functional analysis of English: A Hallidayan approach* (Bloor and Bloor 1995) there is an entertaining political allegory written to persuade the reader of the value of a specialised and technical metalanguage (p13).

Rutherford (1987) in his book *Second language grammar: Learning and teaching* introduces the idea of 'grammatical consciousness-raising'.

Exercises for language teachers

Identify a text which is a good example of the type of text you would like your students to be able to use effectively. The text could be spoken or written. Examine your chosen text using the following questions as a guide.

1   What can you say about the field of this text? (What is the text about?)

2   What can you say about the tenor? (What is the relationship between the speaker and hearer or writer and reader?)

3   What can you say about the mode? (What kind of text is being made, eg face-to-face interaction, book, letter, essay, telephone call, email?)

4   What words and structures in the text gave you clues about each of the above aspects of the context of situation? (This is a preliminary activity only. Just answer with your first impressions. As you continue with your exploration of language through this book, you will learn more detailed and precise ways of recognising the words and structures which put the context of situation in the text.)

5   What activities do you currently design for your students so they learn how to use words and structures like these?

6   How could you extend these activities so your students will learn how to use these words and structures in whole texts in context?

7   What is the overall social purpose of this text? For example, does it tell a story, discuss an issue, organise a body of information or give instructions?

8   How does the beginning of the text contribute to this purpose?

9   How does the middle of the text contribute to this purpose?

10 How does the end of the text contribute to this purpose?

11 What activities do you design for your students so they learn how to construct texts of this type now?

12 How could you extend these activities so students learn how the text structure relates to the text's overall purpose?

13 What kinds of learning activities could you design to assist your students to explore the context of culture and context of situation of this text?

14 What text might you sequence next in your teaching program and why? You might choose this next text because it:
- has the same overall purpose but gives students the opportunity to achieve this purpose in a different context of situation
- has the same field but gives students the opportunity to work with a different tenor and mode
- is different only in terms of field so that the students have the opportunity to use this type of text in a different subject area.

2

Towards a functional grammar

Introducing …

- Notions of grammar
- Building on traditional grammar
- Towards a functional grammar
- Clauses and their constituent parts

Discussing …

- Implications for language teaching

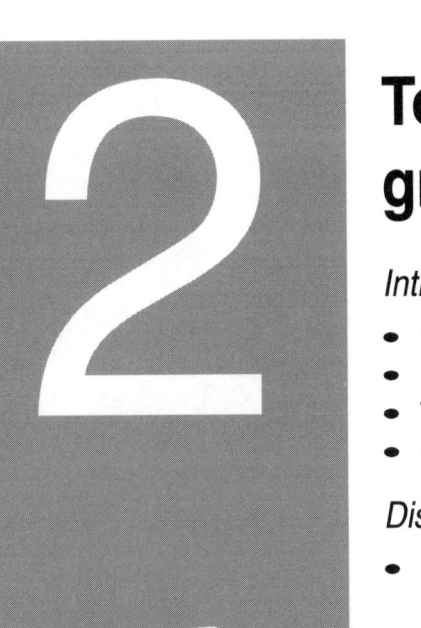

Notions of grammar

One of the first things we need to do in our exploration of a functional aproach to grammar is to explore what we mean by the term *grammar*. To many people the term signifies a fairly rigid set of rules for speaking and writing, the breaking of which will mark you out as uneducated, unsophisticated or even uncouth. Once upon a time you could not finish school in most parts of the English-speaking world without having learned at least a little of this type of grammar. Nowadays many people have had little or no instruction in anything called grammar, but still a kind of mystical importance surrounds the way we talk about grammar. Some people apologise for their written English, explaining that they have never been taught grammar properly; others say that grammar is too technical and difficult for them to handle; still others feel that if they had learnt a foreign language they might have grasped grammar. Even those who have been taught something called grammar in school may have gained the impression that it is indeed a mysterious art in which you learn special terms (such as *verb* and *clause*) and master obscure rules to eradicate such errors as the *split infinitive*.

It is true that 'grammar' can mean something like a grammar book or a set of grammatical rules, particularly rules that people will keep breaking unless they are firmly taught them. But there is another sense in which 'grammar' means something like *the way in which a language is organised*. In this second sense all of us have a command of grammar, even if we speak only one language and have never consciously learned any grammatical rules or terms.

This point is not always readily accepted in English-speaking countries, partly because of an educational tradition of concentrating on only some parts of the language. In speaking English, we all follow rules of grammar, but this rarely, if ever, attracts much attention. Since *rule* may keep reminding us of rules set out in a book, let's drop that word and think instead of patterns of language – and in particular of regular patterns. We all arrange words in certain patterns to construct sentences and, if we grew up speaking English, we don't need formal training in identifying, for example, which of the following is modern English usage:

Did you see Alice's new car?
Did you Alice's new car see?

Did you see car new Alice's?
Saw you Alice's new car?
Did see you Alice's car new?

What speakers of English know, by virtue of being speakers of English, is not just how to put specific words together to create sentences, but how to follow and exploit some very general smaller patterns of language that regularly occur within sentences, as component parts – or CONSTITUENTS – of sentences. *Alice's new car* illustrates a general pattern for expressions such as:

Harry's old typewriter
Mother's dusty books
My sister's lifelong ambition
Someone's dirty shoes

Our first example also points to a fundamental distinction in English between statements and questions, a distinction that is achieved by patterned wording as the following examples demonstrate:

Statement	Question
You saw	Did you see?
You heard	Did you hear?
She laughed	Did she laugh?
You work	Do you work?
Bill paints	Does Bill paint?
They ski	Do they ski?
Carla's working	Is Carla working?
He was laughing	Was he laughing?
They'll write	Will they write?
Denis can hear	Can Denis hear?
I should stay	Should I stay?

These patterns of language can be described as part of English grammar – they are part of how we express ourselves in English. Other languages may or may not have similar patterns. In some languages, for example, the wording of *Alice's new car* may be equivalent to *the new car of Alice*. Interestingly, few languages turn out to have a pattern that matches the English question pattern represented by *Did you see?* In many languages the question pattern is simply a reversal of the corresponding statement; that is, *Saw you?* In fact this was once the pattern in English too but it has been replaced. In 16th century English we do find patterns like:

Know ye what I have done to you?
Died he not in his bed?

while more modern equivalents would be:

Do you know what I have done to you?
Didn't he die in his bed?

Grammar as taught in schools in the past often had little or nothing to say about patterns like these, and in a way this was understandable since most of us learned the patterns quite unconsciously before going to school. What *was* taught as grammar was often directed towards understanding and learning the patterns of other languages, especially Latin. (A grammar school was a school that taught Latin grammar.) That was also understandable, given the importance of Latin in the educational system of the time. It was unfortunate, however, that English grammar tended to be judged in the light of Latin grammar. In general, grammarians and teachers fostered the idea that you needed to learn special rules to be able to speak English properly – or more particularly to be able to produce elegant *written* English. In some instances they actually tried to make English conform to Latin patterns. Thus, many people even today have an uneasy feeling that the way they normally use English cannot be quite right and that they need to remember and apply artificial rules to their written English.

Even more demoralising is the notion held by many speakers of English, native as well as non-native, that their *spoken* language is somehow faulty or improper. The grammatical conventions of face-to-face spoken language and those that apply to formal writing are different in many ways. The grammar teaching of the past tended to obscure this fact, with the result that all too often people – especially those whose spoken variety of English was not that of the dominant middle class – became ashamed of the way they spoke as well as the way they wrote.

Functional approaches to grammar description and pedagogy

A functional approach to grammar description and teaching can help alleviate the irrational feelings of shame identified above, at the same time as it empowers people to look closely at, and feel comfortable about, analysing their own choices and those of others around them. There have been several initiatives in the direction of a functional approach to grammar over the last three decades. Systemic functional linguistics, the approach presented in this book, is one of the most recent – and we would argue one of the most systematically developed – of these initiatives. However, many of the readers of this book will be familiar with other functional grammar initiatives. *Communicative grammars* and *corpus-based grammars*, in particular, are pedagogical grammars claiming a functional approach that have had considerable relevance for English language teachers around the world. We will just mention two such grammars in passing.

In the preface to A *communicative grammar of English*, Geoffrey Leech and Jan Svartvik (1975: 10) describe their book as:

> A communicative grammar of English *is a new kind of grammar. In writing it, we have assumed that studying grammar … makes most sense if one starts with the question 'How can I use grammar to communicate?'. Thus the main part of the book is devoted to the USES of grammar, rather than to grammatical STRUCTURE.*

The *Collins Cobuild English grammar* was published fifteen years later. Compiled by a team of linguists working at the University of Birmingham in Britain, this grammar has strong links to the Bank of English – a computer database (corpus) of English texts, both spoken and written, which seeks to monitor the way in which English is actually used in the modern world. In their introduction the editors make this point (1990: v):

> *People who study and use a language are mainly interested in how they can do things with the language – how they can make meanings, get attention to their problems and interests, influence their friends and colleagues and create a rich social life for themselves. They are only interested in the grammatical structure of the language as a means to getting things done.*
>
> *A grammar which puts together the patterns of the language and the things you can do with them is called a functional grammar.*

Michael Halliday, whose functional approach to grammar description underpins *Using functional grammar*, was a consultant to the Birmingham editorial team, and many of the ideas about language use and grammar choices that are reflected in the *Collins Cobuild English grammar* are shared by grammarians who use Halliday's theory of systemic functional grammar description.

It is important to remember that all functional approaches to grammar description and grammar teaching are firmly steeped in earlier traditions, building on the past not rejecting it. We explain this approach below, with particular reference to systemic functional grammar.

Continuing classical and rehetorical traditions of grammar description

Systemic functional linguists have sometimes been accused of rejecting the strengths of traditional approaches to grammar and to text description. Nothing could be further from the truth. In fact, many of the concepts and goals of systemic functional linguistics incorporate ideas about linguistic philosophy that have carried over from some of the intellectual pre-occupations of the classical world. In particular:

- the concern for turning the study of language back to the applications of speaking, writing, and interpretation
- the treatment of words and grammar as part of a more general study of discourse
- the classification of different registers (or text types) according to the different purposes involved and the different resources used to affect the audience – namely, through *pathos* (emotions), *logos* (reasoning), or *ethos* (personal character)
- the integration of the basic notions of grammar and rhetoric – for example transitivity, mood, modality, theme/rheme, finiteness, tense, voice.

A major concern of linguistic philosophy since classical times has been the consistent separation of function and class labels. Continuing this tradition, systemic functional linguists seek to avoid the contradictions inherent in such grammatical descriptions as SVO; that is, Subject (a functional label), Verb (a class label), Object (a functional label).

The challenge for text linguistics is to explain how a community, a social network, or even two people make use of language across changing contexts, changing social memberships and changing modes (from speech to writing, for example). In the classical tradition the rhetoric of Attic Greek sets out to prepare citizens for public debate and for the evaluation of knowledge. *How different is this in education today* we might ask. Clearly the modes have multiplied (think of the screen and email) but the critical goals of the study of discourse have remained the same.

The crucial difference today, in the context of a language like English (so different from the inflecting forms of Greek and Latin), is that all the concepts of traditional grammar and rhetoric need to be thought through in the specific conditions of English and in the specific registers of a new (once unimaginable) technology. Systemic functional linguistics is a proposal for language description that is consistent with this aim. A dynamic theory, it is itself changing in order to address the changing patterns by which meaning is made.

Building on traditional grammar

If you have had any formal training in grammar, back in primary school for example, you will already be familiar with some grammatical terminology. You may, for instance, have divided a sentence up in terms of its subject and predicate, you may know something about person and tense, and you may be familiar with most of the following words:

adjective	adverb	noun	verb
article	conjunction	preposition	pronoun

In traditional grammatical terminology, these are known as *parts of speech*. You are probably able to suggest useful working definitions for some of them (for example, a *noun* is a naming word, a *verb* is a doing word, an *adverb* adds to the meaning of a verb, a *conjunction* is a joining word, a *pronoun* stands in for a noun and so on).

Now let's, for a moment, look at some rather more technical definitions of these terms. Figure 2.1 contains some definitions from the *Macquarie dictionary* (1997).

Grammatical terms like those in Figure 2.1 are called CLASS terms – they allow us to classify words according to the way they are normally used in the roles they usually play in language. But how useful, and indeed how accurate, is such classification in any quest to describe and explore the grammar of a language?

ADJECTIVE
one of the major word classes in many languages, comprising words that typically modify a noun.

ADVERB
one of the major parts of speech comprising words used to modify or limit a verb, a verbal noun (also, in Latin, English and some other languages, an adjective or another adverb), or an adverbial phrase or clause.

NOUN
(in most languages) one of the major form classes, or 'parts of speech', comprising words denoting persons, places, things, and such other words as show similar grammatical behaviour, as English *friend, city, desk, whiteness, virtue.*

VERB
one of the major form classes, or 'parts of speech', comprising words which express the occurrence of an action, existence of a state, and the like, and such other words as show similar grammatical behaviour, as English *discover, remember, write, be.*

ARTICLE
a. a word whose function is to determine the syntactic scope of the noun with which it is associated.
b. (in English) any of the determiners *the, a* or *an.*

CONJUNCTION
a. (in some languages) one of the major form classes, or 'parts of speech', comprising words used to link together words, phrases, clauses or sentences.
b. such a word, as English *and* or *but.*

PREPOSITION
(in some languages) one of the major form classes, or 'parts of speech', comprising words placed before nouns to indicate their relation to other words or their function in the sentence. *By, to, in, from* are prepositions in English.

PRONOUN
(in many languages) one of the major form classes, or 'parts of speech', comprising words used as substitutes for nouns.

Figure 2.1: Technical definitions of traditional grammar terms
Macquarie dictionary (1997)

If you think of a noun as a naming word, a word that denotes a person, place or thing, it is obvious that the names of concrete, seeable, touchable objects are nouns: *tree, cat, desk, shop, town, teacher, Mary.* But your dictionary (or maybe your own linguistic sensitivity) will tell you that the words *contrivance, emotion, classification, emergence,* and *difficulty* are also nouns. In what ways are the concepts expressed by these words object-like? What qualities are shared by *tree* and *emergence* that allow us to classify each as a noun? Doesn't *emergence* describe a happening or event? How then can it denote a thing?

Similarly, if you were taught that a verb is a doing word, then you will have no trouble identifying the verb in the following sentence: *Most birds build nests in trees.* What most birds *do* is build. But there is no 'doing' word in the following sentence from a well-known song: *I am woman.* Here the speaker is expressing *being* rather than *doing,* and the verb in the sentence is *am,* which those with some knowledge of traditional grammar will recognise as the first person, present tense form of the verb *to be*. It is interesting to note that not all languages express *being* (*existence of a state* according to the *Macquarie dictionary* definition of verb) by way of a verb. In Indonesian, for example, it is normal to say <u>mereka</u> <u>masih</u> <u>di</u> <u>rumah</u> 'they are still at home' (literally: they still at home). In this book we will be making a distinction, in functional terms, between *doing*, *being*, and *saying*, *thinking*, and *feeling* kinds of verbs (see under Clauses as processes in Chapter 3).

Let's now explore some other problems with traditional grammar terminology. First, compare these four sentences:

1 *Bathurst* is a *town* in the *country*
2 Bathurst is a *country* town
3 My cousin has bought a *town* house in Bathurst
4 Stop here for a real *Bathurst* experience

Bathurst, *town* and *country* are all nouns in sentence 1. But what about *country* in sentence 2, *town* in sentence 3 and, indeed, *Bathhurst* in sentence 4? We could say these words are still nouns in terms of CLASS, but in terms of FUNCTION they are playing a different role. In sentences 2, 3 and 4, each of these words plays the role we expect an adjective to play, that is as a describing word to provide additional information about a noun. So *Bathurst* in ... *a real Bathurst experience* belongs to the class *noun*, but it functions to provide information about another noun – *experience*. Usually when a noun acts as if it is an adjective, we apply the functional label CLASSIFIER, but more about that in the next chapter.

Now look at the following pair of sentences:

1 The swallows come to our valley in early spring and we know the warm weather is not far behind.
2 The coming of the swallows in early spring brings a promise of warm weather not far behind.

The swallows do something in early spring and what they do is expressed in each case by the English word *come* (*coming*). In sentence 1, *come* is clearly a doing word and is also clearly functioning in the way we expect verbs to function. However, in sentence 2, the word *coming* looks like a doing word (verb) but is functioning in one of the ways we would expect of a noun; that is, it is preceded by the definite article *the*, and is itself doing something: *The coming ... brings a promise ...* In other words, it is acting like a thing rather than a happening or event.

Another telling example of the problem with traditional grammar terms is the highly colloquial Shakespearian riposte to an argumentative adversary:

But me no buts

In this expression *but*, a word we would normally think of as a conjunction, is used first as an imperative verb and then as a plural noun.

From the examples above, it should be clear that the old classification of words is useful only up to a point. Functional grammarians do not reject, discard or replace the terminology of traditional grammar but, to capture what goes on in language, build on and refine the notions of traditional grammar in several ways. The first way is to recognise that words have functions as well as class and that how a word functions can tell us much more than any description of words in terms of class can about the piece of language, where it occurs, the person who chose to use it in that function, and the culture that surrounds the person and the message. This refinement from word class to word function leads to another refinement of traditional grammar, the RANK SCALE.

Towards a functional grammar: The rank scale

If language cannot be fully explained by labelling words according to their class, if we need to take account of functions as well as classes, then we also need to look beyond mere words. Language is much more than a stringing together of words; we need to be able to analyse and describe patterns of language at several different levels. Just as some scientists look at slides through microscopes with varying degrees of magnification, recognising units at different levels, such as molecule, cell and organism, so linguists look at language at various levels or on various scales. Michael Halliday in *An introduction to functional grammar* (1994) describes language in terms of a RANK SCALE. This concept of a rank scale is very important for an understanding of how a system as intricate as human language works. We present it here, with a brief explanation, and will return to the idea at key points in the book.

RANK SCALE	clause complex
	clause
	group or phrase
	word
	morpheme

The units at each rank are made up of one or more units of the rank below. The highest rank is the CLAUSE COMPLEX and is made up of one or more clauses. (Obviously clause complexes join together to make paragraphs, and paragraphs make up texts, but these are rhetorical and semantic units rather than grammatical or syntactic units.)

A **clause complex**	consists of	one or more clauses
A **clause**	consists of	one or more groups or phrases
A **group** or **phrase**	consists of	one or more words
A **word**	consists of	one or more morphemes

Clause complex is probably a term that needs some explanation. You may already have some ideas about words combining into phrases, phrases into clauses and clauses into SENTENCES. The term sentence is a bit of a problem word in language studies as it has not always been used consistently by linguists in the past. It really relates to a pattern of language that occurs in written texts.

> A **sentence** is a piece of **written** language that in English conventionally begins with a capital letter and ends at the next following full stop.

Spoken language is not divided into sentences, although we often think and talk about it in those terms as the following statements illustrate:

> He never lets me finish a sentence!
> What age does a child begin to talk in full sentences?

Spoken language obviously predates written language – both in terms of human history and in terms of the personal history of any individual – yet prescriptive grammars and grammarians of English in the past have had a tendency to treat spoken forms as if they were imitations or reflections of written forms, as if the written form should be taken as the standard to follow when speaking. This tendency is perhaps understandable when you consider that our culture has been literate for a long time, that writing is such an important part of our lives, and that grammarians of the past based their observations almost exclusively on written texts.

However, there are significant differences between the grammatical norms for speaking and writing, as more recent linguistic research – especially in the latter part of this century – has demonstrated. Since we need a systematic approach that will cover language description for either spoken or written texts, we use the term *clause complex* as an umbrella term for the patterns of language at the level above clause, remembering that in written texts a clause complex often corresponds to a sentence.

> A **clause complex** is a language structure that consists of one clause working by itself, or a group of clauses that work together through some kind of logical relationship (see Chapter 7).

Now let's use a text to explore the different levels on the rank scale using Text 1.

Text 1

> Mr Harper's call for a rise in interest rates should not surprise us. When the national economy is growing fast, many economic analysts will claim that interest rates should rise to prevent a situation of boom and bust. Of greater surprise are his optimistic long-term projections for growth in the Australian manufacturing sector.

Text 1 has three clause complexes; the first and third consist of one clause only while the second consists of four clauses working together. We have used this second clause complex in Table 2.1 to explore the different levels of the rank scale.

Table 2.1: Levels of the rank scale

CLAUSE COMPLEX	When the national economy is growing fast, many economic analysts will claim that interest rates should rise to prevent a situation of boom and bust.				
CLAUSES	1 When the national economy is growing fast 2 many economic analysts will claim 3 that interest rates should rise 4 to prevent a situation of boom and bust.				
GROUPS OR PHRASES	the national economy many economic analysts interest rates a situation of boom and bust		is growing will claim should rise to prevent	fast	when
WORDS *(incomplete list)*	national economic analysts	the claim interest	growing rates situation		
MORPHEMES *(incomplete list)*	nation econom grow situ-at(e)	-al -ic -ing	the claim interest -ion		

Table 2.1 demonstrates the fact that a unit can consist of *one* or *more* lower-level units (just as an organism can consist of a single cell or many cells, or a building may consist of one room or many rooms). In English, for example, many words are single morpheme words (*grow, the, claim, rate, interest, nation, many, you, finger, ticket, mother*), while others can be analysed into two or more morphemes (*growing, rates, national, situation, fingertips, progressing, forgettable, unforgettable, backpack, backpacker, backpackers*).

At word level in our analysis we can recognise words from some classes of traditional grammar such as adjectives, nouns, verbs and adverbs. At group level the picture is somewhat different. Functional grammar recognises the nominal group, verbal group, adverbial group, conjunction group, preposition group, and just one kind of phrase – the prepositional phrase, which consists of a preposition and a nominal group. All other traditional classes are subsumed into these groups with pronouns, adjectives and articles all being considered within normal nominal group structure. Remember that a group consists of one or more words, so a verbal group may have just one word like *eats* (not in this text), or a main verb and several auxiliaries like *is growing, should rise, will claim*, or *might have been going to be caught* (this last not in this text).

A morphological aside

In this book we will focus mainly on the ranks of clause complex, clause, and group or phrase. However, morphemes are part of the rank scale and since the word MORPHEME may be an unfamiliar term a brief discussion of morphemes seems useful at this stage.

Morpheme derives from the Greek word *morphe*, meaning *form*. In linguistics it is the traditional term to describe the most basic building blocks (in terms of meaning) of a grammatical system. A morpheme has been defined as 'the minimal linguistic sign, a grammatical unit that is an arbitrary union of a sound and a meaning and that cannot be further analysed' (Fromkin, Rodman, Collins and Blair 1990: 124). Every word is made up of one or more morphemes, and this is so no matter what language you are looking at.

The division of words into morphemes must not be confused with the division of words into SYLLABLES, which is a phonological division rather than a grammatical one. Some words of more than one syllable are single-morpheme words (*interest, nation, ticket, mother, finger, pocket*), while some words of only one syllable are made up of two morphemes (*rates, boys, things, tried, speaks*). Sometimes the phonological division into syllables does coincide with the grammatical division into morphemes (*backpack, blackbird, friendly*), but there are many words where it does not (*fingered, pockets, oysters*).

In Table 2.2 we analyse some examples of morphemes. Note that where a morpheme has a hyphen mark (-) before or after it, it means that the morpheme is a BOUND morpheme; that is, it cannot function by itself, but rather is attached to a root word to alter its status in some way, for instance to show tense as with *-ed* or to mark a plural noun as with *-s*.

Table 2.2: Division of words into morphemes

one morpheme	the	claim	rate	you	tell
	nation	interest	ticket	mother	finger
two morphemes	rates	=	rate + -s		
	oysters	=	oyster + -s		
	growing	=	grow + -ing		
	tried	=	try + -ed		
	backpack	=	back + pack		
	progressing	=	progress + -ing		
three morphemes	fingertips	=	finger + tip + -s		
	backpacker	=	back + pack + -er		
	unforgettable	=	un- + forget(t) + -able		

The word *progress* illustrates another interesting aspect of morphology (the study of morphemes). In Table 2.2 we have treated *progress* as a single morpheme (thus *progressing* as two morphemes), but someone with a knowledge of the Latin root of this word may very well want to call *progress* two morphemes because they ascribe meaning to the Latin suffix *pro-* and compare *progress* with other words like *congress*, *regress* and *egress*. The division of English words into morphemes is therefore not always absolute but often depends on our depth of historical linguistic knowledge. For most people *progress* will rightly be one morpheme, but for some it will equally rightly be two.

Clauses and their constituent parts

CLAUSE is one of those words that plays several different roles in our language. It is a technical term in the language of law and legal documents, for example:

> A new clause has been written into the contract.
> Clause 5(a) of Regulation 6 states that ...

It is also a technical term in linguistics and it is this sense that concerns us here.

Some of you will already have a fairly clear idea about what a clause is; others may have vague memories about adjectival clauses, noun clauses, adverbial clauses – even perhaps finite clauses – from excursions into grammar in the past. In the following chapters we hope to expand your knowledge of what a clause is and finetune whatever working definition you bring with you.

In all human languages so far studied, the clause is the fundamental meaning structure in our linguistic communication with each other. As anyone who has ever tried to learn another language will know only too well, a dictionary is not a sufficient resource on its own, as words alone are not enough. To communicate effectively we need to know something about how the syntax of the language works; in other words we have to be able to combine words into meaningful message structures, and the most fundamental message structure in any language – in terms of a message that has any sort of completeness about it – is a clause.

An understanding of what a clause is and how to know one when you see it, is essential for both understanding and exploring the workings of the English grammatical system. So we need to spend a little time looking at some clauses and testing our reactions to clause constituency – how would we break any one clause up into its discrete units or component parts. For this task we will use seven-year-old Josephine's text, which she wrote for a second class composition assignment. We will first of all break the text into clauses, and then, in Table 2.3, look more closely at some of the clauses to see what their constituent parts might be.

Text 2: Josephine's text

One day a monster came out of my hot water pipe. I was very frightened. I called my mum and she came and saw the Floogleboogy and ran outside. I wanted to make friends with it and give it a name and so I called it a Floogleboogy and that night it came to bed with me. And I found that a Floogleboogy snores very loud indeed and mum was too frightened to come and kiss me goodnight.

Table 2.3: Clauses from Josephine's text*

1	One day a monster came out of my hot water pipe.	9	and give it a name
2	I was very frightened.	10	and so I called it a Floogleboogy
3	I called my mum	11	and that night it came to bed with me.
4	and she came	12	And I found out
5	and saw the Floogleboogy	13	that a Floogleboogy snores very loud indeed
6	and ran outside.	14	and mum was too frightened to come and kiss me goodnight.
7	I wanted		
8	to make friends with it		

***Note on division into clauses**

You might not agree with this division of the text into clauses. As so often in language description, things are never black and white, and there are several possible 'right' answers here. For instance you might want to call clauses 7 and 8, *I wanted to make friends with it*, one clause not two. Or you might feel clause 14 is actually two clauses: *and mum was too frightened* and *to come and kiss me goodnight*. Then again, you might want *to come and kiss me goodnight* to be two clauses: *to come*; and *and kiss me goodnight*. We have made clause 14 one clause because we are treating *too frightened to come and kiss me goodnight* as a single constituent part of the clause in that it represents a description of what mum was. Compare: *Mum was happy*; *Mum was frightened*; *Mum was too frightened to come and kiss me goodnight*. Exploring such problem areas in grammatical description is one of the fun things about language studies, and one of the skills we hope you will gain from using this book.

The constituents of clauses in Josephine's text

In our analysis of Text 2, the following abbreviations are used to label the constituents of the clauses:

ng	=	nominal group
vg	=	verbal group
conj g	=	conjunction group
adv g	=	adverbial group
pp	=	prepositional phrase

Clause 1 is a complete sentence: recalling our rank scale, it is a one-clause, clause complex. It has four discrete units or constituents and these are labelled according to the class of the group or phrase.

One day	a monster	came	out of my hot water pipe
ng	ng	vg	pp

Clauses 2, 3 and 8 each have three constituents:

I	was	very frightened
ng	vg	ng

I	called	my mum
ng	vg	ng

to make	friends	with it
vg	ng	pp

You might feel that Clause 8 has only two constituents where the phrase *to make friends* acts as a verb, synonymous with *befriend*:

to make friends with	it

And if you disagreed with our division of Clauses 7 and 8 in Table 2.3, seeing them as one clause *I wanted to make friends with it*, then your clause has four constituents:

I	wanted to make	friends	with it

or three constituents:

I	wanted to make friends with	it

As you can see, the division of texts into clauses and clauses into their constituent parts is not always straightforward.

The last clause we will look at from Josephine's text is Clause 11. It appears to have six constituents:

and	that night	it	came	to bed	with me
conj g	ng	ng	vg	pp	pp

One of these constituents (*and*) is rather different to any of the others we have been looking at. Most of our clause constituents can be seen as expressions of our experience in terms of the things, events and happenings of our world, as well as the circumstances under which those events and happenings occur. The word *and*, however, is a conjunction and does not function as an expression of experience in terms of things and events and circumstances. In Clause 11 it is functioning as a linking device that allows us to express some kind of logical relationship *between* clauses rather than within one clause. For this reason we will leave such words out of our constituent analysis of clauses, but come back to them in Chapters 6 and 7.

As we have suggested, the clauses of English typically express our experience of the world in terms of things and events and the various circumstances that surround those events, but it is the event that is central to way we express our experience.

According to Halliday (1994: 106) 'Our most powerful impression of experience is that it consists of "goings-on" – happening, doing, sensing, meaning, and being and becoming'. These 'goings-on' are the events or processes of our experience, and expression of PROCESS or event is the fundamental constituent of a clause.

In traditional grammar terms, every clause must have a verb. In our functional model of grammar, the one obligatory constituent of a clause is the Process, expressed by a verbal group which is essentially realised by a nucleus or head word that belongs to the class verb. Remembering the principles of the rank scale, this verbal group expression of process may consist of one word, for example snores:

   A Floogleboogy <u>snores</u> very loud indeed

or several words, for example *might have been snoring*:

   The Floogleboogy <u>might have been snoring</u> all night

Some clauses will also have constituents that tell us who the PARTICIPANTS in the Process are, and under what CIRCUMSTANCE the process takes place.

Now it's time to test your own reactions to clause constituency. Try your hand on the following clauses. Don't worry too much about attaching labels to the constituent parts for the moment, but just look for what seem to be the natural groupings of words within the clause structures. To get you started we have underlined the process (verbal group) constituent:

   1   The furious child frantically <u>chased</u> our neighbour's cat up and down the street
   2   Pigs <u>might fly</u>
   3   <u>crawling</u> cautiously through the undergrowth
   4   <u>Do</u> you <u>want</u> some more coffee?
   5   <u>Stop</u>!
   6   <u>protected</u> from the wind on three sides ...

Remember that, according to our rank scale, a clause is made up of one or more groups or phrases. We could, of course, say about Clause 1 above that the clause comprises thirteen words, and that those words are thus the constituents of the clause. This is true but not very helpful. We need to look at the way the thirteen words are patterned into smaller groupings in the clause design, each grouping fulfilling a different function:

The furious child	frantically	chased	our neighbour's cat	up and down the street
ng	adv g	vg	ng	pp

We can test the validity of this constituent break down of the clause in a number of ways. Try changing the word order of the clause, presenting the same information while not changing any of the words. There are several possibilities and all involve changing the position of one or both of the following boxed constituents:

frantically		up and down the street

Two possibilities are:

> Frantically the furious child chased our neighbour's cat up and down the street
> Up and down the street the furious child chased our neighbour's cat frantically

If we move anything else around we either get a pattern that is not the norm for English:

> Chased the furious child our neighbour's cat frantically up and down the street

or we get a different message:

> Our neighbour's cat frantically chased the furious child up and down the street

unless we also make certain adjustments to two of the constituent groupings:

> Our neighbour's cat was chased frantically up and down the street by the furious child

A further simple test of clause constituent break down is to see what questions about the message are answered by the different constituents. So, in our example clause:

the furious child	answers the question *who did* the chasing?
frantically	tells us something about *how* the chasing was done.
our neighbour's cat	tells us *who* had the chasing *done to* it.
up and down the street	tells us *where* the chasing happened.

The rank scale and logical meanings

As we've pointed out, a clause complex consists of one or more clauses. When there is more than one clause, the two or more clauses are joined in some sort of logical relation. In Chapter 7 we look in a general way at patterns of clause combination but do not go into all the finer details of clause combinations as set out in Halliday's system (1994: Chapter 7). One of the general principles we do need to appreciate, however, is that sometimes the clauses will be of equal value, while at other times one clause will be dependent on another. Here students of traditional grammar will be remembering principal and subordinate clauses. The terminology preferred in this book is *independent* and *dependent* (see Chapter 7), but many of the principles you are familiar with will be the same.

Conjunctions (and some punctuation devices) express the logical relationships between clauses in a clause complex. For example, clauses joined by *and, but, or, that is,* or even a comma, colon, or semi-colon, are of equal value in the clause complex. But clauses beginning with *although, because, since, if* will always be dependent, even when they come at the beginning of the clause complex.

This notion of complexing, where two or more elements are joined in some sort of logical relationship, can also apply at lower ranks in the rank scale. At group level, two or more nominal groups can join to make a single clause constituent; two or more verbal groups to make a single clause constituent and so on. Here are some examples:

The lion and the unicorn	were fighting	for the crown
ng complex	vg	pp
ng 1 + ng 2		

The answer to the question 'Who were fighting?' is 'The lion and the unicorn', so the two nominal groups join together to make one nominal group complex as a single clause constituent.

The wolf	huffed and puffed
ng	vg complex
	vg 1 + vg 2

If we ask what the wolf did, the answer is *huffed and puffed* as one action, so the two verbal groups join together to make one verbal group complex as a single clause constituent.

Bill, my gardener,	is weeding	the rose garden
ng complex	vg	ng
ng 1 = ng 2		

If we ask *who* is weeding the rose garden, the complete answer is *Bill, my gardener,* so the two nominal groups join together to make one nominal group complex as a single clause constituent. This example is rather different from the previous two – here, instead of two different entities being added to make a group complex, the two parts of the nominal group are different ways of referring to the same entity. That is why we used + between the parts of the group complex in the first two examples, and = between the nominal groups in the last example.

In the following chapters you will learn more about the clause, its constituent elements and its three separate but simultaneous functions. In preparation for this, the last section of this chapter gives a general overview of the three basic functions of language discussed briefly in Chapter 1.

Functions of language

As we saw in Chapter 1, there are three broad functions of language that are central to the way the grammar works in the language system:

> 1   Language has a representational function – we use it to encode our experience of the world; it conveys a picture of reality. Thus it allows us to encode meanings of experience which realise field of discourse (EXPERIENTIAL MEANINGS).
>
> 2   Language has an interpersonal function – we use it to encode interaction and show how defensible we find our propositions. Thus it allows us to encode meanings of attitudes, interaction and relationships which realise tenor of discourse (INTERPERSONAL MEANINGS).
>
> 3   Language has a textual function – we use it to organise our experiential and interpersonal meanings into a linear and coherent whole. Thus, it allows us to encode meanings of text development which realise mode of discourse (TEXTUAL MEANINGS).

Notice that language encodes all three of these kinds of meanings simultaneously. If you say to someone:

The high school students put on a noisy protest.

you are simultaneously representing or describing something, interacting with someone (whoever you are talking to) by telling them something, and organising the linear flow of your message. Each of these aspects of your utterance is achieved through all the linguistic or grammatical options at your disposal. Firstly, you could have said, for instance:

The high school students protested noisily.

or

High school students organised a noisy protest.

and in each case you would have been saying something slightly different. You would have represented a slightly different reality. More on this in Chapter 3.

Secondly, you could have said, for instance:

The high school students put on a noisy protest, didn't they?

or

Did the high school students protest noisily?

in which case your interpersonal meaning would be different. You would be seeking confirmation or asking for information rather than telling or stating. For more on this see Chapter 4.

And thirdly, you could have said:

> A noisy protest was what the high school students organised.
> A noisy protest was organised by high school students.

In this case you have conveyed a different textual meaning by organising the message differently. These last possibilities could be the predicted version in certain contexts. The first might be your choice if the context had already included a discussion of certain groups organising some kind of gathering, and you wanted to emphasise what kind of gathering the students had organised. The second example is in fact the passive voice version of our previous example: *High school students organised a noisy protest*. This version allows you to thematise the protest rather than the protesters. In other words, the textual function has to do particularly with the flow of information and points of departure. More on this in Chapter 6.

Exercises

1. Give two or three English words to illustrate each of the traditional classes of words mentioned in this chapter: adjective, adverb, article, conjunction, noun, preposition, pronoun, verb. If you are uncertain of these terms, check their dictionary definitions again.

2. Find some examples of your own to illustrate the rank scale from clause complex to morpheme. First copy out your sentence (clause complex) then set out your rank scale like the example in Table 2.1.

3. Divide the following clauses into their constituent groups.
   a. Pigs might fly
   b. crawling cautiously through the undergrowth
   c. Do you want some more coffee?
   d. Stop
   e. protected from the wind on three sides …
   f. Next week the committee will announce the winner of the competition
   g. The three wise men of Gotham went to sea in a bowl.

Implications for language teachers

In contrast to thinking about grammar in terms of rules which *prescribe* the way language is structured, in this chapter we have been asked to think about grammar as a way of *describing* regular language *patterns* and the *functions* these patterns achieve.

Some teachers might be uncomfortable with letting go of the idea of grammar rules. Many of their teaching techniques may focus on grammar rules which prescribe 'correct' language use. Other teachers may be equally surprised that they are being asked to think about grammar at all! Their teaching techniques may focus on immersing their students in language as communication. They may believe that learning grammar will prevent their students from using the language fluently and communicatively.

The material in this chapter is of most help to teachers who would like to find a middle way between teaching prescriptive grammar rules and teaching no grammar at all. If teachers think about grammar as a way of describing language in terms of pattern and function, they are inclined to develop teaching techniques that draw students' attention to the regular grammatical patterns which make language use *functional* in its context.

What do teachers want for their students?

Teachers who focus on rules and accuracy want their students to reach an accepted and valued *standard* of language use. This approach, however, may obscure the variation which occurs in real-life language use; it might even imply that some variations are sub-standard. It may also obscure the fact that every language learner progresses via an *interlanguage* towards increasingly effective use of the target language, and that the 'errors' learners make during this process reveal important information about how language learning progresses.

Teachers who focus on communication and avoid teaching grammar want their students to be able to communicate with ease without being burdened with rules and standards. This approach, however, may lead to students being stranded in their interlanguage. They may not be able to use the varieties of language they need, for example, to apply successfully for employment, to write about technical or abstract concepts, to argue their case effectively or to negotiate a delicate personal or business dilemma.

Most language teachers want their students to be both accurate and fluent users of English, but they are faced with an educational paradox. If they demand students use English on the basis of the prescribed rules of traditional grammar, students may be unaware of the variety of language use available to them, and teachers may be unaware of the actual progress students are making with authentic language use. If, on the other hand, teachers expect students to use English without any knowledge of English grammar, students may not have the knowledge they need to use language in a variety of ways and this may restrict the progress students are able to make.

What we have learned in this chapter suggests that one way of resolving this paradox might be to:

- think about grammar in terms of pattern and function
- work with the grammar of whole texts in context.

What do teachers need to know in order to teach about the grammar of whole texts?

In this chapter the traditional view of grammar has been extended in the following four ways:

1   A set of functional labels builds on and enriches the traditional set of class labels.

2   A rank scale allows for a more detailed exploration of clause structure.

3   The constituent parts of the clause can be described in terms of the way each contributes functionally to the message of the clause.

4   The three meanings made simultaneously in clauses are revealed by exploring clause constituents and the way these constituents are organised to reflect the context of situation.

Now let's look at each of these from the perspective of language education. Firstly, we are told not to abandon what we already know about grammar – for example the familiar traditional grammar labels for the parts of speech. These labels describe elements of language in terms of their *class* or, in other words, in terms of what they *are*.

We are shown, however, that identifying parts of speech alone is not enough if we are to describe consistently and fully the grammatical work of words and structures. So next we are shown how these terms can be built on and enriched with a second set of labels which identify what a word *does*; that is, its *function*. This second set of labels extends the metalanguage available to those who teach and study language, allowing them to talk about both the forms that language elements take and the work that language elements do.

Next we are introduced to a series of grammatical units in a *rank scale*. This scale opens up the structure of the English clause allowing us to examine comprehensively and systematically how the parts of a clause are organised. At each rank, functional linguists are able to describe how words are organised into patterns in order to achieve the different functions within clauses. These descriptions reveal the potential for meaning-making available at each grammatical rank.

Using knowledge based on the rank scale, students can structure language patterns at all levels (morpheme, word, group, phrase, clause and clause complex) and strategically organise and integrate all these patterns as they structure clauses. A particularly useful by-product of the rank scale is that students no longer need to talk about spoken language in terms of the sentence – a unit which has never been very compatible with spoken language.

As well as thinking about the clause in terms of its ranks, we are asked to think about the clause as 'a meaningful message structure' with each constituent part playing a functional role in the message. This idea suggests that instead of giving students the rule *Every clause must have a verb*, teachers might more usefully show students how an event takes the central role in constructing the message of a clause. From this starting point, classroom activities can be designed in which students explore:

- how to break a clause down into its parts
- the structure and functional role of each clause part
- how the parts combine into clauses around the central event
- how clauses are combined into clause complexes.

These activities can be designed using the language of real-life texts that are relevant to the students' learning goals.

We are shown how to test whether we have effectively broken a clause down into its constituent parts. This is done by working out the question each part answers about the message. Students can use these questions to guide them as they explore the structures and meanings found in different types of clauses. This idea will be explored further in Chapter 3.

Finally, we are shown how every clause makes three kinds of meanings at once, depending on the constituent parts we choose and how we choose to organise these parts. Every clause (1) represents experience, (2) interacts with someone and (3) organises the message so it makes sense. We know from Chapter 1 that these three kinds of meaning systematically reflect the context of situation. If students know how to choose and structure the parts of a clause to make each of these kinds of meaning effectively and functionally, they will control the full meaning potential of the English clause in whole texts across a variety of contexts.

In the following chapters we will be introduced to different ways of exploring the structure of the English clause to reveal how each of the three kinds of meanings is made in the clause. In addition we will explore the potential different types of clause constituents have for making each of these kinds of meaning.

Further reading

Chapter 2 of *The functional analysis of English: A Hallidayan approach* (Bloor and Bloor 1995) explores class and function labels in some detail.

de Silva Joyce and Burns (1999) in *Focus on grammar* answer the question 'What is grammar?' In Chapter 1 and in Chapter 2 they explore different views of grammar and provide an historical account of the way our views about language standards have changed over time. In Chapter 3 they review the different ways grammar has been used in language teaching.

Exercises for language teachers

1 How would you describe your approach to the teaching of grammar at present?
   For example:
   • You are concerned with developing accurate, standard English based on fixed
     grammatical rules.
   • You are concerned with developing fluent communication rather than grammatical
     accuracy.
   • You try to combine teaching about grammar and structural accuracy with teaching which
     develops fluent communication.

2 How might the ideas about language presented in this chapter influence your approach to
   the teaching of grammar? Use the following text and the questions that follow to explore this
   question.

   There's this girl in my class …
   she tried to do a backward roll
   and she um like her neck clicked or something
   and um she was taken to hospital in an ambulance
   and I had to write down what happened
   because I was in her group
   I've done that before
   and it doesn't hurt that much.
   I think
   she's over-reacting just a bit

   a. Break the clauses in this text into their constituent parts.
   b. Identify whether each constituent is a word, group or phrase.
   c. What question about the message of the clause does each of these constituents
       answer?
   d. Design an activity based on a whole text which would reveal to students how clauses,
       phrases and groups are structured. You can use one of the texts in Chapter 1 or you
       can use a text that is relevant to your students (choose a short text).
   e. Design an activity that would teach students how to work out the questions about the
       message each of the constituents of a clause answers.

3

How speakers represent the world: Exploring experiential meanings

Introducing ...
- The experiential function

Discussing ...
- Implications for language teaching

From Chapter 1

Language has an *experiential* function, so it has *experiential* meanings.
We use the experiential function to encode our experience of the world; that is, we use it
to convey a picture of reality

A landscape of human experience

In Chapters 1 and 2 we introduced you to the notion that language simultaneously performs three functions (experiential, interpersonal and textual). In this chapter we are concerned with the EXPERIENTIAL function; Chapters 4 and 5 will deal with the INTERPERSONAL function, and Chapter 6 with the TEXTUAL function.

Our language builds up pictures of reality – in terms of the things (which as a general term covers people and places as well as concrete and abstract things) and events and circumstances – that form the landscape of our human experience. As we indicated in Chapter 2, these three general categories of human experience (things, events and circumstances) typically occur together in CLAUSES, with the pivotal element of the clause being the expression of event, or PROCESS. In any gathering of functional grammarians, someone is sure to pose the question: *Who does what to whom under what circumstances?* It has become something of a standing joke, but is a neat and brief way of explaining the experiential function of language.

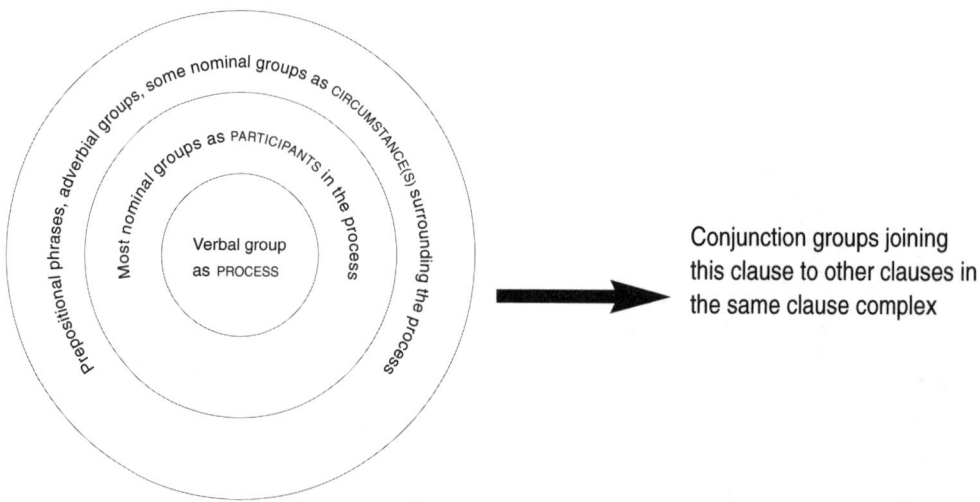

Figure 3.1: Patterns of experience in the clause

Figure 3.1 may be helpful in understanding the experiential function of language. In this diagram PROCESS, realised by a verbal group, is shown as the centre of a clausal solar system. PARTICIPANTS, realised by nominal groups or preposition phrases, revolve around the Process and can interact with it through a variety of PARTICIPANT ROLES. Further out are the CIRCUMSTANCES of human experience (the whys and whens and wherefores), realised by adverbial groups, prepositional phrases and, occasionally, by nominal groups functioning as if they were adverbs. At the outer edge we find the CONJUNCTION GROUPS, not so much a part of this solar system as linking mechanisms ready to help join the various systems (clauses) together in a variety of logical relationships.

The three concentric rings in Figure 3.1 represent the part of the language system that Chapter 3 will explore; the outer edge – the linkages between clauses – will be addressed in Chapter 7.

Metalanguage for discussing language as experience

In describing the experiential function of language we must first have a set of terms to show how the clause can be broken down into three functional constituents: PARTICIPANT, PROCESS and CIRCUMSTANCE. The Participant constituent can be further described in terms of various participant roles such as ACTOR, AGENT, GOAL, CARRIER, SAYER. The Process divides into three basic process types: MATERIAL, RELATIONAL and PROJECTING. There is also a metalanguage that allows us to show finer functional distinctions within the Circumstance constituent.

Other grammatical terms you will find in this and subsequent chapters include labels for the groups and phrases of our rank scale: NOMINAL GROUP, VERBAL GROUP, ADVERBIAL GROUP and PREPOSITIONAL PHRASE. As we look more closely at the structure of the groups and phrases, various function labels such as EPITHET, CLASSIFIER, THING and EVENT will also be introduced.

At this stage we should make clear an important point about the terminology that we will be introducing in the following chapters. You will notice throughout that some terms are always spelled with an initial capital (Actor, Goal, Epithet, Subject, Finite), while others are not capitalised unless they are at the beginning of a sentence (clause, clause complex, declarative mood, embedded clause). The convention we are following is to capitalise function labels and to use lower case for other labels and for the more general grammatical terminology. There are some terms that may be used either as function labels or as more general terms, in which case the presence or absence of an initial capital will indicate the difference (P/participant, P/process, T/thing, E/event). For further reading on labelling as well as other issues arising from a movement from more traditional descriptions of grammar towards the systemic functional approach, see Halliday (1994: Chapter 2).

Packaging experience

It is important to realise that the way we express ourselves is not rigidly determined by an external reality or by universal rules of logic. Suppose, for instance, that you want to draw someone's attention to the fact that a certain shop closes at six o'clock. You might say:

The shop	closes	at six
Participant	Process	Circumstance

But you don't have to present closing as a Process; you could say:

The shop's closing time	is	six
Participant	Process	Participant

Imagine looking at a view or a landscape and wanting to describe what you see. You might want to talk about the sun setting. You could express the setting as a Process:

The sun	is setting
Participant	Process

However, you could also talk about the sun setting in terms of the sun's location. In other words, you could express the setting as Circumstance:

The sun	is	on the horizon
Participant	Process	Circumstance

You might want to treat this event as a thing (Participant) rather than as a Process, as in:

The sunset	's blinding	me
Participant	Process	Participant

It would be difficult to argue that any one way of talking about the sunset is more objective or correct than any other. In fact, given what we know about the movement of the earth relative to the sun, it is just as easy to argue that all of them are inaccurate, as it is to argue that all of them are legitimate (in terms of our perception). Similarly, loving or hating can be things or events. We cannot appeal to any natural criterion to determine that for us as we see in the following examples.

Participant	Process	Participant
The dog	must have hated	that storm
All the world	loves	a lover
Hate	is	a destructive passion
Love	is	a many-splendoured thing
Our greatest need	is	love

Clause constituency in the experiential function

Most English clauses have a constituent structure that can be described functionally in terms of PARTICIPANT, PROCESS and CIRCUMSTANCE, with Process being the essential ingredient. Thus the following clauses all have the structure Participant + Process:

Participant	Process
The chair	collapsed
The water	evaporated
The horse	bolted
He	sneezed
The President	arrived
The truth	will be revealed

Some clauses have the structure Participant + Process + Participant:

Participant	Process	Participant
The water	damaged	the carpet
The horse	kicked	him
She	remembered	his name
The Premier	congratulated	them
Your expression of anger	must have convinced	all the waverers

Some clauses have the structure Participant + Process + Circumstance:

Participant	Process	Circumstance
The chair	collapsed	under him
The President	arrived	by train
The judicial system	works	slowly
Winter	might come	as early as last year

Some clauses have the structure Participant + Process + Participant + Circumstance:

Participant	Process	Participant	Circumstance
The dog	bit	him	on the ankle
I	thanked	her	warmly

Some clauses have only one constituent, the obligatory Process. Reminding ourselves about the rank scale, we find something interesting about the following examples. In each case we have a *clause complex* made up of one *clause*, which in turn is made up of one *group*, which consists of one *word*, which comprises one *morpheme*:

Process
Stop!
Hide!
Run!

Some clauses project another clause:

Participant	Process	Projected clause
She	remembered	that it was his birthday
Chris	said	the VCR wasn't working

Participant	Process	Participant	Projected clause
The manager	told	the staff	that the company was now making a profit

But all of this needs a much closer analysis. We will begin by looking at Process.

Clauses as processes

Processes in English, as we suggested in Chapter 2, are expressions of happening, doing, being, saying and thinking. A Process is realised in the grammar by means of a verbal group, which is either one word, belonging to the class verb, or a group of words with a class verb word as the head or nucleus of the group. Thus the words in the box below are all verbal groups with the class verb word *jump* as head. But more about this later.

Verbal groups with *jump* as head

```
jump
will jump
can jump
ought to jump
might be about to jump
```

In the lists of Processes, Participants and Circumstances on the previous two pages, we have shown that verbal groups realise processes in experiential meanings. Perhaps, like us, you had a primary school teacher who described verbs as *doing words*. These good people were only partly right. If we look at the lists more closely, we can see that not all processes encode *doing*. Rather, they fall into three basic process types (although they can properly be subdivided into more and more subtypes).

1. We could begin the division into three groups by recognising that some verbs are indeed, *doing* words and describe actions and happenings in the outside, material world. A second group can be thought of as projecting processes and might be described as
2. *thinking, feeling* or *saying* words. These words are more to do with the inner world of cognition, perception, emotion and desire and have the potential for projecting our inner world as thought or speech so that it can be apprehended by others. A third
3. group of verbs can be described simply as *being* words.

The first two groups, the doing processes and projecting processes, can be subdivided in the following ways:

The doing verbs can be subdivided into:

1   Processes like *arrived, collapsed, works, bolted,* and *bit* that encode experiences in the external, material world. These are to do with doing and happening and are known as MATERIAL processes.

2   Processes like *sneezed, watched, sang* that encode physiological or psychological behaviour (often the doing equivalent of a mental or even a verbal process). They lie somewhere between material and mental or verbal processes and are known as BEHAVIOURAL processes.

The projecting verbs can be subdivided into:

1   Processes like *enjoyed, remembered* and *overheard* that encode experiences in the inner world of consciousness. These are to do with thinking, wanting, perceiving and emoting and are known as MENTAL processes and, as we have seen, they have the potential to project what is known, remembered or overheard as direct or indirect thoughts. Alternatively, they may use an appropriate nominal group to sum up what is thought or perceived or wanted or liked.

2   Processes like *told* and *said* that encode the experiences of bringing the inner world outside by speaking. These are to do with saying and asking, and are known as VERBAL processes. Like mental processes they have the potential to project the words of the speaker in direct or indirect speech, or they may use an appropriate nominal group to sum up what has been said.

The last group, the being verbs, can first be subdivided into:

1   Processes like *are, was, were,* the function of which is to set up the existence of a sole Participant. These processes are almost always preceded by *there.* They are known as EXISTENTIAL processes.

2   Processes like *are, was, were, seemed, have, became, felt, belongs to,* the function of which is to encode relationships of being and having between two Participants. This group, known as RELATIONAL processes, has to do with the attributes of class membership or with specific identity.

These relational processes can then be further subdivided. Those whose function is to ascribe an attribute are known as RELATIONAL ATTRIBUTIVE processes and those whose function is to identify are known as RELATIONAL IDENTIFYING processes.

The differences among process types have consequences in the wording of clauses. For example, material processes generally distinguish between what is happening now and what is habitual:

He is building a house (<u>at present</u>)
He builds houses (<u>for a living</u>)

But this distinction is not made with all process types. For example, it is usual to say:

I don't believe you

and not:

I am not believing you

The differences among the different process types may also result from the way a particular verb is functioning in a particular clause. The English verb *feel*, for example, can function as a material, a mental or a relational process depending on its relationship with the other elements in the clause or clause complex:

I <u>felt</u> the wood and decided it needed more sanding	material process (doing)
I <u>felt</u> that I was at a crossroads in my life	mental process (thinking)
I <u>felt</u> tired	relational process (a kind of being)

This draws our attention to a point that can not be stressed too strongly: that, rather than thinking of particular verbs as always giving expression to one process type, we should think about how a particular verb is functioning in its context.

Each process type has its own set of participant roles. This means that once the process type has been identified, the function labels for the participant roles fall into place easily. Moreover, the function labels for participants in each process are fairly transparent: when the process is material, the Doer is known as Actor, when mental, the Doer is Senser, when verbal, the Doer is Sayer, and, when behavioural, the Doer is Behaver. We will now look at each process type and its participant roles in more detail.

Process types and participant roles

Material processes

Material processes construe doing; they answer the question 'What did X do?' or 'What happened?' Potential participant roles are: ACTOR (or Doer of the process), a GOAL (or Thing affected by the process), a RANGE (or Thing unaffected by the process), a BENEFICIARY of the process.

Material processes with Actor as the sole participant

Joan	arrived
Actor	Process: material

They	ate	at noon
Actor	Process: material	Circumstance

The army	retreated
Actor	Process: material

Material processes with an Actor and a Goal:

Theo	caught	the cricket ball
Actor	Process: material	Goal

Mother	made		a fruit cake
Actor	Process: material		Goal

The dog	was chasing		the cat
Actor	Process: material		Goal

In English, material processes with a Goal can be either active, as shown above, or passive as shown below:

The cricket ball	was caught		by Theo
Goal	Process: material		Actor

The fruit cake	was made		by mother
Goal	Process: material		Actor

The cat	was being chased		by the dog
Goal	Process: material		Actor

The passive construction presents the Actor and Goal in reverse order to the active construction. The Actor of a passive clause is often described as the Agent rather than the Actor. The passive construction allows the possibility of omitting the Agent altogether (the so-called 'agentless passive'):

The cricket ball	was caught
Goal	Process: material

The fruit cake	was made
Goal	Process: material

An error	has been made
Goal	Process: material

Agentless passives are one way in English of 'losing' the Actor of a process. Whenever you encounter one, it is worthwhile asking just why the Actor has been omitted – is it because nobody knows who did the action, or because everybody knows, or because it is unimportant, or because the writer is purposely not mentioning it for some reason? For example, if you saw a headline 'Man was murdered' (or more likely just 'Man murdered'), it could be that no-one knows yet who did the murder. And if, on the following day, the headline reads 'Suspect arrested', there is no need for the writer to mention who did the arresting because everybody knows that it was done by the police. But if the next headline reads 'Suspect shot', it might be because the writer does not want to draw your attention to who did it. It's always worth asking with an agentless passive!

Material processes with Beneficiary

I	posted	a letter	to a friend
Actor	Process: material	Goal	Beneficiary: Recipient

I	posted	my friend	a letter
Actor	Process: material	Beneficiary: Recipient	Goal

The architect	built	a house	for his mother
Actor	Process: material	Goal	Beneficiary: Client

The participant role Beneficiary may be subdivided into Recipient, the one who receives the outcome of the process, or Client, the one for whom the process is done. All delicate distinctions make the roles more transparent but Client is such a rare Participant role that you may find that Beneficiary is sufficient.

Material processes with Range

Jackson	is climbing	the fence
Actor	Process: material	Range

She	did	some research
Actor	Process: material	Range

These two examples of the participant role Range show that it can be something separate from and unaffected by the process or, as in the second example, it can be more like an extension of the process. In fact, in the second example the verb is fairly empty and gets the bulk of its experiential meaning from the Range.

Behavioural processes

Behavioural processes construe physiological or psychological behaviour. The main participant, the BEHAVER, is generally a conscious being and, if it is not, the clause is considered to be personification. These processes are often the doing version of a mental or even a verbal process. Sometimes there is a Range-like Participant known as BEHAVIOUR, which extends the process; sometimes, especially with relation to those most closely related to mental processes, the Range is a separate entity somewhat like a Phenomenon.

Behavioural processes with a conscious Behaver and with personification

The woman	laughed
Behaver	Process: behavioural

The cat	sleeps	on the back veranda
Behaver	Process: behavioural	Circumstance

Phyllis and Jim	watched	the sunset
Behaver	Process: behavioural	Range

Betty	cried	bitter tears
Behaver	Process: behavioural	Behaviour

The volcano	slept
Behaver	Process: behavioural (personification)

Mental processes

Mental processes encode the inner world of cognition, perception, inclination or liking/disliking (known as *affect*). Potential participant roles are: SENSER (or Doer of the process), which must be realised by a human or at least conscious participant; and a PHENOMENON, realised by a nominal group or embedded clause summing up what is thought, wanted, perceived or liked/disliked. Alternatively, the mental process may project a separate ranked clause. All of these possibilities are illustrated below. Note that where a ranked clause is projected, the clause containing the mental process will be the projecting clause and the other will be a projected clause and can contain any process type.

Mental process with nominal group

In this set the more delicate divisions of mental processes are identified. There may be times when you choose to show this delicacy and others when you simply identify the process as mental:

Annie	knows	the answer
Senser	Process: mental: cognition	Phenomenon

Jessica	likes	icecream
Senser	Process: mental: affect	Phenomenon

Austin	hears	the ice cream truck
Senser	Process: mental: perception	Phenomenon

Henry	wants	an icecream
Senser	Process: mental: inclination	Phenomenon

Mental process with embedded clause

Annie	knows	[[what she wants]]
Senser	Process: mental: cognition	Phenomenon

Austin	hears	[[the ice cream truck coming]]
Senser	Process: mental: perception	Phenomenon

The double square brackets mark a so-called 'embedded clause'. See pages 72ff for further explanation.

Mental process projecting direct thought as a separate clause

'Why am I tired?'	she	wondered
Projected clause	Senser	Process: mental

I	thought,	'He looks ridiculous.'
Senser	Process: mental	Projected clause

She	wondered,	'Why am I tired?'
Senser	Process: mental	Projected clause

Mental process projecting indirect thought as a separate clause

She	wondered	why she was tired
Senser	Process: mental	Projected clause

Hanne	wanted	Jim to go
Senser	Process: mental	Projected clause

Verbal processes

Verbal processes construe saying. Potential participant roles are: SAYER (Doer of the process), RECEIVER (addressee of the speech), TARGET (the participant which is the object of the talk), and VERBIAGE (which corresponds to Phenomenon in a mental process and sums up what is said in one nominal group or embedded clause). A verbal process will most often project what is said in a separate ranked clause. All of these possibilities are illustrated below. Note that where a ranked clause is projected, the clause containing the verbal process will be the projecting clause and the other clause will be a projected clause and can contain any process type.

Verbal process with nominal group

She	said	her piece
Sayer	Process: verbal	Verbiage

Verbal process with embedded clause

Chris	said	[[what he had to say]]
Sayer	Process: verbal	Verbiage

Verbal process projecting direct speech as a separate clause

She	said	'I am tired.'
Sayer	Process: verbal	Projected clause

They	asked,	'Where are you going?'
Sayer	Process: verbal	Projected clause

Verbal process projecting indirect speech as a separate clause

She	said	that she was tired
Sayer	Process: verbal	Projected clause

I	asked	where he was going
Sayer	Process: verbal	Projected clause

Verbal process with Receiver

Isabella	told	the secret	to her best friend
Sayer	Process: verbal	Verbiage	Receiver

Verbal process with Target

Marcus Antonius	praised	Julius Caesar
Sayer	Process: verbal	Target

It's probably worth mentioning that this last example is controversial; some linguists prefer to think of verbs like 'praise' and 'criticise' as behavioural processes.

Existential processes

Because the function of existential processes is to construe being as simple existence, there is only one participant known as the EXISTENT. Existential processes are typically preceded by *there* and occur at the beginning of a text or where the text is moving into a new phase:

Once upon a time there	were	four children
	Process: existential	Existent

There	's	a strange smell
	Process: existential	Existent

There	's been	a bit of a problem
	Process: existential	Existent

There	are	several difficulties
	Process: existential	Existent

Relational processes

The main characteristic of relational processes is that they relate a participant to its identity or description. Thus, within relational processes there are two main types: RELATIONAL ATTRIBUTIVE, which relate a participant to its general characteristics or description; and RELATIONAL IDENTIFYING, which relate a participant to its identity, role or meaning.

In relational attributive clauses the participant carrying the characteristics or attributes is known as the CARRIER and the characteristic is known as ATTRIBUTE. The Attribute is typically an indefinite nominal group or a nominal group with an adjective as Head. Besides the different forms of the verb *be*, other verbs which relate a Carrier to an Attribute may include *seem, look, appear, remain, feel*:

Their office	is	sumptuous
Carrier	Process: relational	Attribute

That bookcase	looks	very heavy
Carrier	Process: relational	Attribute

That bookcase	seems	a fine piece of furniture
Carrier	Process: relational	Attribute

In contrast to attributive processes, relational identifying processes set up an identity, role or meaning. They have been called 'the engine room' or 'power-house' of semiosis. In fact they perform two separate functions and have two sets of labels.

The first function is the one which provides a new identity. If someone asks *Which is my office?* they are looking for the identity of their office, and the question and answer contain an identifying process. Whether it comes first or last in the clause, the nominal group about which the question is asked is labelled IDENTIFIED and the new identity, the answer to the question, is the IDENTIFIER. These function labels are often abbreviated to IFD and IFR:

Your office	is	the room on the left
Identified (IFD)	Process: relational identifying	Identifier (IFR)

The room on the right	is	your office
Identifier (IFR)	Process: relational identifying	Identified (IFD)

The second function of relational identifying processes accounts for the title 'power house of semiosis'. This function allows us to take any form and identify its function and, conversely, to take any function and identify its form. In other words, we take some token and give it a new value, or some value and give its token. Not surprisingly, the participant roles for this function are: TOKEN, the form; and VALUE, the function. It is the function by which we give new Value to a known Token or supply a Token for a known Value.

If all this sounds rather abstract, there is a foolproof way for sorting out which Participant is Token and which is Value. Although the most common relational process is *be*, which has no passive voice, other verbs that can relate a Token and its Value include *mean, spell, express, play, act, show* and *represent*, which do have passive forms. When one of these verbs is in the active voice, the order of the clause will be Token, process, Value; but when the verb is passive, the order is Value, process, Token. In contrast to relational attributive processes, the Participants in identifying processes are typically definite or filled by a proper noun. Compare these examples:

John	is	a leader
Carrier	Process: relational attributive	Attribute

John	is	the leader
Token	Process: relational identifying	Value

Another difference between attributive and identifying processes will become clearer when we reach the discussion of interpersonal meanings but it won't hurt to mention it now. No matter what order an attributive clause takes, the Carrier is always the Subject. But in identifying clauses, the first participant is the Subject whether it is Identified or Identifier, Token or Value.

The following are some examples of Token and Value where both participant roles are filled by nominal groups.

The room on the right   is   your office
                               (represents)

Token	Process: relational identifying	Value

Your office   is   the room on the right
                               (is represented by)

Value	Process: relational identifying	Token

Susanna   acts   the heroine of the story
                               (represents)

Token	Process: relational identifying	Value

The heroine of the story   is acted by   Susanna
                               (is represented by)

Value	Process: relational identifying	Token

D-O-G   spells   dog
                 (represents)

Token	Process: relational identifying	Value

Dog   is spelt   D-O-G
                 (is represented by)

Value	Process: relational identifying	Token

A red light   means   'stop'
                 (signifies)
                 (represents)

Token	Process: relational identifying	Value

'Stop'   is signified by   a red light
                 (is represented by)

Value	Process: relational identifying	Token

The analysis into Token and Value sits alongside the analysis into Identified and Identifier. This double analysis is shown below for the answer to the question *Which is my office?*

The room on the right	is (represents)		your office
Token IFR	Process: relational identifying		Value IFD

Your office	is (is represented by)		the room on the right
Value IFD	Process: relational identifying		Token IFR

There is one more point to mention concerning relational identifying processes, namely that the participant roles may be filled by embedded (rankshifted) clauses. We don't expect you to know what these are yet but they'll be discussed later in this chapter and in Chapter 7. Here is an example with embedded clause enclosed in double square brackets:

[[What I really want]]	is (is represented by)		a good cup of tea
Value	Process: relational identifying		Token

There is more to relational processes than we have discussed so far. The relationships in our set of examples belong to the set of relational processes known as *intensive*, but there are other sets known as *circumstantial* and *possessive*. All we will do here is give one example of relational attributive circumstantial, relational identifying circumstantial, relational attributive possessive, and relational identifying possessive processes. For further examples and discussion of relational processes you may like to read Halliday (1994: 119–138). While looking at the following examples, bear in mind that we can distinguish attributive from identifying processes because the former are about a general category or class and the latter are definite.

Relational attributive circumstantial

The house	was	on a hill
Carrier	Process: relational attributive circumstantial	Attribute: Circumstance

Relational identifying circumstantial

My favourite place	is	at the beach
Value	Process: relational identifying circumstantial	Token

Relational attributive possessive

Maya	has	a beautiful dog
Carrier: Possessor	Process: relational: attributive: possessive	Attribute: Possessed

Relational identifying possessive

That Golden Retriever	is owned by	Gordon
Value: Possessed	Process: relational: identifying: identifying: possessive	Token: Possessor

Table 3.1 provides a summary of the process types and participant roles we have been discussing in this chapter.

Table 3.1 Summary of process types and participant roles

Process type	Domain	Restrictions	Participants
Material *Function:* to construe the material world of doing	outside activities DOING something	none ANYONE/THING can do	Actor = doer Goal = affected Range = not affected Beneficiary = to/for
Behavioural *Function:* to construe conscious behaviour	physiological and psychological behaviour: the doing version of mental or verbal processes	needs consciousness	Behaver = doer Behaviour/Range = done
Mental *Function:* to construe and may project the inner world of consciousness	inside activities thinking, knowing, liking wanting, perceiving	needs consciousness and human characteristics	Senser = doer Phenomenon = thing known, liked/disliked, wanted, perceived

Table 3.1 (continued)

Process type	Domain	Restrictions	Participants
Verbal *Function:* to construe saying	bringing the inside outside: saying something	none anyone/thing can say NB: inanimate saying is close to identifying	Sayer = doer Verbiage = said Receiver = said to Target = said about
Existential *Function:* to construe existence	introduce existence of new Participants	none	Existent
Relational Attributive *Function:* to construe relationships of description	to characterise or assign membership to a class	none	Carrier = thing described Attribute = description
Relational Identifying *Function:* to construe relationships of identification and equation	to decode known meanings and encode new meanings	none	Identified = that which is to be identified Identifier = the new identity Token = form Value = function or role Token represents Value Value is represented by Token

Circumstances

Returning to Figure 3.1 at the beginning of this chapter, we see that a process is at the centre of the world of experience in the orbital diagram. Surrounding that process is an inner orbit of participant roles that answer the questions *Who? Which? What? To whom? For whom?* about the process. This may give the audience sufficient information for some speakers' or writers' purposes, but others may want to fill in more details by telling the audience *where*, or *when* or *how* or *why* or *with whom* or *as what* the process occurred. Sometimes speakers/writers will provide this information in a separate clause or clauses. But very often such circumstantial information is within the clause itself, using a prepositional phrase, an adverbial group, or even a nominal group. Any piece of circumstantial information about the process within its own clause is called a CIRCUMSTANCE.

As we have already said, Circumstances function to illuminate the process in some way. They may, among other things, locate the Process in time or space, suggest how the Process occurs, or offer information about the cause of the Process:

Thing	**Event**	**Circumstance**
The team	practised	in the morning
The Premier	arrived	at the end of the meeting
My mother-in-law	lives	in Perth
Harry	was walking	along the road
The child	was sleeping	soundly
She	signed	with a gold pen
Claudia	plays	brilliantly
My father	suffers	from chronic lower back pain
I	had to sing	for my supper

Of course, a message can contain more than one Circumstance:

Participant	**Process**	**Circumstance**	**Circumstance**
Charles	sings	every week	in a choral group
The Premier	arrived	at ten	in a rented limousine

And Circumstances are rather more mobile than Participants and Processes in English. Compare the positions of *every weekend* and *suddenly* in the following examples:

She works at the service station every weekend
She works every weekend at the service station
Every weekend she works at the service station

Suddenly the driver braked
The driver suddenly braked
The driver braked suddenly

This mobility can be used for specific purposes that will be dealt with more fully when we look at the textual function of language in Chapter 6.

Once you have recognised a Circumstance, you may want to use its proper function label or you may prefer to label it according to the question it answers. In either case what we are always interested in are the types of Circumstance used in a text and how they help us to understand the purpose of a text. You may like to consider what

Circumstances you would expect to find in a biography, a car manual or a travel guide. Table 3.2 lists the type of questions different Circumstances answer about a process and gives examples for each.

Table 3.2 Examples of questions answered by different Circumstances

Type of Circumstance	Answers the question	Examples
EXTENT	How long? How far? How many times?	(for) two hours (for)two miles five times a week
LOCATION	Where? When?	in the yard after dinner
CONTINGENCY	If what?	in case of rain in spite of rain in the absence of fine weather
CAUSE	Why? What for?	because of the rain for a rest
ACCOMPANIMENT	With whom? And who else? But not who?	with a friend as well as Henry instead of Michael
MATTER	What about?	about suffering
ROLE	What as?	as a clown
MANNER means quality comparison	How? What with? How? What like?	by car with a stick quietly like a trooper
ANGLE	According to whom?	to Mary according to Luke

The structure of Participants, Processes and Circumstances

We have seen how clauses as expressions of the experiential function of language are combinations of smaller experiential groups patterned to signify *who did what to whom under what circumstances*. The constituent groups of the clause may be expressed by one word or may themselves have a complex internal structure (whether one word or several words, they are called groups). Thus, our experience is structured by our language into sequences of manageable bundles, each with a distinct outline.

> The Participants in a process are realised in the grammar by
> NOMINAL GROUPS
> (and sometimes by PREPOSITIONAL PHRASES or EMBEDDED CLAUSES)
>
> the Processes themselves by
> VERBAL GROUPS
>
> the Circumstances by
> ADVERBIAL GROUPS or PREPOSITIONAL PHRASES
> (and sometimes by NOMINAL GROUPS)

Participants

Let us now explore what might seem the most straightforward of our three models of experience, namely the notion of a PARTICIPANT.

A participant can be a person, a place or an object (this is the notion of 'thingness'), and in the grammar of a clause the participant is most commonly realised by a NOMINAL GROUP. At the nucleus of the nominal group structure is the word that most generally represents the thingness concept that is being talked about, typically a noun or pronoun. We call this nucleus the HEAD of the nominal group; that is the THING element in the nominal group structure.

Sometimes this single word is all that is needed to signify the concept under discussion, for example when we say 'trees are beautiful' or 'beer tastes bitter'. But we often want to be specific in some way, for example by pinning down some trees as 'those trees' or by qualifying them as 'those trees on the hill'. So the Thing may stand alone or be preceded and/or followed by other words in the group which modify it in some way. In other words, we can have premodification before the Thing and postmodification after it. The whole bundle forms the experiential meaning structure which we call the nominal group.

Premodification

<table>
<tr>
<td>1</td>
<td colspan="2">DEICTICS which point to, or in some way select, the noun functioning as Thing.</td>
</tr>
<tr>
<td></td>
<td>*Deictics include:*</td>
<td>*for example:*</td>
</tr>
<tr>
<td></td>
<td>articles</td>
<td>a, the</td>
</tr>
<tr>
<td></td>
<td>demonstratives</td>
<td>this, that, these, those</td>
</tr>
<tr>
<td></td>
<td>possessives</td>
<td>my, her, their, my father's</td>
</tr>
<tr>
<td></td>
<td>a few non-specific pointers</td>
<td>some, both, all</td>
</tr>
<tr>
<td>2</td>
<td colspan="2">NUMERATIVES which tell how many of the Thing there are or in what order they occur.</td>
</tr>
<tr>
<td></td>
<td>*Numeratives include:*</td>
<td>*for example:*</td>
</tr>
<tr>
<td></td>
<td>cardinal numbers</td>
<td>one, three, a thousand</td>
</tr>
<tr>
<td></td>
<td>ordinal numbers</td>
<td>first, second, third, last</td>
</tr>
<tr>
<td>3</td>
<td colspan="2">EPITHETS which describe a quality of a Thing.</td>
</tr>
<tr>
<td></td>
<td>*Epithets include:*</td>
<td>*for example:*</td>
</tr>
<tr>
<td></td>
<td>adjectives</td>
<td>young, red, dirty, exciting, disgusting, wonderful</td>
</tr>
<tr>
<td>4</td>
<td colspan="2">CLASSIFIERS which establish the Thing as a member of a class.</td>
</tr>
<tr>
<td></td>
<td>*These may be:*</td>
<td>*for example:*</td>
</tr>
<tr>
<td></td>
<td>adjectives</td>
<td>Australian. financial, public</td>
</tr>
<tr>
<td></td>
<td>nouns acting as classifier</td>
<td>cedar tree, car pool</td>
</tr>
</table>

The premodification can be functionally divided into several parts. You will notice that the four broad groups reflect the structure of premodification in a nominal group. In English we put these elements in the order: Deictic Numerative Epithet Classifier. This means we say:

an old timber house	not	a timber old house
those two magnificent cedar trees		those cedar magnificent two trees

There are other constraints and possibilities as well. For instance, it is unusual to have more than one Deictic, but not at all uncommon to have more than one Epithet or Classifier:

a large ferocious guard dog
(two Epithets: large, ferocious)

a new white imported sports car
(two Classifiers: imported, sports)

Epithets can usually be intensified by the word *very*, Classifiers cannot. So, we can talk of *a very old timber house*, but not (normally) of *an old very timber house*.

There are two further points about premodification we need to examine. The first is that the boundaries between these four groups are not watertight. The word *public*, for instance, is commonly a Classifier in nominal groups such as *a public servant* or *public support*, but you can also use *public* in a way that is more like an Epithet, as in *a very public occasion* or *a very public display of emotion*. So we shouldn't think that every word can be labelled once and for all without considering its function in context.

The second point is that we can actually keep refining these categories. For example, we could distinguish between Epithets expressing size (*big, small*) and colour (*red, white*), noting that the former typically precede the latter (*a big red car*) and that it seems more normal to intensify size (*a very big dog*) than colour (*a very brown dog*). However, in this discussion we'll confine ourselves to the four basic categories.

Postmodification

Postmodification functions to qualify the Thing in more detail. It is functionally labelled as QUALIFIER and it gives more detail about the Thing by means of a clause or prepositional phrase. As the clause or prepositional phrase is functioning as a Qualifier within a group, it is said to be embedded in that group and has no independent status as a phrase or clause. Here are examples of nominal groups containing Qualifiers (the Qualifiers are in bold type):

the house **on the hill**
snow **on Mount Kosciusko**
the car **that came hurtling down the road**
the tall woman **who parks her car outside number 16**

In fact, the Qualifier is by far the most intricate part of a nominal group, and it can be extremely complex. Take the following example:

the desk **which you bought at that shop near the bakery which sells those cakes your father likes**

All of this is a nominal group. Its Head is *desk* and everything after that is qualifying the desk. But there are Qualifiers within Qualifiers here. We could show the structure like this, where each Qualifier is on a new line.

the desk
   which you bought at that shop
         near the bakery
            which sells those cakes
               your father likes

Or we could show the nesting like this:

the desk [[which you bought at that shop [near the bakery [[that sells those cakes [[your father likes]]]]]]]

The convention here is to use a pair of double square brackets [[...]] for a clause Qualifier and a pair of single square brackets [...] for a prepositional phrase Qualifier. In the example above, you read the pairs of brackets from the outside in. So:

everything after **desk** qualifies the desk, [[**which you ... father likes**]];
everything after **shop** qualifies the shop, [**near ... father likes**];
everything after **bakery** qualifies the bakery, [[**which sells ... father likes**]];
and the last embedded clause qualifies the cakes [[**your father likes**]]

Table 3.3 Some example nominal groups

Deictic	Numerative	Epithet	Classifier	Thing	Qualifier
the	many	long	broadleaf	weeds	in my garden
my		friendly		dog	
the hitchiker's				guide	to the galaxy
that		extremely dangerous	Alpine	route	that we took last summer

Processes

We will now look at the way PROCESS is realised in the grammar of the English clause. Here verbal groups model the experience of eventness in English – whatever is happening, acting, doing, sensing, saying, or simply being. As with the nominal group, the verbal group may consist of one word or of a group of words.

Just as the Head of a nominal group (which expresses thingness in English) typically involves a noun or pronoun, the word at the heart of the verbal group (which expresses eventness) most generally represents the concept of eventness. This is typically a member of the word class verb, and is known as the Event in the verbal group structure. The Event is thus the central verb and signifies the activity taking place.

In an English verbal group, the Event may stand alone or be preceded by other words in the group. The Event is shown in bold in the examples below:

Participant	Process
Nominal Group	Verbal Group
	Event
The string	**broke**
The cat	has been **sleeping**
My car	was being **towed**
The other team	might have been **slacking**
The premises	could have been being **watched**

The elements that precede the Event itself are a quite limited set of forms known as auxiliary verbs or auxiliaries. They express aspects of the event such as:

Location in time (tense)	will eat, did eat
Completeness or continuousness of the event (aspect)	has eaten, was eating
The speaker's judgment of the certainty of the event (modality)	may eat, must have eaten
Active or passive (voice)	was eaten (by someone)

The first auxiliary in the verbal group is sometimes called the FINITE, because of its special role in the grammar of English. Note, for example, that it is the Finite that is echoed in tag questions:

> Your car **was** being towed at the time, **was**n't it?

and that it is the Finite that moves position to make the difference between a question and a statement:

> Your car **was** being towed at the time
> **Was** your car being towed at the time?

The auxiliary verb(s) and the main Event verb are sometimes separated in the word patterning of the English clause. In each of the following examples there is just one Process realised by a verbal group, but in each case there is an adverb functioning as circumstance intervening in the linear structure of the verbal group. The verbal groups are in bold type:

> I **can** clearly **remember**
> They **seem to have** totally **lost** the plot
> They **must have been** completely **confused** by your directions

The functions of auxiliary verbs in general, and the role of the Finite in particular, relate much more to the interpersonal aspect of grammar than to the experiential. They will therefore be dealt with more fully in Chapters 4 and 5.

Circumstances

Circumstances are realised by adverbial groups, prepositional phrases and even by nominal groups. We will look at the structures of each of these in turn.

Adverbial group

The adverbial group, like any other group, can be one word or several. It has an internal structure that allows some premodification and postmodification as demonstrated in the following list:

	quickly
fairly	quickly
very	quickly
ever so	quickly
so	quickly [[that we couldn't catch him]]
as	quickly [[as she could]]
as	quickly [as possible]

At the head of the adverbial group is an adverb. This may be premodified by some kind of INTENSIFIER (a word that modifies the meaning of the head adverb). Words like *quite, so, very, too, all too* are among the common Premodifiers of adverbial groups.

The Postmodifier in the adverbial group is similar to the Qualifier in the nominal group in both structure and function. Structurally it may be an embedded clause or, less commonly, a prepositional phrase, and it functions to extend the definition of the Head word in the group or to pin down its meaning more specifically. However, unlike the nominal group, as you'll notice from the examples above, there is often a structural relationship between the Pre- and Postmodifiers in the adverbial group, for example *so …* *that, as … as.*

Prepositional phrases

The *prepositional phrase* has the structure PREPOSITION + NOMINAL GROUP. The nominal group may be quite simple:

Preposition	Nominal group
in	the morning
on	Wednesdays
at	home

or may contain embedding:

Preposition	Nominal group
in	the house [[that had been their home for 20 years]]
on	that fateful Wednesday [[which changed their lives]]
under	the flag [[that fluttered bravely in the breeze and that seemed to them a symbol of their endeavour]]

Remember that a prepositional phrase can serve not only as Circumstance in a clause but also as Qualifier within a nominal group or as Postmodifier in an adverbial group. Notice that inside the prepositional phrases in these examples there are four other prepositional phrases, three of them within the one overarching prepositional phrase structure:

for 20 years
in the breeze
to them
of their endeavour

Nominal groups

Finally, there are some groups of words that function as Circumstance but do not appear to fit the pattern of either adverbial group or prepositional phrase. For example:

all week	three weeks ago
six months later	some time recently
all the time	home
many times	a different

Some of these look like, and indeed are, nominal groups (*all week, many times, home*), others seem to be adverbial groups with premodification by a nominal group instead of by an intensifier of some kind (*three weeks ago, some time recently*). What is important here is to be able to recognise a Circumstance element of a clause by its function; that is, the role it is playing in conveying the meaning of the message. Compare, for instance, the function of the word *home* in the following two messages:

Home is a cave in the hills
The troops are coming home

In the first of these clauses, *home* is a nominal group functioning as Thing; in the second it is functioning as Circumstance.

Structures within structures

The patterning of meaning in the experiential function of English offers many examples of structures within structures. Each structure has its own function. Take as an example the following sentence incorporating one of the prepositional phrases discussed above:

They stood under the flag that fluttered bravely in the breeze and that seemed to them a symbol of their endeavour.

This has the structure Participant + Process + Circumstance, where the Location Circumstance is realised by the prepositional phrase *under the flag that fluttered bravely in the breeze and that seemed to them a symbol of their endeavour*. The prepositional phrase has the expected structure, preposition (*under*) + nominal group (*the flag* [[*that fluttered bravely in the breeze and that seemed to them a symbol of their endeavour*]]). Now notice that this nominal group has two embedded clauses functioning as equal status Qualifiers of the Thing – it is a flag [[*that fluttered bravely in the breeze*]], and a flag [[*that seemed to them a symbol of their endeavour*]]. Inside each embedded clause there is a prepositional phrase functioning as Circumstance in the clause structure. *In the breeze* tells us where and by what means the flag fluttered; *to them* tells us for whom the flag was symbolic.

The second of these embedded clauses has a Participant realised by the nominal group *a symbol of their endeavour* with the prepositional phrase *of their endeavour* functioning as Qualifier. An important point to remember is that when a prepositional phrase functions as a Circumstance, it is acting in its own right as a consituent of its clause:

Participant	Process	Circumstance
They	work	in the factory
The accident	occurred	in the factory

But as Qualifier inside a nominal group, the prepositional phrase becomes part of the description of the Thing. In the following examples the relevant nominal groups realise a Participant constituent of a clause:

Participant	Process	Circumstance
The workers in the factory	were meeting	yesterday
The accident in the factory	is being investigated	

In the examples above the prepositional phrase is said to be embedded or rank shifted – embedded because it is now inside a clause constituent element, and rank shifted because it is lower in rank than when it functions as Circumstance; that is, it now functions merely as part of a clause constituent rather than as the clause constituent itself.

Sometimes an utterance may be ambiguous if it is not clear at which rank a prepositional phrase is functioning. Consider for example the following clause: *Did you hear about the accident in the factory?* The speaker may mean to ask whether it was in the factory that you heard about the accident. In this case *in the factory* is intended as Circumstance within the clause, designed to locate the Process *did hear*. But if the speaker is asking whether you heard about the accident which took place in the factory, then *in the factory* describes or limits *accident* and is a Qualifier in the nominal group *accident in the factory*.

Experiential meanings and clause constituency

If you have been dividing clauses into their constituent parts and labelling them with class labels before you examine experiential meanings, you may have noticed that not all clause constituents figure in the experiential analysis. Conjunction groups, for instance, are only relevant in the textual analysis and when you are examining how clauses fit together in clause complexes. They should therefore be omitted from your experiential analysis.

Similarly, some prepositional phrases and adverbial groups are important for interpersonal and textual meanings but will not figure in your experiential analysis. To help you sort out the various functions of prepositional phrases and adverbial groups a help list is included as Appendix A. The following analysis of a clause shows the constituency and what is relevant for the experiential analysis.

	And	actually	the monster	probably	burped	after his meal
constituency	conj g	adv g	ng	adv g	vg	prep phrase
experiential			Behaver		Process: Behav	Circ: When

Nominalisation

We now return to the idea that clause patterning is a variable model of experience. Consider a clause like this:

Excessive consumption of alcohol is a major cause of motor vehicle accidents

If you were to ask what events or processes are important in this message, you might think of *drinking too much alcohol* or *heavy drinking causing accidents* or *drivers having accidents* or even *cars hitting people or other cars*. Yet none of these events is presented here as a Process. The only Process here is the simple relation *is*; the clause is actually structured as *something is something*, and all of the potential events and happenings are packaged not as Processes, but as Participants. The process of drinking is presented here as a Participant (*consumption*); the process of *causing* is packaged as *a major cause*, another Participant structure; and so on. If you try rewording this clause to bring out the events as Processes you might come up with clauses like these:

People who drink too much alcohol and drive often cause motor vehicle accidents
If you drink too much alcohol when you drive your car, you are likely to have an accident
Motor vehicle drivers often have accidents because they have been drinking too much alcohol

If you reflect on these possibilities you realise that the paraphrases are not identical in meaning, that each attempt at rewording brings different aspects of the message into prominence, and in some cases changes the message substantially. Does *major cause* actually mean the same as *causes a lot of accidents* or *often causes accidents* or even *increases the risk of an accident*? In other words, the packaging expressed through the clause is part of the way in which we represent or model what is going on, what is at stake, what we take to be reality.

The particular phenomenon illustrated by the Participant *excessive consumption of alcohol* and *a major cause of motor vehicle accidents* is known as NOMINALISATION. Through nominalisation, events and even entire clauses are repackaged as Participants. Other examples of nominalisation are:

Clause		Thing
The plane leaves at 9.00	**Repackaged as**	The plane's 9.00 departure
She wrote this poem	**Repackaged as**	Her writing of this poem

Functional grammarians sometimes call nominalisation an ideational or experiential grammatical metaphor. Like the more familiar lexical metaphors, grammatical metaphors represent a shift or transference of meaning. Lexical metaphors often do this using relational processes which, as we said earlier in this chapter, can be used to describe or define. We can tell that the clause is metaphorical because the truth would be impossible or incongruent.

The girl was tiny   possible or congruent meaning
The girl was a doll   incongruent or metaphoric meaning.

The occurence of shifts of meaning from the congruent to the incongruent create lexical metaphors. Similar shifts from congruent to incongruent meanings also occur in the grammar. We've already seen this shift in the example *The volcano slept* in the discussion of behavioural processes on page 55. This clause is incongruent because behavioural processes require a conscious Senser (which a volcano clearly is not) and this shift into personification is an experiential grammatical metaphor. In fact, any mismatch of processes and participants is a shift in experiential meanings, and this is what happens in nominalisations.

When the event is realised in a verbal group it is congruent with experience, but when we turn the event into a noun expressing a participant role, the event has become an object and the language is no longer congruent with our experience. We have made an experiential shift and, because we are functional grammarians who regard all choices as meaningful, we look for some reasons for the shift.

One explanation is that we want to freeze that event in time and make it an object that participates in a different sort of process. Furthermore, as we saw in our discussion of nominal group structure, turning an event into a noun offers opportunities to point out, count, describe, classify and specify further and further. Another reason for the re-packaging lies in the shift from spoken to written language or from one register to another. You could compare the spoken language used during a scientific experiment, taking place in primary or secondary school, at university or in the workplace, with the nominalised language used to write up the research. You can read more about ideational (experiential) grammatical metaphor in Halliday (1994: Chapter 10).

To sum up

English speakers and writers manipulate the experiential meanings of their language in order to encode their experiences of the world around them. Every clause in English can be seen in the experiential function to be made up of combinations of Participant(s) and Circumstance(s) revolving around the obligatory Process. But within this seemingly narrow framework there are almost endless possibilities as to how we encode our experience. Just what part of our experience goes into which constituent part of the clause structure is by no means fixed, and will vary widely from speaker to speaker, writer to writer, and situation to situation. If you want to find out more about language as experience read Chapters 5 and 6 in Halliday (1994).

After you have analysed a text clause by clause you will want to sort out the various process types used by the speaker or writer. This will help you to see just what kind of a world has been constructed, a world of doing or being or thinking or saying. You will want to know what nominal groups are selected as Actor, Senser, Carrier or Token. You will want to know, for example, which material processes have Goals and which do not. You will want to know how the speaker/writer constructs nominal groups so that you can identify how the world of experience has been constructed in the text. You will ask whether the nominal groups are abstract or concrete, whether they are people or animals and in what field of experience they belong. In Appendices D (Templates for summarising experiential meanings) and G (Template for exploring nominal group structures) there are some charts to help you in your investigation.

Exercises

1 Create clauses of your own that have the following patterns:
   a. Participant Process Circumstance
   b. Participant Circumstance Process
   c. Circumstance Participant Process

2 Identify the Participants, Processes, Circumstances in these clauses:
   a. Harry loves the bush
   b. In the aftermath of Christmas festivities I left
   c. Mr Bird wiped his tea wet lips on the back of his hand
   d. The King was walking on the terrace

3 Label the constituents in these nominal groups:
   a. a small gnome in the garden
   b. three tall gum trees
   c. clear water cascading over the rocks
   d. that big guard dog that lives over there

4 Create nominal groups to fit these patterns:
   a. Deictic Epithet Epithet Thing
   b. Numerative Thing Qualifier
   c. Epithet Classifier Thing Qualifier

5 List each Circumstance in the following passage and indicate whether it is an adverbial group or prepositional phrase.

   He pushed his chair back angrily and strode from the room. The other members of the committee watched him in silence. The president waited for a few seconds, then smiled reassuringly. She calmly sorted her notes and turned to the secretary.

6 Of what type is each Process in the following passage?

   I was driving down the Buchan to Orbost road on my way to another cave when I noticed a dark cleft in a cliff near the top of a hill. I thought there must be a dry cave, so I abandoned my previous plans and headed across the paddocks up to the cliff. Outside the cave was a rockshelter with a roof that had been blackened by the smoke of many campfires. A short rocky passage led into a dimly lit inner cavern with a high cathedral-like roof. I had feared that there would be a rock-strewn floor; instead the earth was soft and dry, perfect for prehistoric and indeed modern campers.

Implications for language teachers

This chapter describes the potential of the English clause to make meaning about human experience. It also describes how each speaker represents their experience differently by packaging it in different ways, in other words, by choosing different clause constituents.

How is knowledge of experiential grammar useful to teachers?

The value of describing language in terms of experiential grammar is that it makes it possible for teachers to introduce students explicitly and systematically to the array of choices available for making meanings about human experience in an English clause. These choices include:

- the types of Process which can be at the centre of an English clause
- the Participant roles which can be related to each process type
- the types of Circumstances which can illuminate processes.

A study of these choices reveals how meaning, function and structure are interrelated. As students explore the functions of each of these choices in authentic language, they are exploring experiential meaning and the structures which express experiential meaning.

The structure of the clause itself can be described in terms of the potential 'slots' it has available for making experiential meaning. The Process slot must be filled for a clause to come into being, then one, two or even three Participants can be added and one or more Circumstances. The choices we make to fill these slots are motivated by:

- the purpose we are using the text to achieve
- the field of the immediate situation.

Each of the possible 'slots' in the clause can be described in terms of its meaning potential and in terms of the structures which can realise that potential. For example the event or Process slot in the clause has the potential to achieve a material, relational or projecting function. Verbal groups are the structures which realise this potential.

Distinguishing between different types of Processes draws attention to structural patterns in the clause which may otherwise be considered by some students as arbitrary rather than related to meaning and function. Often in language classrooms the first examples of English clauses which students meet are built around material processes. The structures of these clauses, and of the verbal groups which realise material processes, tend to be held up as the norm. As a result, the structures of clauses built around relational and projecting processes can seem somehow 'irregular' and 'difficult'. If students are aware from the beginning that there are different types of clauses making different types of meaning, the differences in structure will be revealed as functional.

Verbs expressing mental processes are an interesting example of how an apparently arbitrary 'rule' of English grammar appears to be functionally motivated when viewed in terms of experiential meaning. In standard dialects of English, verbs expressing a mental process are less likely than those expressing a material process to be used in a continuous form. Consider the following clauses:

> I'm finishing now. (material process)
> [Compare: I finish now.]
> I think that it's time to finish now. (mental process)
> [Compare: I'm thinking that it's time to finish now.]

How does knowledge about experiential grammar help language learners?

Language learning activities designed around the categories of Process, Participant and Circumstance and their different sub-categories have been very effective. In these activities colour and shape are sometimes used to symbolise and reinforce the metalanguage (Williams, in press). In some teaching contexts, time or syllabus constraints make using the metalanguage for these categories impossible. In all teaching contexts, however, these categories provide language teachers with many ideas for experiential probe questions that students can use as they explore English clauses in whole texts. The following are examples of experiential questions that can be used to probe the structures of a clause:

- What is the process (or verb)? What work is it doing? Is it telling about a material or physical action, or is it relating (ie identifying or describing), saying or sensing?
- Who or what is doing the action, relating, saying or sensing?
- Who or what is being done to or related to, said/said to or sensed?
- Is the saying or sensing clause projecting another clause? Is this clause direct (or quoted) speech or is it indirect (or reported) speech? Is this clause direct (or quoted) thought or is it indirect (or reported) thought?
- When, where, how, why, with whom or what, for how long has all this been going on?

If we ask students to search for the answers to these questions in real texts in context, we will reveal many of the structural patterns language learners are aiming to control, including some of the structures that are especially challenging for students of English. Probing for experiential meaning, for instance, can show two things. First, the way that an extremely long and complex noun group with one or more clauses in the Qualifier remains a single functional unit within the clause, only filling the meaning potential of one slot:

She	saw	the desk which you bought at that shop near the bakery which sells those cakes your father likes
Participant	Process	Participant

Second, a clause (traditionally known a noun clause) can take up the meaning potential of a participant slot inside another clause, thus becoming a constituent of that clause:

[[What I really want]]	is	a good cup of tea
Participant	Process	Participant

The section on nominalisation at the end of this chapter introduced you to grammatical metaphor, a process in which there is a shifting in the alignment between a meaning and its grammatical expression. In the case of nominalisation, the metaphor occurs because a phenomenon which we experience in real life as an event – and which might more 'naturally' be expressed in language as a Process (for example the verb *drink*) – is instead expressed in language as a Participant (for example, the noun *consumption*). Understanding the way nominalisation works and how it impacts on clause structure is important knowledge for students working with written English.

How can knowledge of experiential grammar enhance teaching programs?

As we have seen, the experiential grammar we choose when we produce texts is motivated by:

- the purpose we are achieving with the text
- the field of the immediate context of situation.

Language teaching activities can be designed which draw students' attention to how both these aspects of context find their way into the clauses of a text.

Experiential grammar and text structure

In Chapter 1 we were told that the structure of a text is related to its overall purpose. In fact, the structure of a text emerges from the way words and grammar structures are used as the text unfolds. Students can undertake activities that explore the way words and structures expressing experiential meanings contribute to the structure and purpose of different types of texts.

In Narratives, students might look:

- in the Orientation for
  - existential processes which introduce people, places and things into the story

- Circumstances which set the story in a time and place
- relational processes used to identify and describe the characters
- material processes which introduce the typical action of the characters
- in the Complication for
  - sequences of material processes which keep the action going
  - verbal processes to slow the action down while projecting what characters are saying
  - relational and mental processes to freeze the action, build suspense, reveal the characters' thoughts and feelings and evaluate what is happening
- in the Resolution and/or Coda for
  - relational processes that reveal the message of the story.

This kind of exploration builds knowledge about the grammar patterns which typically structure different types of texts. Students can consciously and strategically draw on this knowledge as they structure their own texts.

Experiential grammar and field

Being able to control the expression of field through experiential grammar greatly enhances students' ability to manage:

- the language of specialised academic disciplines
- the imaginary worlds of literature and creative writing
- strategic and relevant vocabulary building.

Studying a specialised discipline is all about learning how to perceive and experience the world in a new way. For those who are learning English in order to study within a specialised discipline, it is essential to be able to manage the expression of field through experiential grammar. In everyday contexts grammatical structures encode specific, everyday experiences of the world. In specialised academic disciplines experience is analysed and organised in generalised, systematic and technical ways. If students are to manage specialised varieties of English, they must manage the relevant grammar necessary to encode generalised, systematic and technical knowledge in a specific discipline. For example, to produce the language of disciplines related to the sciences, students must:

- select technical, rather than everyday, words and put these words into groups, phrases, clauses and clause complexes which encode the specialised relationships of the subject they are studying
- choose Participants which represent general categories, concepts and processes rather than specific people and things
- use nominalisation so that
  - events and series of events are encoded as (often technical) nouns

- these nouns become the Thing in a nominal group so the event or process can be quantified, classified, described and/or evaluated
- the nominal group based on the nominalisation takes a Participant role in the clause
- use relational processes to identify, describe, classify and define
- use relational processes in clauses where the actual events have been encoded as Participants and can no longer be represented as Processes
- use Circumstances to enhance precision and to identify conditions or constraints.

The way experiential grammar represents field is also important for working with literary texts and for creative writing. In language programs that focus on literary texts, students can investigate how writers use experiential grammar to build a story world for their readers and to develop the characters in their stories. Students can investigate how, for example:

- Circumstances are used to set the story in a time and place
- existential processes are used to introduce the reader to people, places and things in the story world
- relational processes are used to identify and describe characters
- nominal groups expressing Participant roles are used to reveal the qualities of the characters
- material processes are used to reveal what happens in the story world
- projecting processes are used to reveal the inner world of the characters
- the writer uses experiential grammar to blend two fields in the same story (eg an everyday world and a fantasy world, a real world and a dream world, a domestic world and a specialised world).

Whether students are learning the language of everyday contexts, a specialist discipline or literary texts, an exploration of the field helps them to build vocabulary which is relevant to the course content and to their learning needs and goals.

Using experiential grammar to build a critical response to text

Experiential grammar is also useful for helping students to respond critically to the texts they encounter. The words and structures chosen by producers of texts reveal how they perceive and experience what is going on in the world. An exploration of experiential grammar therefore reveals a great deal about the worldview expressed in a text.

The following are examples of activities that can help students to explore the world-view expressed in the experiential grammar of a news story:

- Students consider the incident on which the news story is based. They think about all the events which might have constituted or contributed to this incident or happened as a result of this incident. They then note how these events are represented in the story as Processes:

Are there any events which are not represented in the story at all? Why might this be so? What effect does this have on the reader's perception of the incident?

- Students note how the journalist represents events in terms of material, relational or projecting processes:

Is the news story mostly representing actions, relating identities and descriptions or projecting people's words and thoughts? Are people's words and thoughts quoted directly or reported indirectly?

What effect does the representation of events in the grammatical structures have on the reader's perception of the incident?

- Students consider all the people who might have a stake in the events of the news story. They then note who are represented in Participant roles in the news story and who are not.

Why are some people represented and others not?
What effect does this have on the reader's perception of the incident?

- Students identify the type of Participant roles used for different categories of people revealing, for example:
  - which people are represented as Actor (ie people who do things) and what these people get to do
  - which people are represented as Sayer (ie people whose words are listened to) and what these people get to say
  - which people are represented as Senser (ie people whose thoughts and feelings are revealed) and which of their thoughts and feelings are revealed
  - which people are represented as Goal (ie people who have things done to them) and what these people have done to them
  - which people are represented as Receiver (ie people who are spoken to) and what these people have said to them
  - which people are represented as Phenomenon (ie people who are projected into the text by someone else's thoughts) and how these people are projected
  - the way Relational Processes are used to identify and describe different people

How does the way people are represented in the grammatical structures affect the reader's perception of the incident and the people involved in it?

- Students note the words used inside the nominal groups expressing the Participant roles. This investigation reveals at a more delicate level how different people are represented in the text. For example, students might note whether certain types of people are represented:
  - with words which have a positive or a negative feel (eg *chief executive* or *boss*, *guerilla* or *freedom fighter*)

- in terms of family relationships (eg *wife, mother, brother, son*) or community role (eg *mayor, doctor, builder, artist*).

How does the selection of words affect the reader's perception of the incident and the people involved in it?

- Students note whether the Circumstances illuminate the Processes largely in terms of, for example, time, place, manner or cause and the effect this has on the reader's perception of the incident.

Exercises for language teachers

1 Identify a good example of a type of text you would like your students to be able to use effectively. The text might be spoken or written. If you wish, you may choose one of the texts in Chapter 1.
   - Look for patterns of experiential grammar which:
     - contribute to the structure and purpose of the whole text
     - build the field of the immediate situation
   - Relate what you have discovered about the experiential grammar of the text to your students' learning needs and goals.

2 Use what you have discovered about the experiential grammar of the text to design activities which support your students' progress towards their learning goals. These activities might draw your students' attention to:
   - the purpose and structure of the text as revealed in experiential grammar
   - the nature of the field (eg Is it an everyday or technical field? Is it a literary field or combination of fields?)
   - how the field is represented in the vocabulary and grammatical structures of the text
   - the worldview represented in the experiential grammar of the text.

4

How speakers interact with language: Exploring interpersonal meanings

Introducing …

- The interpersonal function

Discussing …

- Implications for language teaching

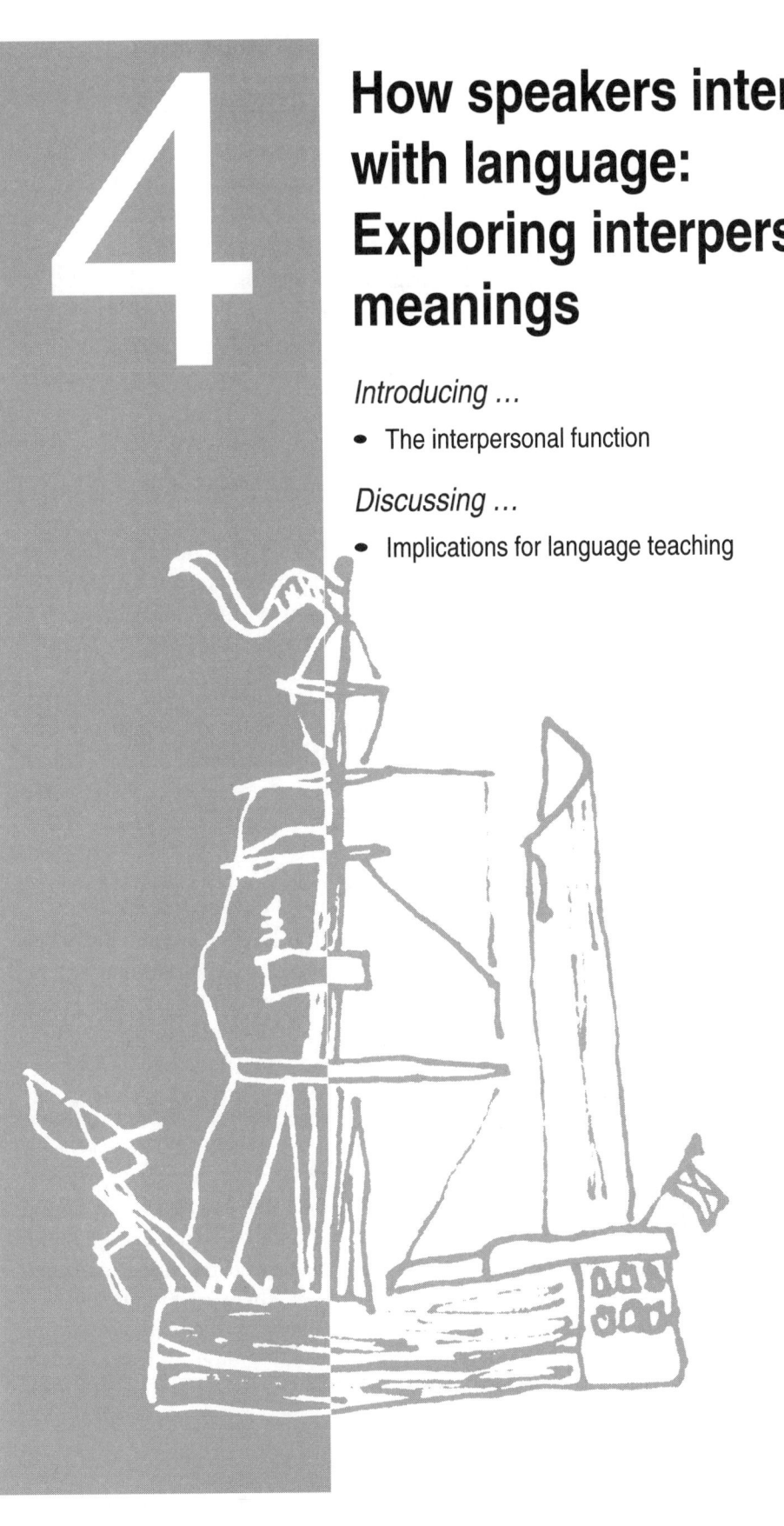

From Chapter 1

Language has an *interpersonal* function, so it has interpersonal meanings.
We use language to encode our interaction.

If we see people talking together, we may wonder what they are talking *about*. This experiential aspect of their talk is, of course, realised in the lexicogrammar of Participants, Process and Circumstance as we discussed in Chapter 3. But speakers do more than talk about experience; they also use language to *interact* with language and to express interpersonal meanings. In this chapter and the next, the focus is on the lexicogrammatical resources available to realise these interpersonal meanings.

Interpersonal meanings cover two main areas: one concerns the type of interaction taking place and the kind of commodity being exchanged, and the other concerns the way speakers take a position in their messages. We will discuss the former in this chapter and the latter in Chapter 5.

Interacting with language

One of the most basic interactive distinctions concerns the kind of commodity being exchanged; that is, the difference between using language to exchange information and using it to exchange goods and services. A second distinction concerns the type of interaction taking place; that is, the difference between demanding and giving. In other words, we can demand information or we can give it and we can demand goods and services or give them. These interpersonal meanings from the semantic level of language are realised in the wordings of the lexicogrammatical level (refer to Figure 1.3 on page 7).

It is important to remember that there is not a one-to-one relationship between semantics and lexicogrammar. What someone says may look like demanding or giving information but could be an oblique way of demanding goods and services. For example, we recognise that if someone says, 'Are you thirsty?', or 'It must be afternoon tea time', they may actually be asking us to make the tea. Nevertheless, there are predictable and straightforward ways to create meanings in the lexicogrammar and we will see in our observations of the following texts that the most usual way of giving information is a statement, the most usual way of demanding information is a question and the most usual way of demanding goods and services is a command or order. There is, however, no linguistically straightforward way of giving goods and services.

Giving and demanding information

Demanding and giving information are meanings at the semantic level which are most often realised at the lexicogrammatical level by asking questions or making statements. Certain contexts will motivate these meanings in a text. In a lecture, for example, we expect that most of the clauses will be giving information. The same is the case in a recount, an information report or a discussion. In a law court transcript, however, we expect that information will be demanded by a barrister and given by a witness or defendant. Likewise, in classrooms, teachers often check what pupils know by demanding information and, hence, there will be sequences of questions and statements. Text 1, a Year 3 Social Studies text, is a good example of exchanging information.

Text 1: Mike's text

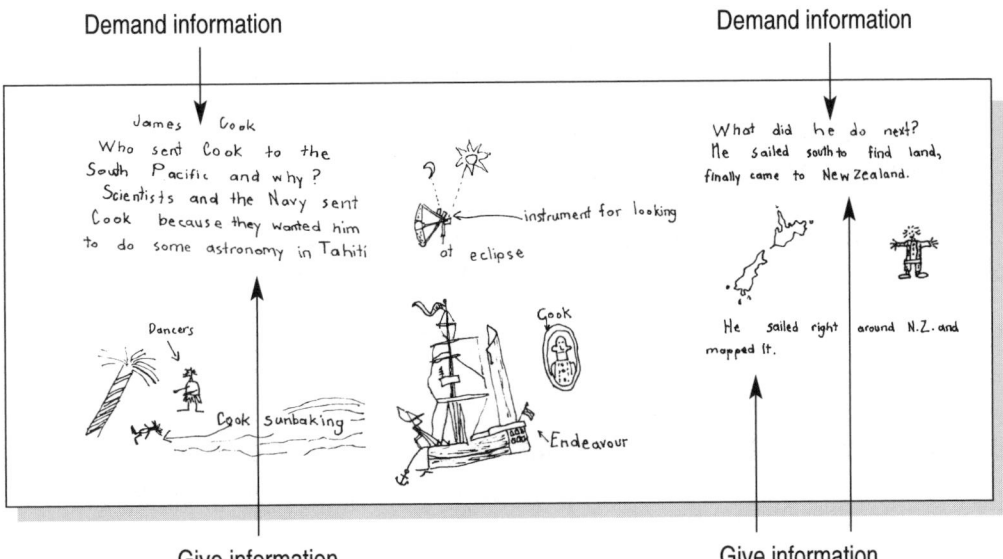

Another good example of the exchange of information is the nursery rhyme below (Text 2).

Text 2

Demand information:	How many miles to Babylon?
Give information:	Three score miles and ten.
Demand information:	Can I get there by candlelight?
Give information:	Yes, and back again.
Give information (dependent clause):	If your heels are nimble and light,
Give information:	You may get there by candlelight.

Demanding goods and services

In contrast to the exchange of information, the exchange of goods and services involves using language to get things done, either by offering to do them ourselves or ordering someone else to do them. Demanding goods and services are meanings at the semantic level which are most often realised at the lexicogrammatical level by giving orders or instructions. Certain contexts where power or knowledge is unevenly distributed motivate the giving of orders and instructions. Procedural texts commonly contain a number of orders. Although these are not really authoritative demands, they are presented to us as orders which are to be obeyed if we want to achieve the intended results.

Text 3

	To Government House from Circular Quay
'Demand' service	From Circular Quay, follow the waterfront for a short distance
'Demand' service	then cross the road
'Demand' service	and go up the Moore Stairs
'Demand' service	cross Macquarie Street
'Demand' service	and enter the park opposite
'Demand' service	walk some distance to the right towards the Conservatorium
Give information	you will then find yourself at the Government House gates

Metalanguage for discussing language as interaction

The metalanguage of interaction

Finite
Subject
Mood
Modal Finite
Polarity
Residue
Predicator
Complement
Adjunct
Vocative
Person
declarative mood
interrogative mood
imperative mood

In our exploration of the experiential function, we found that the crucial meanings were the relationship between the groups and phrases functioning as the Process, the Participants in the process, and the Circumstances. For interpersonal meanings the crucial relationship is between *grammatical functions*. The two grammatical features that carry the main burden of interpersonal meanings are the SUBJECT and the FINITE. They combine to make the MOOD of the clause. By the end of this chapter, we will see that the order of Subject and Finite is a grammatical sign of the kind of exchange taking place. We will begin our exploration by examining the grammatical resources to express interaction.

The Finite

In our discussion of clause constituents we saw that a verbal group is made up of one or more words. Whereas experientially the EVENT is the most important part of the verbal group, it is the Finite which is the *focus* for the *expression of interpersonal meanings*. The Finite is that part of the verbal group which encodes primary tense or the speaker's opinion. Thus, the Finite has two main interpersonal roles in the verbal group – it can be a sign of TIME in relation to the speaker, or a MODAL sign of the speaker's opinion.

If we were looking for experiential meanings we would decode all the following verbal groups (underlined) as encoding the material process *eat*:

  1   The three little kittens soon <u>ate</u> up the pie
  2   Jack Sprat <u>could eat</u> no fat
  3   The pig <u>was</u> not <u>eaten</u>
  4   Why is he <u>eating</u> the pie?
  5   You <u>will eat</u> strawberries, sugar and cream

The Finites in the clauses, however, are quite different, for instance: the time (tense) of Clauses 1 and 3 is in the past; in Clause 3 there is a separate word *was* to tell us this, but in Clause 1 the pastness of the activity is mapped on to the single word *ate*, making this word a double sign – for the process itself and for the Finite telling the time of the process. In Clause 4 the separate Finite *is* is the first word in the verbal group, signifying present tense; and in Clause 5 the separate Finite *will* tells us that the Event will take place some time after the talk about it.

Whether an Event has occurred, is presently occurring, or is yet to take place is obviously very important if we are to argue about a clause, and in the next chapter we will be exploring the notion of arguability. With this in mind, we notice that in Clause 2 the definiteness of the clause has been moderated by the speaker's opinion about Jack Sprat's ability to eat fat so that the debate rests not on whether or not he *did* but whether or not he *could*. Finites that encode the speaker's *opinion* rather than *tense* are known as MODAL FINITES. The argument of Clause 3 is a negative one – the pig was *not* eaten. All English clauses have either positive or negative POLARITY, but only negative polarity is shown – positive polarity is assumed unless negativity is marked.

So now let's look at the five clauses again with just the Finite and negative polarity underlined:

  1   The three little kittens soon (<u>Finite past</u>) <u>ate</u> up the pie
  2   Jack Sprat <u>could</u> eat no fat
  3   The pig <u>was not</u> eaten
  4   Why <u>is</u> he eating the pie?
  5   You <u>will</u> eat strawberries, sugar and cream

Where the Finite is mapped on to the same word as the Event, we regard the word as two separate signs and draw a line through its centre, marking one side as Finite and tense, and the other as Predicator.

There is a way to double check that we have identified the Finite correctly. If the verbal group contains more than one word, the Finite will be the first word in the verbal group but, if the verbal group is only one word, a Finite signifying tense as well as the Event itself, will be mapped on to that one word:

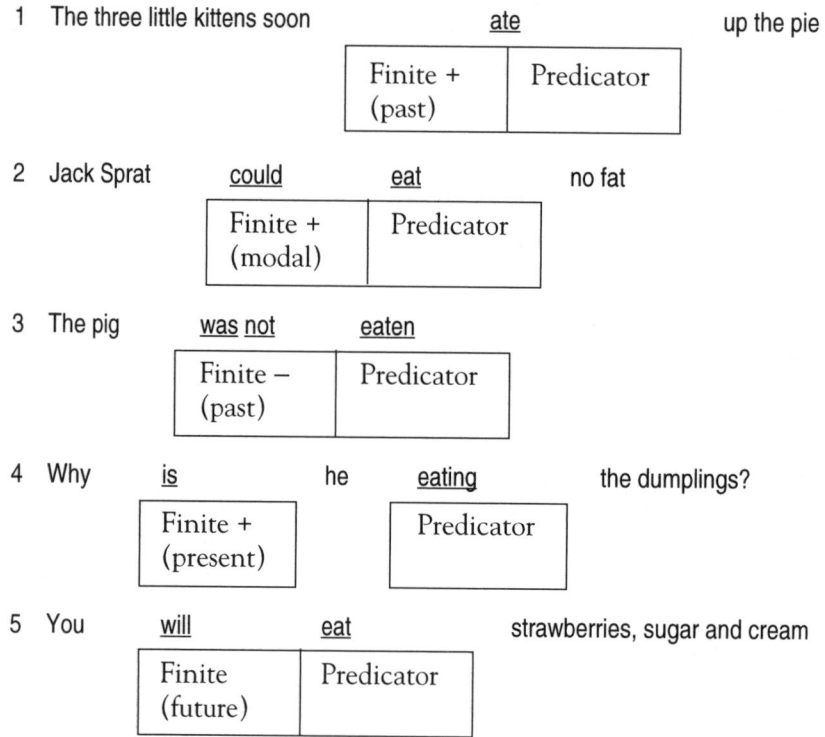

1 The three little kittens soon   ate   up the pie

Finite + (past)	Predicator

2 Jack Sprat   could   eat   no fat

Finite + (modal)	Predicator

3 The pig   was not   eaten

Finite − (past)	Predicator

4 Why   is   he   eating   the dumplings?

Finite + (present)	Predicator

5 You   will   eat   strawberries, sugar and cream

Finite (future)	Predicator

The Subject and Subject-Finite relationship

The nominal group which interacts most closely with the Finite is known as the SUBJECT. The strong interaction between this and the Finite is a fundamental relationship in English grammar. The significance of the Subject-Finite relation can sometimes be seen in the effect of the Subject on the Finite. When the nominal group in the Subject role changes, from singular to plural or from first person (*I, we*) to third person (*she, the team, they*), the Finite may reflect the change in its form. The verb *to be* signals the Subject-Finite relation most strongly:

I   am

Subject	Finite (present)

you/we/they   are

Subject	Finite (present)

he/she/it	is
Subject	Finite (present)

This overt marking of the relationship is repeated in all verbal groups where part of the verb *to be* is the Finite:

He	was	walking
The buns	were	eaten
Subject	Finite (past)	Predicator

Whether or not it is overtly signalled by changes in the verbal group, the relationship between the Subject and Finite is what counts. It is such a strong bond that it intersects normal group boundaries so that the nominal group functioning as Subject and the Finite from the verbal group function together as the Mood (or Mood Block) of the message, leaving any other auxiliary verbs and the process itself as Predicator in the less important Residue of the clause. We'll define these terms properly after a discussion of Mood.

He	was	walking
The buns	were	eaten
Subject	Finite (past)	Predicator
Mood Block		Residue

Mood

The MOOD or MOOD BLOCK is the name given to the Subject and Finite plus the polarity (plus, as we shall discover in the next chapter, any other modality). One way to test a message for its Mood Block is to add a brief check, or MOOD TAG, to the message, as if we are checking that we have understood the message. After a message like: *Jack Sprat could eat no fat*, we add a tag: *could he?* The tag we add will contain the Subject and Finite in the reverse order from the original clause.

So, once we have constructed the Mood tag, we can return to the original message to identify the Mood Block, and the separate Subject and Finite within it become very obvious. The Subject is the whole nominal group referenced by the pronoun in the Mood tag and the Finite is that part of the verbal group which occurs in the Mood tag. Where the Finite is mapped onto the same word as the process itself, adding a Mood tag will show us whether the Finite is past or present. In the case of *the three little kittens ate up their pie*, we add a tag *didn't they?* This demonstrates that the Subject of the message is the whole nominal group referenced by *they*, so the Subject is, of course, *the three little kittens*. Because *did* is past tense, the Finite is past.

The following clauses show an interpersonal analysis including the Mood tag check to find Subject and Finite. Note that the + symbol next to the Finite indicates positive polarity and the − indicates negative polarity. Other parts of the interpersonal analysis are also labelled and will be discussed directly below.

They	open		on Friday,	don't	they?
Subject	Finite + (present)	Predicator	Adjunct	Finite	Subject
Mood Block		Residue		Mood tag	

You	liked		the film,	didn't	you?
Subject	Finite + (past)	Predicator	Complement	Finite	Subject
Mood Block		Residue		Mood tag	

He	had	swum	there,	hadn't	he?
Subject	Finite + (past)	Predicator	Adjunct	Finite	Subject
Mood Block		Residue		Mood tag	

The doctor	will	sign	the script,	won't	she?
Subject	Finite + (future)	Predicator	Complement	Finite	Subject
Mood Block		Residue		Mood tag	

Predicator

The rest of the verbal group, including any other auxiliaries, is simply described as the Predicator because, as we shall discover in the next chapter, it is the basis for the predication, or validation, of the rest of the clause.

Adjunct

Adverbial groups, nominal groups and prepositional phrases that acted as Circumstances for the experiential meaning of a clause are now simply known as Adjuncts because they are added on to the interpersonal meanings.

Complement

Other nominal groups may be regarded as Complements because they *complete* the argument set up in the clause.

Residue

The Predicator, Complement(s) and Adjunct(s) make up the Residue of a clause.

Extra elements

Vocative

Especially in spoken language, speakers may add a direct address of some kind as in:

Andrew, did you borrow my stapler?
Hey, Alex, you've left your keys over here!

Elements like these, which directly address someone, are known by the traditional grammatical term VOCATIVES. They are additional to the clause structure and, although they are labelled in the interpersonal analysis, do not form part of the Mood Block or Residue.

Person

In describing interaction we are never very far away from the interactants themselves, the speaker as *I* or *we*, and the addressee as *you*. As speakers and addressees interact in conversation they take up different roles – the speaker of one clause becomes the addressee of the next as, in turn, the first addressee becomes the next speaker.

The traditional way of describing the interactants is first person (singular: *I, me, my*; plural: *we, us, our*) and second person (singular and plural: *you, your*). Third person is the persons and things spoken about. In English first person plural may either include or exclude the addressee, so grammarians refer to *inclusive* or *exclusive we*.

Although person is not a labelled part of our interpersonal analysis, any investigation must be concerned with the interplay of first and second person and whether the addressee is included in first person plural pronouns. The identity of *I* and *you*, and the expression of solidarity or distance by inclusive or exclusive first person plural pronouns, are expressions of the relationship between speaker and addressee. These important realisations of the tenor of discourse will be discussed again in Chapter 8.

Metalanguage for analysing and describing interaction

At the beginning of this chapter we drew on Halliday's discussion of *exchange*, which distinguishes the exchange of information from the exchange of goods and services. In both types of exchange it is possible to demand or give. The Subject/Finite relationship becomes a sign of the interaction taking place in the discourse by establishing the message as statement, question, command. We will now look at each of these in greater detail.

Exchanging information

In the exchange of information, the Subject and Finite are both present or can be easily recovered from the preceeding text. The order of Subject and Finite in the Mood Block shows whether information is given or demanded.

Giving information

The Medea text (Text 4) is taken from a Year 12 English essay where, in the way of all such essays, the writer is presenting information to the reader. Speakers and writers giving information most normally make statements. In clauses giving information, the Subject *precedes* the Finite, and this configuration of the Mood Block is known as DECLARATIVE MOOD. In this text the Subject always preceeds the Finite, and the Finite, which is always present tense, is usually mapped on to the same word as the Event.

Text 4: The Medea text

> Medea is a strange and complex character. She is inexplicable because of the extremities of emotion she displays. Both her love and her hate are awesomely powerful, almost too powerful to be human. In the final scene, Euripides displays this by placing her in a blazing chariot above the stage. By this action, she is transformed into a quasi-divine figure. But, at the same time, she remains a savage and her barbarian qualities, her 'fierce, resentful spirit', continue to govern her actions and emotions.

	In the final scene	Euripides	displays	this
declarative mood demand information	Adjunct	Subject	Finite + (present)	Predicator	Complement
	Res-	Mood Block		-idue

	By this action	she	is	transformed	into a quasi-divine figure
declarative mood demand information	Adjunct	Subject	Finite + (present)	Predicator	Adjunct
	Res-	Mood Block		-idue

Demanding information

Speakers demanding information normally ask questions. Sometimes they ask in polar interrogatives which expect a yes/no response. In a polar interrogative question the

Finite comes before the Subject, and this order is the signal of the INTERROGATIVE mood. For example:

Does	Penny	play	squash?

interrogative mood demand information	Finite + (present)	Subject	Predicator	Complement
	Mood Block		Residue	

Can	I	get	there	by candlelight?

interrogative mood demand information	Finite (modal)	Subject	Predicator	Adjunct	Adjunct
	Mood Block		Residue		

In information-seeking questions, if the question word is *Who?*, *Which*, or *What?* functioning as Subject, then the Finite follows it. For example:

Who	killed	Cock Robin?

interrogative mood demand information	WH- Subject	Finite + (past)	Predicator	Complement
	Mood Block		Residue	

Who	has	taken	my pen?

interrogative mood demand information	WH- Subject	Finite + (present)	Predicator	Complement
	Mood Block		Residue	

What	was	making	that noise?

interrogative mood demand information	WH- Subject	Finite + (past)	Predicator	Complement
	Mood Block		Residue	

Otherwise, if the question word is not the Subject, or if any other question word is used, the sequence in the Mood Block is Finite followed by Subject. For example:

Who	did	you	see?

interrogative mood demand information	WH- Complement	Finite + (past)	Subject	Predicator
	Res-	Mood Block		-idue

	Where	has	my little dog	gone?
interrogative mood demand information	WH- Adjunct	Finite + (present)	Subject	Predicator
	Res-	Mood Block		-idue

	Why	didn't	she	leave?
interrogative mood demand information	WH- Adjunct	Finite - (past)	Subject	Predicator
	Res-	Mood Block		-idue

	How	does	Heidi	know?
interrogative mood demand information	WH- Adjunct	Finite + (present)	Subject	Predicator
	Res-	Mood Block		-idue

	When	will	they	arrive?
interrogative mood demand information	WH- Adjunct	Finite + (present)	Subject	Predicator
	Res-	Mood		-idue

There are exceptions to this typical realisation. In English the Finite may precede the Subject in exclamations or inverted declaratives, as shown in the following two examples (we'll find out what to do with *never* in the next chapter). In Chapter 5 we will investigate exceptions to this order in some other languages.

	Never	**had**	**she**	seen	such power [[invested in one woman]]
declarative mood give information		Finite	Subject	Predicator	Complement
		Mood Block		Residue	

	'Stuff and nonsense'	said	Alice	loudly
declarative mood give information		Finite	Predicator	Subject	Adjunct
		Mood	Res-	Block	-idue

As you can see, the clauses above remain declarative mood in spite of the reversal of Subject and Finite which more typically realises interrogative mood.

Exchanging goods and services

Demanding goods and services

Speakers demanding goods or services may give orders or commands. In the most straightforward and easily recognised form of this type of exchange there is no apparent Subject or Finite, but speakers can, if they wish, make their demands more emphatic by adding a Subject or a Finite. These configurations of the Mood Block are known as IMPERATIVE MOOD.

If we add a Mood tag at the end of each message, the result is *will you?* or *won't you?* Because of this, some linguists would prefer to say that the Subject is the addressee (you) and that the Finite must contain some idea of futurity. On the other hand, the suggestion that the Subject and/or Finite need not be present in the imperative highlights the difference between demanding information and demanding goods and services:

			Play	squash!
imperative mood demand goods and services	No Subject	No Finite	Predicator	Complement
	Mood Block		Residue	

			Do	play	squash!
imperative mood demand goods and services	No Subject	Finite		Predicator	Complement
	Mood Block			Residue	

			You	play	squash!
imperative mood demand goods and services	Subject	No Finite		Predicator	Complement
	Mood Block			Residue	

Remember that in English there is no one-to-one correspondence between meanings and the way they are encoded in the grammar. We may also find a demand for goods and services encoded as a declarative or interrogative and in such cases the Subject/Finite follows the normal pattern of declarative or interrogative mood, for example:

I need to see your passport

or

Can I see your passport?

Giving goods and services

Speakers who are offering goods and services do not have recourse to any special configuration of the Subject-Finite relationship, so this type of exchange does not have a special mood but is identified through the context of the message.

	I	'll	make	the tea
declarative mood give goods and services	Subject	Finite	Predicator	Complement
	Mood Block		Residue	

	Shall	I	make	the tea?
interrogative mood give goods and services	Finite	Subject	Predicator	Complement
	Mood Block		Residue	

Exchange in context

At the beginning of this chapter we talked about the ways in which certain contexts raise strong expectations about whether information or goods and services will be given or demanded. We can now return to an examination of texts to explore the meanings realised in their mood choices.

Texts like the Year 12 essay on Medea (Text 4) are concerned with giving information. This meaning is realised in the writer's choice of declarative mood. On the other hand, speakers and writers of procedural texts usually select imperative mood because they are giving orders which should be followed to accomplish the task. In Text 5 the verbal groups in imperative mood are underlined.

Text 5: Recipe for Sticky Date Pudding

Ingredients
200 g dates
1 cup water
60 g butter
2 eggs
190 g white sugar
190 g SR flour
1 tsp bicarb. soda
1/2 tsp vanilla essence

Equipment
small saucepan
wooden spoon
round or ring pan
baking paper

Method
<u>Put</u> dates and water in saucepan, and <u>heat</u> until jammy.
<u>Beat</u> in the other ingredients.
<u>Line</u> pan with greased baking paper.
<u>Bake</u> at 19°C for 30 minutes.
<u>Serve</u> with caramel sauce and cream.

In conversation, in the real world or in the dialogues of plays and narratives, we demand information as well as give it, and we often give orders. The relative status of the interactants is often disclosed by just *who* demands the information in questions, or demands goods and services in orders. In Text 6, from a conversation between a mother and her child over afternoon tea, the mother demands goods and services and demands information, thus controlling both the activity and the flow of the conversation. By now you should be able to label the mood of each verbal group in this text.

Text 6: Conversation between mother and child

Mother:	Ben, hop down please
	No, don't do that
	You'll break the plant
	Now, what did you do at kindy today?
Child:	(I) Played
	(I) Had a drink
Mother:	What did you have a drink of?
Child:	(I had) A drink of water
Mother:	And what did you have to eat?
Child:	(I) Ate a 'nana
Mother:	Don't give your sandwich to the cat
	She's had her dinner

To sum up

English speakers and writers manipulate the Subject-Finite relationship of Mood to indicate whether they are giving or demanding information or demanding goods and services. However, the relation between lexicogrammar and interpersonal meanings is not always straightforward – information can be sought using the imperative and declarative moods as well the interrogative; and there is no 'normal' way of encoding an offer of goods and services. In spite of this, there are very few misunderstandings: listeners are perfectly able to distinguish a demand for goods and services mapped on to an interrogative from a genuine question.

Exercises

1 Add a Mood tag to each of the following clauses and then underline the Subject of each clause and circle its Finite.
   a. The gardens are irrigated with recycled water
   b. Dr Foster went to Gloucester in a shower of rain
   c. But the pig would not jump over the fence
   d. On solemn festivals many people will visit the temples of the gods
   e. The truth of the matter was becoming evident

2 Mark whether the mood of the following clauses is declarative, interrogative or imperative. Underline the Subject and circle the Finite and comment on the way they are ordered.
   a. Will you join the dance?
   b. This is a fine example of Goya's early style
   c. Why are you crying so?
   d. Stop that nonsense immediately
   e. Everybody must leave the theatre at once

3 Change the interpersonal meanings of the clauses in Exercise 2 by manipulating the Subject and Finite.

4 Find short texts where the main type of meaning is:
   a. demanding goods and services
   b. giving information
   c. giving and demanding information
   How is the context of situation reflected in the meanings and lexicogrammar of the texts?

Implications for language teaching

This chapter describes the potential of the English clause to exchange meaning. It is this potential that makes it possible for us to use language to interact with each other. Specifically the chapter explores:

- the types of meanings we exchange when we use language to interact with each other (when exchanging information or goods and services)
- how we exchange these meanings (by giving or demanding them)
- the interpersonal grammar we use to exchange these meanings in these different ways.

How is knowledge of the interpersonal grammar of exchange useful to teachers and learners?

Knowledge of the interpersonal grammar of exchange makes it possible for teachers to introduce students explicitly and systematically to the grammar they can use to **exchange meanings** with others.

Language teachers are already familiar with the grammar of the types of clauses discussed in this chapter; that is, declarative, interrogative and imperative. This chapter introduces the metalanguage for talking about the way the parts of these clauses function so we can interact with each other.

In some texts, for example many written texts, only declarative clauses are used. Readers are not usually able to exchange meanings with writers in an interactive way, so this one-way grammar of declaration remains constant throughout the text (though electronic communication is changing this). Some writers, however, do include questions in their texts to encourage a kind of interaction in the reader's mind, although natuarally they don't expect to hear the reader's response. These questions are called rhetorical questions. (Have you noticed whether the authors of this book use rhetorical questions?)

When we are exchanging meanings face-to-face in spoken interactions, the grammar of interaction is critical to the effectiveness of the texts we construct. We draw on this grammar from moment to moment as the interaction unfolds. Let us now consider how knowledge about grammar can assist language learners to manage spoken interactive texts more effectively.

As we have been reminded in this chapter, the meanings we make when we interact – that is when we are giving or demanding information or goods and services – are at the semantic level of the language map, while the patterns we use to realise these meanings at the level of lexicogrammar will not necessarily be aligned to these meanings. Students must initially learn to manage effectively **the most straightforward grammatical** realisations of the interpersonal meanings used in interactions. They need to understand that:

- the most straightforward way to demand information is to use interrogative clauses to ask questions
- the most straightforward way to give information is to use declarative clauses to make statements
- the most straightforward way to demand goods and services is to use imperatives to give instructions
- although there is no straightforward way to give goods and services, we often temper an interrogative or a declarative with a modal Finite in order to make offers.

Students also need to learn how to respond in an exchange to each of these. In other words they need to learn how to:

- respond to a question by, for example, giving or withholding information
- respond to a statement by, for example, acknowledging or contradicting the information
- respond to instructions by, for example, complying or not
- respond to offers by, for example, accepting or declining.

In addition, they need to learn how to manage the exchange by:

- confirming, clarifying or checking what they have heard and asking for repetition or more information when necessary
- deflecting, contradicting or challenging meanings made by other speakers in the interaction.

The Subject and Finite in the Mood Block are the pivotal elements of the clause that make all these types of interaction possible. The order of the Subject and Finite is the 'grammatical sign of the type of exchange taking place'. It determines whether the clause will be declarative, interrogative or imperative. The turns of an exchange are generated and sustained by the way speakers manipulate the Subject and Finite in clauses from one turn to the next. Teachers and students can use this knowledge to distinguish and manipulate the elements of the clause which are at stake whenever a speaker initiates an exchange or responds to someone else. They can also distinguish those elements that remain constant as the exchange unfolds. Often the constant elements are left out, or ellipsed. This moves the interaction along at a cracking pace, a pace that can be difficult for language learners to manage. In addition, knowing what to leave out of the clauses in an interaction can be just as difficult for language learners as knowing what to put in.

The elements of the Mood Block are often small, especially if the Finite is an auxiliary verb and the Subject is expressed as a pronoun. It can be difficult for people learning English to hear the Mood Block in spoken language if they do not know to listen for it. It is very important that students are conscious of this element if they are to learn to interact effectively. Awareness of the Mood Block and the work it does makes it possible for students to 'catch the ball' in an interaction as speakers toss meanings backwards and forwards. They can then either return the same meanings back into the flow of the interaction or they can introduce new meanings and take the interaction in a new direction.

At the expression level of English different **intonation patterns** are used with declarative, interrogative and imperative clause structures depending on the meaning being made. It is important that students learn the intonation patterns at the same time as they learn the grammatical patterns if they are to control the full interpersonal potential of spoken clauses in interactions.

Manipulating the parts of the Mood Block is what keeps an exchange going. In fact quite lengthy exchanges can keep going with Mood Blocks alone, something which we hear in children's arguments and comedy routines. Have you ever heard children forget what they were arguing about? They can be so busy keeping the interpersonal meanings going, they forget the experiential meanings which began the argument in the first place! Text 7 is an extract from a transcript of a children's argument (the transcript of this conversation appears in full in the next chapter). The Mood Block is in bold to show how:

- the order of the Subject and Finite determines the type of exchange
- the Mood Block is tossed back and forwards from one speaker's turn to the next
- the Mood Block keeps the interaction going even when the rest of the clause is left out (or ellipsed).

Text 7: The Mars Bar argument

John:	Where **did** (F) **you** (S) get that Mars Bar?	interrogative
James:	**Bill** (S) **gave** (F) it to me at lunch time.	declarative
John:	No, **he** (S) **didn't** (F).	ellipsed declarative
James:	Yes, **he** (S) **did** (F).	ellipsed declarative
John:	**He** (S) **did** (F) **not**.	ellipsed declarative
James:	**Did!** (F).	ellipsed declarative

The Mood Block accounts for some of the structural features of English which are most challenging for students aiming for **accurate language use**. These include:

- subject-verb agreement (which reflects the interdependence of the Subject and Finite)
- auxiliary verb
- tense (expressed in the Finite)
- Mood tags (based on the Subject and Finite)
- negatives (an aspect of polarity)
- modal verbs (which are usually the Finite in a clause)
- contractions (which involve the Subject and Finite or the Finite and a negative)

- the way parts of clauses are ellipsed in spoken language (*Hot, isn't it? Yes, it is.*)
- many dialectal and non-standard variations in structure (*Ain't it the truth!*).

Understanding the function of the parts of the Mood Block in English helps students to understand, for example, that the morphological agreement between Subject and Finite is a reflection of the way their functional roles are intertwined in the Mood Block. Being aware of the structure of the Mood Block also helps students to explore the English tense system. For example, it helps students to understand the way the interpersonal meaning (Finite) and experiential meaning (Process) in a verb group can be fused in one word (eg *runs*) or teased apart in two or more words (eg *is running*) depending on the time of the event from the speaker's point of view.

In summary, understanding the grammar of the Mood Block shows students that some of the apparently arbitrary rules of English grammar have a functional motivation. The grammar of the Mood Block is often manipulated in what may appear to the learner very small and apparently insignificant changes in morphemes or words. If students learn to control this grammar they are able to control many of the resources in English that allow speakers to finetune, in subtle yet powerful ways, the language they use to negotiate relationships with others. We will explore this aspect of interpersonal grammar further in the next chapter.

We have already seen that students can begin working with the interpersonal meanings and grammar patterns which converge on the Mood Block by building a repertoire of the most straightforward ways of expressing meanings in an exchange. But being straightforward is not always the most useful way to interact in English, especially if we are asking people to give us something or do something for us; that is, if we are demanding goods or services. As students develop their knowledge of interpersonal grammar they will notice the way English speakers regularly finetune interpersonal meaning by shifting between structures that are straightforward ways of demanding or giving information or goods and services to those that are less straightforward. This is another example of grammatical metaphor, but in this case it is the alignment between interpersonal meaning and grammatical expression that shifts.

This shift to less straightforward structures increases the interpersonal distance between the speaker and the person they are speaking to, which is often an expression of politeness. For example, in most social settings English speakers will rarely use the imperative (eg *Open the door!*) to demand goods and services. Instead they usually shift their demand to an interrogative based on a modal finite (*Could you open the door? Would you mind opening the door?*). We will explore modality in more detail in Chapter 5.

The grammar of many of these shifts in expression is too complex for a beginner to unravel, but even beginners need to be able to express politeness in their exchanges so some of these 'shifted' expressions have to be learnt as whole 'gambits' at first. Students should also be aware that there are times when speakers of English are even less straightforward. For example they might even shift a demand for a service to a declarative clause (*It's stuffy in here, isn't it?*).

How can knowledge of the interpersonal grammar of interaction enhance teaching programs?

The interpersonal grammar speakers choose as they interact, is motivated by the tenor of the immediate context of situation. Language teaching activities can be designed to draw students' attention to this aspect of context and how it finds its way into the clauses of an interaction.

If teachers are aware of the functions of the clause parts that express interpersonal meaning, they will be able to help students analyse authentic interactions to discover how people use interpersonal grammar to take part in the interaction. Unfortunately, many of the dialogues in language teaching textbooks do not reflect the way people use language to interact in real life. A knowledge of interpersonal grammar helps teachers select the most authentic interactions for students to work while exploring the way speakers of English use this grammar. Teachers may also want to carry an audio or video recorder with them to capture authentic interactions. Some teachers even use their children's arguments, workplace negotiations, extracts from soap operas, or even the famous Monty Python *Argument* skit! Bear in mind, however, that teachers should seek the permission of the participants before using a recorded interaction in the classroom.

The interpersonal grammar of interaction and tenor

Students can explore how the tenor of the context of situation is expressed in interactions by exploring what the grammar reveals about:

- the relative power of the people taking part (*who does most of talking, who shares the talking, who merely listens and acknowledges*)
- the relative status of the people taking part (*who does what when they talk – for example who initiates by demanding or giving information or instructing or offering and who merely responds; who has to shift the grammar the greatest interpersonal distance from the meaning*)
- the level of personal involvement between the people taking part (For example: *Do they see each other regularly? Do they have a strong emotional bond?*).

Learning how to build and maintain social relationships in interactions can be one of the most challenging aspects of acquiring a new language. Conscious knowledge of the interpersonal grammar of interactions makes it possible for students to explore interactions used in contexts of situation relevant to their learning needs and goals. For example, if students wish to gain employment in a particular workplace, an exploration of interactions that take place in that workplace, or similar workplaces, will reveal the most effective ways for the student to interact with management and fellow workers.

Students might also think about the effect of interpersonal meanings on experiential meanings in interactions. For example, students might investigate:

- what speakers talk about in different types of interactions
- whether different relationships between speakers influence what the speakers talk about and how they talk about it.

For example, the two speakers arguing about the Mars Bar (Text 7) are likely to be children who are brothers or schoolmates. In a work place employees do not argue like this with their manager about confectionery. They may, however, argue about work matters although they are likely to use grammatical metaphor to shift the interpersonal grammar away from the meaning and create some interpersonal distance.

Teachers can also use their knowledge of interpersonal grammar to reflect on the way they interact and build relationships with their students in the classroom. Teachers are more powerful and have a higher status than students, so it seems 'natural' for them to dominate classroom interaction. Analysing typical classroom interactions can give teachers ideas for making more space for student contributions in class and for building relationships with students which might lead to more effective learning outcomes.

Using the grammar of interaction to build a critical response to text

Systemic functional linguists have undertaken interesting research into the roles different types of people play in interactions. For example, they have used interpersonal grammar to analyse the different roles men and women play in casual conversation.

Students might like to undertake small research tasks in which they analyse the different ways various types of people participate in interactions. They could, for example, explore interactions between young people and older people, men and women or adults and children. On the basis of their findings they might consider:

- who has the most power and status and who has the least power and status in different types of interaction
- how speakers can challenge or change relationships of power and status in different kinds of interactions.

Further reading

For more about language as interaction, read Chapter 4 of An *introduction to functional grammar: 2nd edition* (Halliday 1994).

Chapter 2 of *Focus on speaking* (Burns and Joyce, 1997: 17–38) is titled 'Producing and negotiating spoken language'. In this chapter the authors explore different types of spoken interactions that can be used in the classroom. *Focus on speaking* also includes transcripts of authentic spoken language as well as a whole chapter on classroom activities.

If you want to read how systemic functional linguists use the grammar of exchange to analyse the way tenor is expressed in interaction, read Chapter 5 of *Analysing casual conversation* (Eggins and Slade 1997).

For more about how intonation patterns are mapped onto clause types, see *In tempo: An English pronunciation course* (Zawadzki 1994).

Exercises for language teachers

1 Locate, and if necessary, record and transcribe a text which is a good example of the type of interaction you would like your students to be able to take part in effectively.
   - Look for patterns of interpersonal grammar that answer the following questions:
     – What types of meanings are exchanged in this interaction? (information or goods and services?)
     – How are these meanings exchanged? (giving or demanding?)
     – What interpersonal grammar is used to exchange these meanings? (declarative, interrogative, imperative)
   - Relate what you have discovered about the interpersonal grammar of the interaction to your students' learning needs and goals.

2 Use what you have discovered about the interpersonal grammar of the interaction to design activities which support your students' progress towards their learning goals. These activities might draw your students' attention to:
   - how speakers initiate, respond to and manage meanings exchanged in an interaction
   - the order of Subject and Finite in declarative, interrogative and imperative clauses
   - how the Mood Block is used to generate and sustain the exchanges in an interaction
   - how the constant elements of the clauses in an exchange are often left out
   - how the Mood Block accounts for many of the grammatical patterns that demand attention to detail if language use is to be accurate and relationships are to be negotiated effectively
   - how speakers shift the grammatical expression of some of the meanings they exchange in order to be polite
   - how the relative power and status of the speakers and their involvement are expressed in the vocatives
   - how the relative power and status of the speakers and their involvement are expressed in the interaction
   - how the expression of tenor in the interaction influences the experiential meanings people make in interactions.

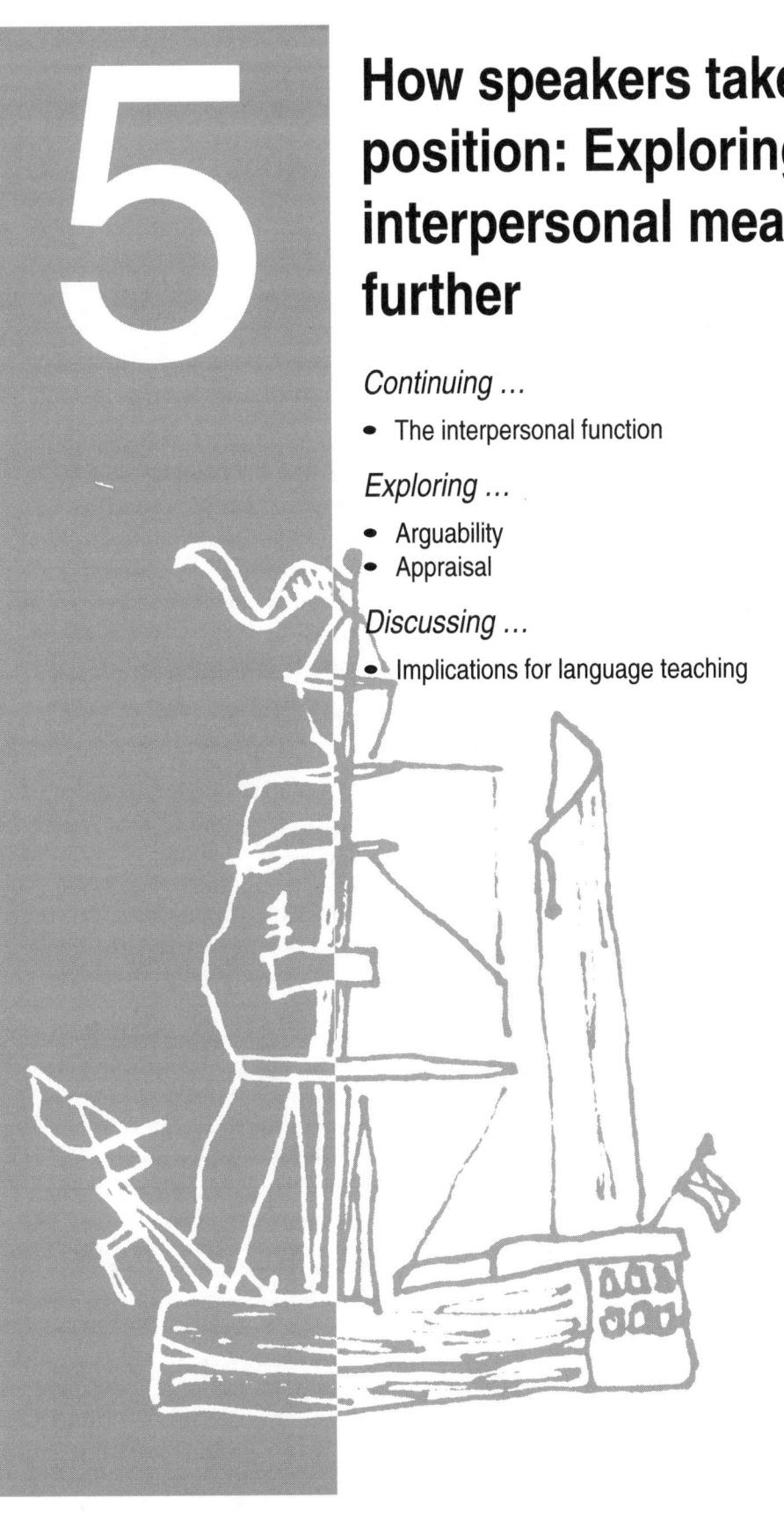

5 How speakers take a position: Exploring interpersonal meanings further

Continuing …

- The interpersonal function

Exploring …

- Arguability
- Appraisal

Discussing …

- Implications for language teaching

From Chapter 1

We use language to position ourselves (and our audience) to show how defensible we find our propositions, to encode our ideas about obligation and inclination, and to express our attitudes.

In the last chapter we discussed the interactions construed by different configurations of the Subject and Finite in the Mood Block. We noticed that the configuration of the Mood Block is a pattern in the lexicogrammar whereas what is being exchanged is a meaning in the semantics. Exchanging information operates quite differently from exchanging goods and services and what is at stake for argument or discussion in each type of exchange is therefore understandably different. In each case the addressee can accept or reject the speaker's proposition or proposal but in the former it is the information that is up for discussion while in the latter it is the proposed action.

In this chapter we explore the two main resources through which speakers take a position in their messages:

- adjustment of the Mood Block (the nub of the message available for argument or discussion)
- positive or negative appraisal of experiential meanings.

Speakers can position themselves in an argument or discussion by taking a definite stand or by adjusting their stand to a position between a definite *yes* and an equally definite *no*.

The main topics for discussion in this chapter are the speaker's resources for definiteness and adjustment (although we also explore meanings that are not available for argument ot discussion). We conclude by exploring the second resource available to speakers – the attitudinal positioning by positive or negative appraisal of their experiential meanings. We will begin by separating the two main types of exchange – exchange of information and exchange of goods and services.

Exchange of information

Taking a definite stand

Whenever speakers assert their propositions they put them up for agreement or disagreement by their hearers. In any discussion, argument or quarrel, it is the contents of the Mood Block which are at stake. This includes the Subject, the Finite and whether the proposition is positive or negative. When speakers are definite about their propositions, the Finite encodes information about whether an Event has occurred, is presently occurring, or is yet to occur. Text 1 is an example of an argument in a child's play. For our discussion we have numbered the clauses (this is always a good idea when exploring texts because it makes reference easy). In Clause 2 James takes a definite positive stand while in Clause 3 John takes an equally definite negative position.

Text 1: Felicity's play

Scene:		A suburban garden. After school.
		John and James are having an argument.
John:	1	Where did you get that Mars Bar?
James:	2	Bill gave it to me at lunch time.
John:	3	No, he didn't.
James:	4	Yes, he did.
John:	5	He did not.
James:	6	Did!
John:	7	Did not. (8) I saw you take it from mum's secret hiding place.
James:	9	You did not.
John:	10	Yes, I did.
James:	11	It's mine anyway.
John:	12	I want one too. (crying)
Mum:	13	What's all this noise about? (14) If you can't play outside (15) without fighting, (16) come inside (17) and do your homework.

We already know the metalanguage needed to discuss what's going on here. In Clauses 2 to 10 each boy is quite definite about what has happened, although they do not always need a full clause to say so. Clauses 2 and 8 each contain a complete proposition but in Clauses 3, 4, 5, 7, 9 and 10 the argument is maintained by the simple repetition of Subject, Finite and Polarity. In Clause 6 only the Finite is necessary to maintain the argument.

If we want to disagree with a speaker's positive proposition, we simply add a negative such as *not* or *n't* into the Mood Block after the Finite. This gives the clause NEGATIVE POLARITY. If the original proposition was negative, we show our disagreement by changing the polarity of the message to positive:

| Speaker 1: | Tom was beaten. |
| Speaker 2: (disagreeing) | Tom was not beaten! |

| Speaker 1: | I haven't seen him. |
| Speaker 2: (disagreeing) | You have seen him! |

The analysis of the first exchange is:

| Tom | was (positive polarity) | beaten |
| Tom | was not (negative polarity) | beaten |

Subject	Finite (past)	Predicator
Mood Block		Residue

In the examples above the second speaker repeats the whole clause of the first speaker while reversing the polarity. This sounds very emphatic. Normally we would not repeat an entire clause. It is enough to repeat the Subject and Finite. In most cases, the speaker would also substitute an appropriate pronoun for the nominal group filling the Subject slot, for example:

Speaker 1:   Your car's blocking the driveway.
Speaker 2:   No, it isn't.

It's worth repeating that in any argument or quarrel about the information in a message, it is the relation between the Subject and Finite in the Mood Block which is at stake. It carries the argument and allows discussion. In fact it is not unusual to hear a quarrel reduced to an exchange of opposing Finites as it was in Text 1. Here is another example:

		Mood Block		
		Subject	Finite	
Speaker 1:		Hector Protector	was	dressed all in green
Speaker 2:	No	he	wasn't	
Speaker 1:	Oh yes	he	was!	
Speaker 2:			Wasn't	
Speaker 1:			Was!	

Meanings that are not available for argument or discussion

If a clause does not have a Mood Block, there is nothing on which to base an argument. We are not talking about the clauses where the Subject-Finite relationship is ellipsed, that is omitted but recoverable from previous clauses, but about clauses that never had a Finite and are therefore non-finite clauses.

Examples of non-finite clauses

| Shaken | at last | out of his complacency |

Predicator	Adjunct	Adjunct
Residue		

Eating	an apple
Predicator	Complement
Residue	

You may know the grammatical term *infinitive*. An infinitive verb is the most basic form of the verb which signifies the Event without specifying a Subject and without indicating any time or duration of the Event. An English infinitive such as *to eat* corresponds broadly with the Latin *edire*, the German *essen* and the French *manger*. While we can contest the proposition being made in a Finite clause, there can be no argument about the general idea *to eat*. Thus, one function of the Finite is to tie down the verb to its Subject so that the proposition in the clause is debatable or arguable. In English the infinitive *(to) eat* is non-finite, as are past and present participle forms such as *eaten* or *eating* when they are without a Subject and thus they are not open to debate or argument, nor tied to a relationship with the here and now.

In the following clauses the verbal groups which include a Finite are underlined and those which are non-finite are in bold:

> **Going** upstairs, I <u>discovered</u> my two cats, who <u>had been missing</u> for some time, **disembowelling** my lace cushion.
>
> The city **having been** well and truly **sacked**, the Visigoths <u>retired</u> to their own territory.
>
> To **err** <u>is</u> human; **to forgive** divine.

Without a Finite, a clause has no clear-cut place in the arguability of things. It is difficult to argue with *Going upstairs*, or *To err* or *to forgive*, or even with *having been sacked*. Each has an Event but not a real Finite or Subject and it is the Subject/Finite relation, the Mood, which allows discussion.

Adjusting one's stand: probability, usuality, obligation, inclination, typicality and obviousness

Sometimes speakers want to signal that they are not definite about their messages, that is, they are looking for a position between a definite *yes* and a definite *no*. They do this by changing the configuration of the Mood Block in some way. Their range of options for doing this is known as MODALITY and it has its own metalanguage.

The metalanguage of adjustment

Modality
Modal Finite
Mood Adjunct
Interpersonal grammatical metaphor

We use the term MODALITY to refer to all positioning by speakers about probability, usuality, typicality, obviousness, obligation and inclination. There are three ways of doing this:

- by a Modal Finite
- by an adverbial group or prepositional phrase, here known as Mood Adjunct
- with an interpersonal grammatical metaphor.

Because any expression of modality affects the arguability of a proposition, Modal Finites, Mood Adjuncts and interpersonal grammatical metaphors all belong in the Mood Block. The kinds of modality we shall explore in most detail in this section are those which position speakers between a definite *yes* and a definite *no* – whether this is possibly *yes* or possibly *no* (where the uncertainty is to do with probability) or sometimes *yes* and sometimes *no* (where the uncertainty is to do with usuality). Modals of obligation and inclination will be discussed in more detail later in this chapter.

Modal Finites

Let's go back to Felicity's play (Text 1) and imagine that Clause 2 now says:

> James: Bill might have given it to me at lunch time

Here the Finite expressing past time has been replaced by a Modal Finite and James is now expressing an opinion about probability. Notice how this will change the subsequent argument from whether Bill did or didn't give James the Mars Bar to whether he might or might not have. The Modal Finite indicates that James has modified the force of the proposition from a definite polarity to the grey area between *yes* and *no*. All speakers and writers use the Finite to position themselves, and can choose whether to express time or opinion in their Finites just as they can choose positive or negative polarity. In the following examples, Finites expressing time are contrasted with Finites expressing modality.

Examples of clauses with Finite expressing time

The dunce	was	going	to school
They	will	be staying	with us
I	have	been courting	for six years

Subject	Finite	Predicator	Adjunct
Mood Block		Residue	

Examples of clauses with a Finite expressing modality of possibility or usuality
For this illustration, the details of the Residue are not significant and have been omitted:

The child	might	have fallen into the water
The cattle	could	have drowned during the storm
They	would	go to the market
I	will	see justice done

Subject	Finite (modal): probability/usuality	Residue
Mood Block		

The distinction between Finite expressing time and Finite expressing modality is not always as clear cut as we may have made it seem. Sometimes only the tone of voice and overall context indicate whether *will* and *shall* express future time or the speaker's determination – what we might call willpower. Can you distinguish futurity from certainty in the following clauses? Does it matter?

She	shall	have music wherever she goes
I	will	win the race tomorrow
He	'll	come back again

Mood Adjuncts

In Chapter 3 we explored the way that experiential meanings are realised in the patterns of nominal groups, verbal groups, adverbial groups and prepositional phrases. But not all adverbial groups and prepositional phrases are relevant for the analysis of experiential meanings and any box diagrams underneath them are left blank. At this point we need to investigate whether they are realising the interpersonal meaning of modifying the argument expressed in the Mood Block. They may do this by expressing usuality, probability, typicality or obviousness.

It may suit our purposes to be aware of these sub-categories of modality, or it may be enough just to recognise modality without any more delicate analysis. In any case, without some metalanguage it is hard to provide a delicate analysis. For more details about modality, consult Halliday (1994: 82, 83).

Here are some examples of Mood Adjuncts:

Georgie Porgie	always		kissed	the girls
Subject	Mood Adjunct (usuality)	Finite + (past)	Predicator	Complement
Mood Block			Residue	

The team	probably		couldn't	have beaten	the grandfinalists
Subject	Mood Adjunct (probability)	Finite – (modal)	Predicator	Complement	
Mood Block			Residue		

Do	you	come	here	often?
Finite + (present)	Subject	Predicator	Adjunct	Mood Adjunct (usuality)
Mood		Residue		Block

The family	generally		has	coffee	after dinner
Subject	Mood Adjunct (typicality)	Finite + (present)	Predicator	Complement	Adjunct
Mood Block			Residue		

Of course	the boy	will	play	soccer
Mood Adjunct (obviousness)	Subject (future)	Finite + (future/modal)	Predicator	Complement
Mood Block			Residue	

Interpersonal grammatical metaphor

Sometimes we use a whole clause in a text to express our opinion of the proposition in a neighbouring clause. We are using the grammar metaphorically when we say, for example, *I think* when we mean *probably*; or, *I believe* when we mean *almost certainly*; or *don't you think?* when we mean *definitely*.

The last example is a bit problematic: The Finite before the Subject shows that the speaker is demanding an agreement. It encodes both the speaker's demand for a *yes* response and the speaker's opinion. The best way of handling a modal grammatical metaphor in a detailed analysis is to analyse it twice, first as a separate clause and then as a Mood Adjunct within the clause it expresses an opinion about. But at this stage it's much more important to recognise it as a kind of modality than to analyse it in detail.

Just as an ideational grammatical metaphor uses the experiental resources of the grammar to shift meaning, so interpersonal grammatical metaphors shift meaning from a separate mental process clause to an expression of modality in the projected clause. Take for example the following sentence:

I think he's coming to the party.

We would of course analyse this as a projecting clause (*I think*) followed by a projected clause (*he's coming to the party*).

But now check what the Mood tag would be for this sentence, not *Don't I?* but *Isn't he?* This suggests that what looks like a projecting clause is actually functioning as a Mood Adjunct within the second clause. Imagine this now being reworded as:

Probably he's coming to the party.

Exchange of goods and services

Demands realised in declaratives with modals of obligation

In Chapter 4 we noticed that the imperative mood is the most straightforward and easily recognised way of demanding goods and services and that imperatives may be positive or negative. In most positive imperatives there is no Subject and no Finite in the clause. In spite of this absence we still describe the verb in imperatives as a finite verb because we can recover the Subject and Finite in a Mood tag. What is interesting is that the Finite in the Mood tag always expresses modality rather than time:

	Open	the door	will can't can	you? you? you?
	Predicator	Complement	Finite (modal)	Subject
Mood Block	Residue		Mood tag	

What is at stake here is not the definiteness of a proposition but whether the addressee will do what has been asked in the proposal. If addressees do not wish to comply with the demand, their response takes up the Mood tag, arguing:

No,	I	won't can't	(open	the door)
	Subject	Finite – (modal)	Predicator	Complement
	Mood Block		(usually ellipsed) Residue	

Similarly, in an imperative with negative polarity, while there is a Finite in the Mood Block of the clause itself, it is not the same as the Finite in any added Mood tag:

Don't	open	the door,	will	you?
Finite – (present)	Predicator	Complement	Finite (modal)	Subject
Mood Block	Residue		Mood tag	

Once again, if addressees do not wish to comply with the demand, they can argue by using the Finite in the Mood tag, not that in the original clause:

Yes	I	will	(open	the door)
	Subject	Finite + (modal)	Predicator	Complement
	Mood Block		(usually ellipsed) Residue	

What is at stake is whether the addressee will or will not perform the demanded action. For some people and in some contexts the use of an imperative seems too bossy, not sufficiently polite or otherwise inappropriate. You might think of people and places when you yourself would not choose the imperative to demand goods and services but would choose something softer and more polite. For example, instead of an imperative, you could demand goods and services with an interrogative or with a declarative using a Modal Finite to express obligation.

Up to this point we have only mentioned modality of probability, usuality, obviousness and typicality, which go by the collective name of MODALISATION, but obligation can also be expressed through MODULATION. Perhaps using a declarative with a Modal Finite expressing obligation doesn't seem any less bossy to you but at least rather than ordering the addressee to do something, the speaker is putting forward an opinion about whether or not that something should be done. A declarative also allows speakers to suggest that persons other than the addressee should embark on some form of action. The following are clauses with a Finite expressing modality of obligation and necessity. For this illustration, the details of the Residue are not significant and have been omitted:

The author	should	have checked her facts
You	have to	eat your dinner first
All nonmembers	must	be signed in
She	ought	to visit the dentist
You	need	to go to the library

Subject	Finite (modal: obligation)	
Mood Block		Residue

Offers realised in declaratives and interrogatives with modals of inclination

As we saw in Chapter 4, there is no special configuration of the Mood Block for offering a service. What is at stake here is whether the offer will be accepted or rejected and this may explain why there is no special form for giving goods and services as there is with demanding goods and services or giving or demanding information. Perhaps there is a need to save the face of the one who makes the offer and the one who may reject the offer? Indeed the three examples of offers below could possibly be mistaken for demands or gifts of information. However, there are two pointers to the fact that they are offers – one in the making of the offer and the other in its reception; that is, the Finite in this type of exchange is usually a modal and, rather than a simple *yes* or *no*, the response is usually *yes*, *please*, if the offer is accepted, and *no*, *thank you*, if the offer is rejected:

	Would Can		you I	like carry	a chocolate? your case?
I'	II		do	that	
Subject	Finite (modal: inclination)		Subject	Predicator	Complement
Mood Block				Residue	

Modality in context

The following three texts have different purposes. Text 2 (Cherie's text) is written by a primary school child after a session on how to write an exposition. She has been taught that this text type should include a point of view. Text 3 is from the conclusion of an investigative report. The writer knows that, after being objective about his purpose, methods and results in the body of the report, it is now appropriate to make recommendations. Text 4 is from a courtroom cross-examination in which the second speaker is trying to avoid giving definite answers.

In each text we recognise that the speakers and writers are including their own opinions. This is a very useful device because it sometimes allows a speaker to stand apart from the action as if to say, 'Well, it's only my opinion. You don't have to agree with me. I could be persuaded otherwise'. In other situations, it allows a speaker to appear openly persuasive, or even downright bossy, about how the world could, or should, or ought to be arranged. We can see from Text 3 how useful modality is at the end of a discussion text because it allows the writer to conclude with an opinion or recommendation.

Text 2: Cherie's text

> **What Makes a Good Teacher?**
>
> A good teacher needs to be understanding to all children. He or she also must be fair and reasonable. The teacher must work at a sensible pace and not one thing after another. The teacher also needs to speak with a clear voice so the children can understand. If the children have worked hard during the week there should be some fun activities. Thats what I think a good teacher should be like.
>
> by Cherie.

Text 3: From a discussion on the future of suburban estuaries

In conclusion, estuarine waterways within an urban environment could add a special dimension to daily life. An expanse of safe water would provide additional opportunities for recreation. These are values which ought to be preserved. Unfortunately, our social and community life is sometimes hostile to these values. While urban subdivision, traffic, refuse disposal and industry may all be essential parts of our daily life, we must pursue these activities without unnecessary environmental degradation. Different conflicting interests must be resolved so that our many, proper aspirations may be accommodated both now and in the future.

Text 4: Cross examination of Mr L

Speaker 1:   After that meeting with Mr S, when was the next time that you saw him?
Speaker 2:   Approximately September or October or maybe November of 1976.
Speaker 1:   Come, come, Mr L, can't you be more accurate than that?
Speaker 2:   No, I can not. I think it was most likely the end of October.

Appraisal

The resource of APPRAISAL is one of the ways speakers position their audience. In other words, their choice of lexicogrammatical patterns influences the audience's personal reaction to the meanings in a text. We have only to think of the positive or negative spin put on the 'same information' by opposing sides of a debate to see how this positioning works. However, if the colour or flavour of the text is very strong, the audience may interpret the text as being very emotional, judgemental or critical, so lexicogrammatical resources for creating and interpreting appraisal and attitude are important tools in our exploration of text.

The metalanguage of appraisal

Attitude, including judgement, affect and appreciation
Graduation, including force and focus
Engagement

Much recent work, notably by J R Martin (Christie and Martin 1997) and Peter White (www.grammatics.com/appraisal/), has focused on the different lexical and grammatical systems available to speakers and writers for including their emotions (affect), judgements of people's behaviour, and their appreciation of phenomena in the world. In spoken texts, speakers can also position themselves by using such phonological systems as voice quality.

This recent work is a vast contribution to the way we understand texts, although its details are beyond the scope of this book. However, even though we are watering them down, they are worth mentioning because of the exciting way different appraisal motifs build up patterns across a whole text. These patterns align speakers with listeners around a set of values to produce a sense of belonging and community. In other words, effective speakers and writers are able to spread appraisal meanings across a whole text so that the audience is drawn to a particular point of view or interpretation of the content which seems natural. Effective listeners and readers need to realise that they are being positioned by these patterns of meaning so that they can choose whether or not they wish to align themselves with them.

Perhaps the most accessible appraisal motifs are lexical systems of GRADUATION (amplification), where the volume of a lexical item is turned up or down in positive or negative appraisal. We can think of graduation as options of FORCE and FOCUS – force adjusts the volume of gradable meanings while focus grades ungradable experiential meanings. As an example of force, we could change the verb *walk*, enriching it positively by choosing instead the verbs *stroll* or *saunter*, or by adding a Circumstance: manner: quality such as *walk gracefully*, or we could enrich it negatively by choosing *shuffled* or *like a hippopotamus*.

As another option, if we were to take the adjective *beautiful*, already an enriched word, we could amplify its intensity by repeating it, as in:

The painting was beautiful, beautiful, beautiful

or we could expand it with synonyms as in:

The painting was beautiful, inspired, magnificent

or we could premodify the adjective in some way as in:

It was very beautiful

or:

It was bloody beautiful

Focus, on the other hand, is concerned with blurring or sharpening. Examples are expressions like *kind of woozy*, *a true friend*, *effectively signed his death warrant* and *pure folly*.

Some words, such as *clean* and *dirty*, have an experiential meaning as well as an interpersonal, attitudinal one and properly belong in our experiential analysis as well. But other words, such as *splendid*, *lousy*, *fabulous* and *gross*, are more often used simply to convey a positive or negative attitude. These Epithets, which map the subjective and interpersonal on to our modelling of experience, are examples of appraisal. In any analysis it is worth keeping track of who does the appraising, whether it is positive or negative, and what items are appraised.

In the area of ATTITUDE appraisal resources include lexical items for judging people's behaviour in terms of social esteem and social sanction. Under the heading of social esteem, Martin includes lexical items for assessing normality and luck, capacity and dependability. Under the heading of social sanction are assessments of honesty and integrity or propriety.

Another of Martin's networks collects together the grammatical resources speakers use to position themselves in relation to experiential meanings. This ENGAGEMENT system brings together items that we have met elsewhere in the grammar. For instance, Circumstances of angle (for example *according to John*) and Circumstances of abstract location (for example *In Freud's psychoanalytical theory*) allow writers to disclaim or distance themselves from the views expressed in the experiential meanings.

One resource for appraisal particular to the interpersonal metafunction is the COMMENT ADJUNCT, which allows speakers to comment on experiential meanings. Because Comment Adjuncts represent the intrusion of a speaker into a clause, they are important enough to be included in the Mood Block even though they do not modify the argument in any way. The Comment Adjuncts in the first and third of the following examples express Attitude while that in the second expresses Engagement:

Unfortunately	we	can't	come	to the party
Comment Adjunct	Subject	Finite – (modal)	Predicator	Adjunct
Mood Block			Residue	

The committee	is	apparently	working	all weekend
Subject	Finite + (present)	Comment Adjunct	Predicator	Adjunct
Mood Block			Residue	

Hopefully	the missing puppy	will	be found
Comment Adjunct	Subject	Finite	Predicator
Mood Block			Residue

More about Adjuncts

In the metalanguage for interpersonal meanings, all adverbial groups and prepositional phrases that are not embedded are known as Adjuncts. In fact there are four different types of Adjunct:

Adjunct: those prepositional phrases, adverbial groups and even nominal groups that realise Circumstance and those prepositional phrases that realise Participant in experiential meanings are known simply as Adjuncts and form part of the Residue for the interpersonal analysis.

Mood Adjunct: those which are not relevant to the experiential analysis but modify the argument of a clause are known as Mood Adjuncts and are included in the Mood Block.

Comment Adjunct: those which comment on the experiential analysis but do not form part of it are known as Comment Adjuncts and are included in the Mood Block.

Conjunctive Adjunct: those which form a connection or bridge to a previous clause are known as Conjunctive Adjuncts and are excluded from the experiential analysis and are labelled in the interpersonal analysis but excluded from the Mood Block and Residue.

Appendix C contains a prepositional phrase and adverbial group help list.

Mapping experiential and interpersonal meanings on the same clause

Earlier chapters of this book have indicated that different metafunctions map different meanings on to a clause, so it is not surprising that we use different metalanguage in analysing and describing the metafunctions. The metalanguage for the description of the experiential function focuses on the various possible combinations of Processes, Participants and Circumstances, while the metalanguage for the description of interpersonal meanings focuses on the Subject/Finite relationship, Mood and Comment Adjuncts in the Mood Block and the Predicator, Complement and ordinary Adjuncts that make up the Residue. Not every word in a clause will be relevant to the description of each function.

In the following analysis we have also labelled the class of the basic clause constituents.

	And	apart from that	hopefully	we	might	make	it
constituency	conj	prep phrase	adv g	ng	vg		ng
experiential				Actor	Process: material		Range
interpersonal	Conjunctive Adjunct		Comment Adjunct	Subject	Finite (modal)	Pred	Comp
			Mood Block			Residue	

	although	perhaps	the pie	was eaten		by the dog
constituency	conj g	adv g	ng	vg		pp
experiential			Goal	Process: material		Actor
interpersonal			Mood Adjunct	Subject	Finite +	Predicator	Adjunct
			Mood Block			Residue	

	And	actually	the monster	probably		burped	after his meal
constituency	conj g	adv g	ng	adv g	vg		prep phrase
			Behaver		Process: behav		Circum: when
interpersonal		Conj Adj	Subject	Mood Adj Prob	Finite + (past)	Pred	Adjunct
			Mood Block			Residue	

To sum up

In Chapters 4 and 5 we have explored how interpersonal meanings express interaction and positioning. In Appendix E you will find charts for summarising your interpersonal analysis, which you will need to expand or contract for different types of text. If you are analysing dialogue, for example, you will want to include a column to identify each speaker and you may even want separate charts for different speakers. If you have studied conversation analysis, you may choose a more delicate way of charting interaction, such as whether the speaker initiates, continues or concludes a topic, whether a clause is a demand or a response, and whether the response is the one the demander wanted. It's entirely up to you. We simply offer you some basic templates as tools to summarise the interpersonal meanings uncovered by your analysis.

Exercises

1   Identify the ways the speakers have encoded their positions in the following text. What can you say about the relationship between the speakers (ie the tenor) in the context of situation?

Speaker 1:   And then at that time did you give him the gun?

Speaker 2:   It was probably about that time.

Speaker 1:   Did you have at that time some talk about the incident?

Speaker 2:   Yes, I think I did.

Speaker 1:   And, at that time, was the man R still in the back room?

Speaker 2:   Yes, I think he was.

Speaker 1:   Perhaps I should ask you as a matter of finality, were you in the lounge room when Mr R was escorted through the house?

Speaker 2:   No sir, I don't think so, no.

2   Take another look at the sample text types in Chapter 1. Pull out all examples of modality and appraisal in these texts and describe each as delicately as you can.

3   Take a simple sentence such as *The house is empty* or *She works in Newcastle* and consider all the ways you might modify the wording to play with the polarity, modalisation and modulation of what is being asserted. Think also about how statements like these might be modified by a Comment Adjunct or an Attitudinal Epithet.

4   Return to Text 4 (The Medea text) in Chapter 4 and explore the following questions.
    a.   Which lexical items show the writer's appraisal of Medea?
    b.   What kinds of adjustments are made in this text? eg polarity, non-Finite clauses, modality, appraisal
    c.   How are these adjustments spread across the text?
    d.   What position (or positions) is the writer taking?
    e.   Is this position explicit or is it made to seem 'natural'?
    f.   Do you agree with this position?

5   Redraft the text, readjusting the meanings so that the position the text takes is changed. What do you notice as you do this activity?

Implications for language teaching

This chapter sketches in an outline of the rich and complex language resources English speakers have for putting themselves into their language and adjusting the worldview, that is, the experiential meanings, they are making. These resources include:

- varying how definite the speaker is about experiential meanings through:
  - the tense and polarity of the Finite
  - making the meanings unavailable for argument in non-Finite clauses
  - finding ground between positive and negative with modality
- appraising experiential meanings.

How is knowledge of the interpersonal grammar for taking a stand useful to teachers and learners?

Speakers of all languages want to be able to put themselves into the meanings they make with language. When we learn a new variety of our own language, for example when we first learn to write our own language, or when we learn a new language, we feel frustrated because it is so difficult to express exactly how we view things. We don't know how to make a meaning unavailable for argument, to hedge our bets when we want to, to turn the volume of what we are saying up or down or to reveal just a little bit of our point of view at a time.

Students are usually given support with expressing experiential meanings and with some of the meanings of exchange. They have traditionally been taught how to add a negative to the Mood Block, but have rarely been shown, explicitly and systematically, how to express and finetune their own points of view, positions and opinions. In language teaching this has traditionally been an under-described area of the grammar and teachers have not had the resources to address it fully.

If we want to infuse, temper, negotiate, constrain or challenge the experiential meanings in a message with our own point of view, it is the Mood Block which is in focus. Speakers of English use the **Finite** in the Mood Block to reveal:

- *either* – the time of the event from their point of view
  - whether they are positive or negative about the information in the clause
- *or* – the degree to which they are definite about the information in the clause

In English **tense** gives the timing of an event in a clause from the point of view of the speaker. Tense in English is relative not absolute. The interplay of tense and aspect, which generates so many verb forms in English and which can be so confusing to language learners, is used to update and refine this timing as a text unfolds, often from one clause to the next. Armed with this information the language learner may still find the English tense system complex, but perhaps more meaningful and therefore more understandable – and ultimately, more manageable and useable. In Chapter 9 we will explore a whole text approach to thinking about tense.

In the Mood element a Finite with tense can be replaced by a MODAL FINITE if the speaker wants to adjust their perspective on the meanings in the clause to fall somewhere between absolute *yes* and absolute *no*. Many otherwise quite fluent speakers of English as a second or foreign language never quite master this area of English grammar and are thus denied the rich potential that Modal Finites have for tempering and finetuning exchanges. If they are not using Modal Finites effectively, speakers can seem either overemphatic or imprecise, even if that is not how they wish to be perceived. The information in this chapter makes it possible for teachers to map this ground for students, showing them how modality works when exchanging information (modalisation) and when exchanging goods and services (modulation).

Putting meanings into NON-FINITE clauses is a way of making meanings unavailable for argument or discussion. This resource is especially useful for students learning to write English for academic purposes. The grammar of non-Finite clauses, however, can be quite challenging for language learners. This is especially so because these clauses always have to be combined with a main clause and, if the writer is not careful, this can lead to some infelicitous meaning combinations, for example:

Having been damaged in the rear, the driver eased his car gently off the road.

Another common error that language learners make is to write non-Finite sentence fragments. If language learners know the functions of non-Finite clauses, they are more likely to manage their use effectively.

MOOD ADJUNCTS are also introduced in this chapter as an important aspect of modality in English. Students rarely find these words difficult to learn and often favour them over Modal Finites. It is important that students come to use these two aspects of the Mood element in a balanced way.

This chapter also illustrates how modal meanings are often made in English by using grammatical metaphor. It is important that language learners understand this metaphorical shift if they are not to misinterpret or ignore it, and thus fail to recognise that a meaning has been tempered or constrained.

Interpersonal meaning may converge on the Mood Block, but students need to know that it also spreads out across other parts of the clause. As we make experiential meanings about the world, we are also appraising them. English has an array of resources which make it possible to appraise experiential meanings anywhere in the clause.

This chapter shows how English speakers drop COMMENT ADJUNCTS into any part of the clause to show their attitude to experience. In addition, it shows how speakers and writers often incorporate attitude and point of view into words used to represent experience. It is important that an exploration of these more scattered, but nevertheless systematic, interpersonal resources are included in a language education program.

The expression of interpersonal meaning in English is a very complex area of grammar, and very hard to pin down. This complexity may be seen as a functional characteristic because, after all, the negotiation of our relationships with others and the expression of our points of view are fluid and everchanging areas of our lives. We need a language resource which can refine and rework our interpersonal meanings to a very high degree of delicacy and with a great deal of flexibility.

How can knowledge of the interpersonal grammar for taking a position enhance teaching programs?

Most English speakers are unconscious of the nature of the interpersonal grammar for taking a position, even though they use this resource with such finesse everyday of their lives. It is, therefore, one of the most difficult areas of English to teach others. Exploring the interpersonal meanings of English clauses in terms of function will give students a feel for the way these resources are used across different contexts. In this way learners are more likely to build a viable repertoire of workable language resources for making interpersonal meaning even while they are gaining control of the whole system.

We saw how experiential meanings in the clause can be explored in terms of structure and how students can explore the different 'slots' of the clause in terms of their meaning potential, using WH-questions to probe for these meanings. In contrast, interpersonal meanings are often more usefully explored in terms of their spread across the clauses of text. Coloured highlighters can be a very useful resource for revealing the stand a speaker or writer is taking towards the experiential meanings in a text. For example, students might use different colours to bring out the use of polarity, the two types of modality and different types of appraisal across the clauses of a text.

Modals have always been given a great deal of attention in traditional language classrooms, but the functional description in this chapter provides the teacher with a comprehensive framework that captures all the grammatical expression of modality in terms of the way it is used rather than in terms of the word class (for example verb or adverb) which expresses it. For instance students can explore the different ways English has of expressing modality (for example, *must, should, probably, the possibility, I think*) in order to increase their repertoire beyond the overused and inflexible *maybe*.

Students can also explore the elements of experiential grammar that can be used to express point of view. These include:

- mental processes (for example *I think, I want*)
- material and verbal processes (for example *slammed* instead of *put*, *shrieked* instead of *said*)

- mental and verbal processes which attribute and report point of view (for example *They believed ...*)
- Attitudinal Epithet (realised as adjectives like *ugly, wonderful, courageous*), Numerative (*more than a million*) and Thing (realised as nouns like *saint, idiot*) within a Participant or Circumstance.

There are also experiential meanings that will have a predictable impact on particular audiences. For example, in the following clause:

She rescued the child from the fire

most people will think that the rescuer is courageous, even though this word is never used (or some people may think she was foolhardy).

Students can highlight words in a text using shades of different colours, or different font styles, to reveal how interpersonal meanings for taking a position are graded from:

- positive to negative (*happy* → *sad; honest* → *dishonest; good* → *bad*)
- strong to weak (*certainly* → *perhaps; absolutely terrified* → *mildly anxious; abhor* → *hate* → *dislike*)
- the subjective to the objective (*I think* → *the significance of*)
- the explicit to the implicit (*She was courageous* → *She rescued the child from the fire.*)

When teaching vocabulary, teachers usually present words to students in sets organised according to field. In other words, vocabulary is presented to help learners make experiential meanings. Students also need vocabulary for making interpersonal adjustments to their experiential meanings. New research by Martin and by White (cited in this chapter) provides teachers with ideas for organising vocabulary lists that help learners include and adjust point of view in their texts. For example, teachers might organise vocabulary in the following sets:

- lexical items for expressing attitude
  - lexical items for responding emotionally (*happy/sad; safe/dangerous*)
  - lexical items for judging people's behaviour in terms of its normality (*unlucky, eccentric, unfashionable*) dependability (*brave, reliable, flighty, lazy*), capacity (*talented, strong, stupid*), honesty (*genuine, deceitful*) or integrity (*saintly, unethical*)
  - lexical items for appreciating the aesthetics and value of phenomena (*stunning, harmonious, insignificant*)
- lexical items for grading point of view (*slightly, a bit, somewhat, quite, very, a true friend*).

It is very important for students to experiment in the relative safety of the classroom with different ways of adjusting the position they are taking in their language. People outside the classroom are likely to be much more aware and understanding of the errors learners make with experiential meaning than they are of the errors learners make as they adjust that meaning interpersonally.

What other features of interpersonal grammar for taking a stand are useful in the classroom?

Taking a position and text structure

The way speakers and writers adjust their point of view is spread across a text. This spread is aligned to the purpose and structure of the text. A speaker or writer can spread interpersonal meanings across a text to give it a particular colour, flavour or perspective. If the colour or flavour of a text is very strong, the audience may interpret the text as being very emotional, judgemental or critical. For example we often interpret certain types of journalism as 'sensational' and in this case what we are responding to is the way the journalist has adjusted the experiential meaning in order to spread a certain kind of interpersonal meaning across the text.

Effective speakers and writers are able to spread explicit and implicit interpersonal meanings across texts so that the audience is drawn towards a particular point of view or interpretation of the content. This position may be interpreted as 'natural'. This is particularly true of stories and of texts which are structured to persuade. As the text unfolds, the impact of these meanings accumulates from stage to stage, until the desired 'volume' is reached. The accumulated meanings can be capitalised on by the speaker or writer in the final stage of their text to enhance the achievement of the text's purpose.

Taking a stand and tenor

We have already seen that expressions of tenor in grammar reveal the relative power and status of the people taking part and the level of their personal involvement. This is also true of the interpersonal meanings used to adjust experiential meanings in texts. At first these adjustments can be invisible to language learners and if they are not made explicit, learners are denied the language resources which make it possible to build solidarity, persuade or challenge in relationships which are important to them in the community, at work or in education.

If language learners have the opportunity to explore the language resources used to make these adjustments, these resources become visible and potentially useable. Control of these resources can greatly ease a learner's entry into different communities of English speakers.

Using an understanding of how speakers and writers take a stand to build a critical response to text

Effective listeners and readers recognise that they are being positioned by the patterns of diffused interpersonal meanings layered over a text and they can choose whether they wish to align themselves with the speaker's or writer's position or not.

Language learners can be helped to develop this awareness by being shown how to look for expressions of point of view in the texts they are working with. They can note how these expressions of point of view adjust experiential meaning and how these meanings are spread over the structure of the text.

Further reading

For more on the uses of appraisal resources in education see Christie and Martin (1997).

You can find out more about the appraisal resources of English in White (1998) [Online].

Exercises for language teachers

1   Identify a good example of a type of text you would like your students to be able to use effectively. You might like to choose a text in which the adjustment of experiential meanings is critical; for example, a text designed to persuade people to a particular point of view, or a news story in which language is used to enhance the 'newsworthiness' of an event. The text could be spoken or written. If you wish, you can choose one of the texts in Chapter 1.
    a. Look for words and structures that adjust the experiential meanings interpersonally.
        –   What kinds of adjustments are made in this text (eg polarity, non-Finite clauses, modality, appraisal)?
        –   How are these adjustments spread across the text?
        –   What position (or positions) is the speaker/writer taking?
        –   Is this position explicit or is it made to seem 'natural'?
        –   Do you agree with this position?
    b. Redraft the text, readjusting the meanings so that the position the text takes is changed. What do you notice as you do this activity?
    c. Relate what you have discovered about the interpersonal resources for taking a position to your students' learning needs and goals.

2   Use what you have discovered to design activities that support your students' progress towards their learning goals. These activities might draw your students' attention to:
    •   the way these interpersonal meanings can be aligned to the purpose and structure of texts
    •   the nature of the tenor (eg Is the relationship between the people taking part equal or unequal? Is their level of involvement close or distant?)
    •   how the tenor is represented in the vocabulary and grammatical structures which interpersonally adjust the experiential meanings in the text
    •   the position taken in the text
    •   the interrelationship between experiential and interpersonal meaning.

6

How speakers organise their message: Exploring textual meanings

Introducing …
- The textual function

Discussing …
- Implications for language teaching

From Chapter 1

Language has a *textual* function: so it has *textual* meanings.We use it to organise our experiential and interpersonal meanings into a linear and coherent whole.

To organise any text into a coherent whole, writers and speakers need to keep their readers and listeners well informed about where they are and where they are going. Fortunately there are grammatical resources to signpost the way through clauses, clause complexes and paragraphs, from the beginning to the end of a text. The first signpost must be at the beginning of a text, paragraph or clause: it tells readers and listeners what the speaker or writer has in mind as a starting point. The signposts realise our textual meanings.

The four clauses analysed below are each signposted differently although they have the same experiential meaning. You will notice that in all four clauses *the lion* is Actor; *the unicorn* is Goal; and the Circumstance gives the same spatial information wherever it occurs. The interpersonal meanings of clauses 1 and 2 are the same; as are the interpersonal meanings of 3 and 4 – in the first two clauses, *the lion* is Subject as well as Actor while in the second two *the unicorn* is Subject as well as Goal. But each of the clauses is arranged in a different order.

1

	The lion		beat		the unicorn	all round the town
experiential	Actor		Process: material		Goal	Circumstance
interpersonal declarative mood give information	Subject	Finite (past)	Predicator	Complement	Adjunct	
	Mood Block		Residue			

2

	All round the town	the lion		beat		the unicorn
experiential	Circumstance	Actor		Process: material		Goal
interpersonal declarative mood give information	Adjunct	Subject	Finite (past)	Predicator		Complement
	Res-		Mood Block		-idue	

3		By the lion	the unicorn	was	beaten	all round the town
experiential		Agent	Goal	Process: material		Circumstance
interpersonal declarative mood give information		Adjunct	Subject	Finite (past)	Predicator	Complement
		Res-	Mood Block		-idue	

4		The unicorn	was	beaten	all round the town	by the lion
experiential		Goal	Process: material		Circumstance	Actor/Agent
interpersonal declarative mood give information		Subject	Finite (past)	Predicator	Adjunct	Adjunct
		Mood Block			Residue	

Notice that in each clause the speaker has made different choices about how the first position in the clause should be filled. Because we know that all choices are meaningful, we need to ask what has motivated the change, so let us examine each one:

1	The lion	beat the unicorn all round the town
2	All round the town	the lion beat the unicorn
3	By the lion	the unicorn was beaten all round the town
4	The unicorn	was beaten all round the town by the lion

The change in linear order changes our perspective about the concerns of the clause. As speakers of English, we interpret clause 1 as a message about the lion, clause 4 as a message about the unicorn. On the other hand, clause 2 is more likely to be part of a conversation about where various actions took place, and clause 3 is about the agency of the action. At this point you may also be wondering about the function of final elements in each clause. We will return to this at the end of the chapter.

Metalanguage for discussing the first element(s) in a clause

The metalanguage of first position

Theme
Rheme

simple Theme
multiple Theme
topical Theme
interpersonal Theme
textual Theme

What comes first in a clause expresses an important and separate kind of meaning. English speakers and writers use the first position in the clause to signal to their audience what the message is about. In English the first position in a clause contains *textual meanings* because it signposts the development of a text. To analyse and discuss textual meanings we need a simple and distinct metalanguage: we call the first element THEME and the rest of the clause RHEME.

In *An introduction to functional grammar* (1994: 38), Halliday characterises *Theme* as 'what the message is concerned with: the point of departure for what the speaker is going to say'. In other words, it functions as a starting point or signpost, that is, the frame the speaker has chosen for the message. Returning to our four clauses, we can apply Theme and Rheme categories to each one:

Theme	Rheme
The lion	beat the unicorn all round the town
All round the town	the lion beat the unicorn
By the lion	the unicorn was beaten all round the town
The unicorn	was beaten all round the town by the lion

Identifying Theme

Topical Theme

Because the Theme is the starting point from which experiences are unfolded in a clause, it must include the whole of the first item in the experiential meanings. This means that the division between Theme and Rheme in a Finite clause always comes at the end of the first group or phrase relevant to the experiential function and meaning, whether this first element is Participant, Process or Circumstance. Because it is the place (Greek *topos*) where the experiences in the clause begin, this first element is known as the TOPICAL THEME.

It is, of course, the *whole* nominal group, verbal group, adverbial group or prepositional phrase filling the first Participant, Process or Circumstance slot that functions as topical Theme. When the Theme slot is filled by a nominal group, the Theme includes all premodification, postmodification, and even all group complexing. All of the nominal group is included in Theme in these examples:

The man in the moon	came down too soon
The lion and the unicorn	were fighting for the crown
The man who came to dinner	stayed for breakfast
Little Brown Betty	lived at the Golden Can
Robbin and Bobbin, two great Belly'd men	eat more Victuals
Three wise men of Gotham	went to sea in a bowl

Theme	Rheme

Quite often, the first element in the experiences encoded in a clause is a Circumstance. In this case, whether the Circumstance slot is filled by an adverbial group or a prepositional phrase, the topical Theme again includes all premodification, postmodification and group complexing. The whole of the circumstance element is included in Theme in the following examples:

On the first day of Christmas	my true love sent to me a partridge in a pear tree
On Sunday morning	my love will come in
In a cottage in Fife	lived a man and his wife
Merrily, merrily	shall I live now
At Stow-n-the-Wold	the wind blows cold
In marble halls as white as milk	a golden apple doth appear

Theme	Rheme

A SIMPLE THEME, like those in the examples above, contains only an experiential or topical element. But in some clauses the topical Theme may be prefaced by inter-personal and/or textual elements. The Theme can then be subdivided into *textual*, *interpersonal* and *topical* elements and the clause is said to have MULTIPLE THEMES. If the topical Theme is the *only* Theme in a clause, there is no real need to label it as anything more than Theme.

Textual Theme

Quite often we preface our experiential meanings with a group or phrase whose function is to connect our message to the previous text. When we do this, we create a cohesive text with well-signposted connections between messages. Conjunctions are most likely to occur at the beginning of clauses and when they do they must be considered thematic. Even so, they do not fulfil the primary requirement of Theme which is to signal the point of departure for the experiences in the clause. We refer to these text-creating meanings as TEXTUAL THEMES in order to distinguish them from the experiential meanings in the topical Theme. Each of the following clauses begins with a textual Theme which connects its experiential meanings to the meanings of neighbouring clauses.

But	the pig	would not
Nevertheless	the alternative	was not an alluring one
And	Jill	came tumbling after
When	the prince	saw Cinderella
And so	the teacher	turned it out

textual	topical	
Theme		Rheme

It is often possible to tell something about the purpose of a text by examining its textual Themes. In a simple narrative, such as 'The day I was lost' (Text 1) the main textual Themes are often *and* and *then*. In other text types, however, the textual Themes are likely to come from a different set of connecting words. In discussion text, for example, conjunctions such as *if*, *although*, *unless*, *because*, and *in order to* are likely to introduce dependent clauses which enhance the argument. Other Conjunctive Adjuncts such as *therefore, nevertheless, in addition, finally*, and *in conclusion* may also be thematic if they are used at the beginning of a clause to signpost the development of the discussion. In the two following texts, the textual Themes are underlined. Notice how, even taken alone, the textual Themes are signposts to the purpose of the text.

Text 1: The day I was lost

> (1) I went over to my friend's house (2) <u>and</u> I said (3) 'We'll go for a walk'. (4) <u>And</u> we went far away (5) <u>and</u> I said (6) 'I don't know our way home'. (7) <u>And</u> we kept on walking (8) <u>and</u> we were hungry. (9) <u>And</u> we saw a village (10) <u>and</u> we went (11) to talk to them (12) <u>and</u> we said (13) 'We are hungry'. (14) <u>And</u> they gave us some food (15) <u>and</u> we thanked them (16) <u>and</u> we went walking off. (17) <u>And</u> then we stopped (18) <u>and</u> sat down. (19) <u>And then</u> we saw a giant (20) <u>and</u> I screamed (21) 'Cooee'.

Text 2: Iain's text

> A good parallel in terms of qualitative research is the written survey method which poses questions <u>and</u> has a selection of answers from which to choose. <u>Although</u> problems can obviously arise <u>when</u> the respondent can not identify an adequate response from the selection, face-to-face informants will be able to respond in a way that is appropriate for them. <u>However</u>, it is the depth-interview methodology that has been most criticised for its lack of reliability and validity.

Interpersonal Theme

There are also times when we begin clauses with interpersonal meanings indicating the kind of interaction between speakers or the positions which they are taking. At these times, we are using INTERPERSONAL THEMES. The most common interpersonal Theme is the Finite in interrogative clauses where it precedes the Subject and immediately signals that the speaker is demanding information. Other interpersonal Themes include initial Vocatives, and Mood and Comment Adjuncts. Once again, we do not consider the thematic potential of an English clause to be exhausted until we have reached the end of the topical Theme, so we look for the first experiential meaning before marking the division into Theme and Rheme.

The following examples have an interpersonal Theme combined with a topical Theme:

May	we	have some butter for the royal slice of bread?
Jennifer,	come	here
Could	the team	have beaten the grand finalists?
Probably	they	could

interpersonal	topical	
Theme		Rheme

Note that a distinction can be drawn between textual and interpersonal Themes that come at the beginning of clauses simply because the English language places them in that position, and those where speakers and writers exercise a valid choice. Textually, we are constrained to put conjunctions at the beginning of English clauses but have more freedom about the placement of Conjunctive Adjuncts such as *nevertheless*, *however*, or *in addition*.

Similar distinctions can be drawn with interpersonal Themes. Here the Finite-Subject order of interrogatives is set by the pattern of English clauses but speakers may exercise discretion about the placement of Vocatives and Mood and Comment Adjuncts such as *probably*, *sometimes*, *thankfully* and *apparently*. The WH- element at the beginning of a non-polar interrogative can also be considered an interpersonal Theme over whose placement we have little control. Unlike the Finite, this element also plays an important part in experiential meanings.

The notion of markedness and its application to Theme: Typical Themes for different mood types

When linguists say that some state of affairs is UNMARKED, they mean it is the most expected, common and unremarkable case. Conversely, when they say that something is MARKED, they mean that it is unusual and should be noticed because of the way it stands out. Applying this concept to Theme, we can separate the typical and expected patterns from the atypical and unexpected. Because all choices are meaningful, when we find marked Themes we look for the purpose behind the speaker's patterning. The purpose may be to draw the addressee's attention to a particular group or phrase but more often it is to build a coherent text that is easy to follow. Because of the influence of Mood on the choice of Theme, our exploration of marked and unmarked Themes should look at each kind of interaction separately.

Giving information in declarative mood

The unmarked Theme for this mood has Actor (or Sayer, Behaver, Senser, Carrier or Identified), Subject and Theme all mapped onto the same nominal group. For example:

	The little dog	laughed
experiential	Actor/Behaver	
interpersonal	Subject	
textual	Theme	

Where the Goal, Subject and Theme are mapped onto the same nominal group, the Theme is said to be more marked:

	The pig	was eaten
experiential	Goal	
interpersonal	Subject	
textual	Theme	

Where the first group or phrase is Circumstance, the Theme is said to be even more marked and we look for the speaker's purpose for this choice:

	Up street and down street	each window	's made of glass
experiential	Circumstance		
interpersonal	Adjunct	Subject	
textual	Theme (marked)		

Where the first group is Complement, the Theme is extremely marked, and once again we look for the reason for the choice.

	Happy	is	the bride [[the sun shines on]]
experiential	Attribute		
interpersonal	Complement		
textual	Theme (marked)		

Demanding information in interrogative mood

Where the speaker requires a yes/no answer in a polar interrogative, an unmarked Theme combines an interpersonal element (the Finite) with an experiential element and follows the pattern above where Actor, Subject and topical Theme are all mapped on to the same nominal group:

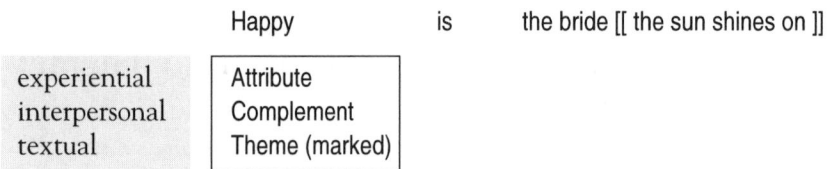

	Are	you	going to Scarborough Fair?
experiential		Actor	
interpersonal	Finite	Subject	
textual	interpersonal Theme	topical Theme	

Where the speaker requires specific information in a WH-interrogative, the WH-word is the unmarked Theme and fuses interpersonal and experiential meanings:

	Who	goes there?

experiential	Actor
interpersonal	Subject
textual	interpersonal
	topical Theme

Where the Circumstance precedes the Finite or the WH-word as the first element in the clause, it takes up the full thematic potential and displaces the Finite or WH-word as theme:

	In the spring	shall	we	go shearing?

experiential	Circumstance		Actor
interpersonal		Finite	Subject
textual	Theme (marked)		

Demanding goods and services in imperative mood

In this mood, the first position in the clause is most commonly filled by the process, so Process and Predicator as Theme is the unmarked pattern:

	Put	the kettle on!

experiential	Process: material
interpersonal	Predicator
textual	Theme

Any variation from this pattern is more marked, with Circumstance as Theme the most marked:

	You	tidy your room!

experiential	Actor
interpersonal	Subject
textual	Theme (marked)

	Under no circumstances	open the door

experiential	Circumstance
interpersonal	Adjunct
textual	Theme (marked)

In every mood there is a cline in markedness from unmarked to most marked rather than any clear cut division.

Extending the notion of Theme to clause complex, paragraph and text

At the level of *clause complex* the first clause can also be regarded as thematic. In the following example the entire first clause can be regarded as Theme for the second:

| When she got there | the cupboard was bare |

Theme	Rheme

Each paragraph may also be said to have a Theme: the first clause or the first clause complex signals what the paragraph is concerned with, the writer's point of departure for what will come next. This part of the paragraph is often called the **topic sentence**. Texts also have a point of departure – the first paragraph generally frames the rest of the text and introduces the main thrust of what is to follow.

Thematic progression

If the Theme is the signpost for a speaker or writer's point of departure, then each Rheme is the temporary destination. Usually the bit of the message that the writer or speaker considers interesting or important comes in the Rheme. While the first clause or clause complex in a text will probably contain all new meanings, the thematic choices for the following clauses should not be unexpected. They should be connected with ideas that we have already met in the Theme or Rheme of a clause not too far before.

Because readers and addressees need to be reassured that they are following the development of the text, many texts are signposted by placing elements from the Rheme of one clause into the Theme of the next, or by repeating meanings from the Theme of one clause in the Theme of subsequent clauses. The following examples demonstrate different styles of thematic progression.

Text 3: Cherie's text (first encountered in Chapter 5)

1		A good teacher	needs to be understanding to all children
2		He or she	must also be fair and reasonable
3		The teacher	must work at a sensible pace and not one thing after another
4		The teacher	also needs to speak with a clear voice
5	So	the children	can understand
6	If	the children	have worked hard during the week
7		there	should be some fun activities
8		That	's what I think a good teacher should be like

textual	topical	
Theme		Rheme

In Cherie's text, *a good teacher* and *the teacher* are the predominant Themes, appearing in clauses 1, 2, 3 and 4. *All children*, which first appears in the Rheme of clause 1, becomes Theme in clauses 5 and 6. *That*, the Theme of clause 8, refers to the whole of the previous text. This thematic progression is illustrated in Figure 6.1. The only Theme which is at all unexpected is the existential *there* in clause 7, which breaks the well signposted progression of the text. Figure 6.1 shows how we could draw the patterns of thematic progression in Cherie's text.

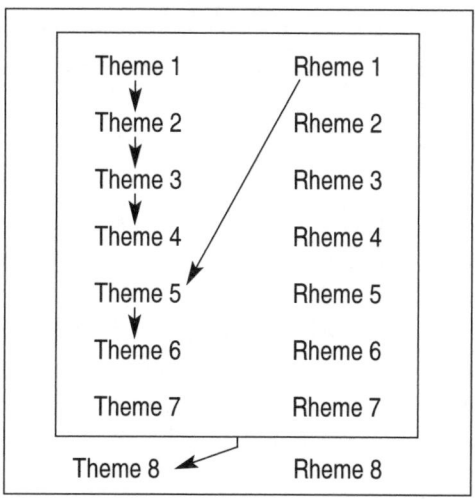

Figure 6.1: Thematic progression in Text 3

Similar patterns of thematic progression occur in Texts 4 and 5, both from *An introduction to phonology* (Clark and Yallop: 1995).

Text: 4

Theme	Rheme
1 Phonetics and phonology	are concerned with speech – with the ways in which humans produce and hear speech.
2 Talking and listening to each other	are so much part of human life
3 that they	often seem unremarkable.

In Text 4, *humans produce and hear speech* in the Rheme of clause 1 becomes *talking and listening to each other* in the Theme of clause 2 and *they* in the Theme of clause 3. The patterns of thematic progression in Text 4 are represented in Figure 6.2.

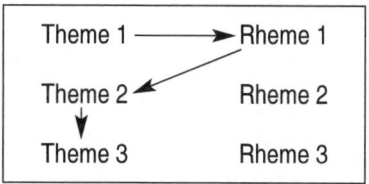

Figure 6.2: Thematic progression in Text 4

Text: 5

	Theme	Rheme
1	It	is possible to distinguish three auditory dimensions or parameters of phonation: loudness, pitch, and a quality of sound that is some times called 'timbre'.
2	Perceived loudness	is related to subglottal pressure.
3	Pitch	is the perceptual correlate of the frequency of vibration of the vocal folds.
4	The frequency	is determined by subglottal pressure and by laryngeal adjustments governing the length, tension and mass of the vocal folds themselves.

In this text, three elements of phonation – *loudness, pitch* and *timbre* are introduced in the Rheme of clause 1. The first of these (*loudness*) becomes Theme in clause 2, and the second (*pitch*) becomes Theme in clause 3. *Frequency*, part of the Rheme in clause 3, becomes Theme in clause 4. When the writers have finished the discussion of frequency, we should not be surprised to find *timbre* in thematic position – the path through a technical discussion has been well signposted. The patterns of thematic progression in Text 5 are represented in Figure 6.3.

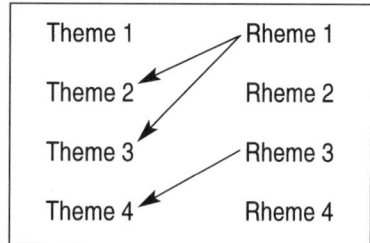

Figure 6.3: Thematic progression in Text 5

Thematic drift

A full grammatical analysis of any text allows us to comment on the meanings the speaker/writer has accumulated. After we have divided any text into clauses and set out our analysis of transitivity, Mood and Theme, we should be able to notice these accumulated meanings emerging as overall patterns in the text.

Text 6 is a procedure, although in the last sentence the writer has broken away from the conventional structure and included her own opinion. Text 7, a letter from a school camp, can be seen as a kind of recount even though the writer includes future events as he counts through his week's activities. In these two texts, the textual Themes have been set in italics and the topical Themes are underlined.

Text 6: Procedural text

Mango salad
Peel the mango *and* cut into 1cm cubes. In the bowl from which you will serve the salad lightly beat the yoghurt until creamy. Add the chilli, salt and sugar. Put the mango on top of the yoghurt. Heat the oil in a little pan, *and* when hot put in the mustard seeds. They will start popping within seconds. Immediately put in the dried red chilli. As it darkens add the chopped shallots. Stir *and* fry *until* the shallot is just browned. Pour quickly over the bowl of mango and yoghurt. I don't mix the salad together *as* it looks beautiful *as* is – the red chilli and black mustard seeds glisten on top of the luscious golden mango, which is in turn set off by the creamy yoghurt below.

Text 6 varies in its choice of Theme for the different clauses. Predictably, many begin with the Process; that is, the writer presents the next action as the point of departure. Some messages, however, foreground the Circumstance. Then, after all the instructions have been presented, we find the expert presenting her own angle on the task. We could summarise the Themes in the Mango Salad text like this.

Textual Themes:	and, and, and, until, as, as
Topical Themes:	
Process:	Peel, cut, add, place, heat, stir, fry, pour
Circumstance:	In the bowl from which you will serve the salad, when hot, Immediately, As it darkens, until the shallot
Participant:	They, I, it, the red chilli and black mustard seeds, which

Text 7: Recount text

Dear M & D,

Tomorrow's an early rise *because* we failed our last inspection *so* tomorrow morning we have to get up at 5am to prepare the unit for 6am inspection. Yesterday was the Combined School Sports – fun to be in. I ran about 2.13, which wasn't too bad *as* it was my second race for the season. Today we walk up Mt Stirling. *Then* tomorrow we have 10 hours of orienteering. What fun! I'd better get some sleep.

love you both,

We can summarise the Themes in the school letter like this:

Textual Themes:	because, so, as, then
Topical Themes:	
Circumstance:	tomorrow, tomorrow morning, yesterday, today, tomorrow
Participant:	we, I, which, it, I

From this examination of thematic choices, we can see that the writer is concerned with time and with himself as Actor, both singularly and as part of a group. His textual Themes show concern with providing reasons for his actions.

There is a template in Appendix F to help you summarise your analysis of Theme.

Other textual meanings

This book is largely about analysing clauses into experiential, interpersonal and textual meanings. Eventually we put these meanings together so that we can talk about a text as a whole – its overall patterns of experiential meanings, overall patterns of interaction and opinion, and overall patterns of thematic drift and thematic progression. We can go on to investigate the relation between the lexicogrammar, meanings, context, and structure, and these are the focus of Chapters 8 and 9. However, it's worth noting here that there are other textual resources which are not limited to individual clauses. One relates to the text as a whole (cohesion) and the other to its division into information units (the organisation into Given and New information).

Given and New information

A parallel textual system to Theme/Rheme is the organisation into Given and New information. Speakers divide their texts into information units, each of which peaks with a change of pitch, or loudness, signalling what they think is the point of their message, that is, its NEW and exciting bit of information. Any other information in the unit is GIVEN. There is no necessary one-to-one relationship between a clause and an information unit, and speakers may foreground any element in a clause as New information. Nevertheless, the unmarked pattern is that Given information is included in the Theme of a clause and New information somewhere in the Rheme.

Speakers and writers choose their Themes and their New information to guide their audience effectively through their texts. This choice influences the organisation of experiential and interpersonal meanings. One reason for passive clauses is thematic selection; another is to put the Actor as New information. We can see the patterns emerging in these lines from the nursery rhyme *The farmer in the dell*. We'll give the main narrative clauses in the rhyme and analyse just one clause.

Text 8: The farmer in the dell

1   The farmer takes a wife
2   The wife takes a child
3   The child takes a nurse
4   The nurse takes a dog

5   The dog takes a cat

6   The cat takes a mouse

7   The mouse takes the cheese

Analysis of clause 5

| The dog | takes | a cat |

The dog		takes	a cat
Actor	Process: material		Goal

Subject	Finite	Predicator	Complement

Theme	Rheme

Given..New

Cohesion

COHESION deals with devices that give a text *texture*. While it may appear that linguists have appropriated 'texture' from the field of textiles along with terms like 'ties', 'close knit', and 'weaving', in fact, 'text', 'texture', and 'textile' all come from the same Latin root meaning 'that which is woven', so it is entirely appropriate for linguists to talk about meanings being woven together and about lexical and grammatical ties between clauses as *cohesive devices*. Cohesive devices include the *lexical* devices of repetition, semantic relations, equivalence and semblance and the *grammatical* devices of reference, substitution and ellipsis (see pages 165 ff). Thematic progression from Theme to Rheme or from Theme to Theme is a *structural* expression of cohesion.

You can read more about cohesion and information units in Halliday (1994: Chapters 8 and 9) and Halliday and Hasan (1985).

It's possible to make a simple but effective diagram of the ties between clauses by listing elements with the same referent in columns or chains. Text 9, from Lewis Carroll's *Through the looking-glass*, is shown first as a block, then divided into clauses with different cohesive devices listed immediately after, then set out in lexical chains.

Text: 9

> So Alice got up and walked about – rather stiffly at first, as she was afraid that the crown might come off; but she comforted herself with the thought that there was no-one to see her. 'And if I really am a Queen,' she said as she sat down again, 'I shall be able to manage it quite well in time.'

Text in clauses

1   So Alice got up
2   and (she) walked about – rather stiffly at first
3   as she was afraid [[3.1 that the crown might come off]]
4   But she comforted herself with the thought [[5.1 that there was no-one
     [[5.1.1 to see her]]]]
5   'And << 6, 7, 8 >> I shall be able to manage it quite well in time
6   if I really am a Queen'
7   she said
8   as she sat down again

In the following table various cohesive devices are separately listed. Notice also that, in one form or another, Alice is Theme for almost all the clauses.

cl#	Conjunctions/ Conj. Adj	Repetition	Pronominal reference	Ellipsis	Sense relations Movement	Royalty
1	so	Alice			got up	
2	and			she (Alice)	walked about rather stiffly	
3	as		she (Alice)			the crown
4	but		she, herself, her (Alice)			
5	and		I (Alice) it (the crown)			
6	if		I (Alice)			Queen
7		Alice				
8	as		she (Alice)		sat down	

Lexical chains

Lexical chains are an excellent way of exploring the main preoccupations of speakers and writers and the way their texts develop. In this analysis referential pronouns are replaced by their relevant nouns, and, if Alice 'really is a Queen', the Alice and Royal chains would combine in Clause 6.

	Chain 1: Alice	**Chain 2: Movement**	**Chain 3: Royal**
1	Alice	got up	
2	Alice	walked about rather stiffly	

3
| Alice | | crown |

4
| Alice |
| Alice |
| Alice |

5
| Alice | | crown |

6
| Alice | | Queen |

7
| Alice |

8
| Alice | sat down |

The Alice chain is an identity chain of identical meanings passed from clause to clause using the proper noun *Alice* and the referential pronouns *I*, *she*, *herself* and *her*, each referring to Alice. The second chain is a similarity chain of Alice's movements. Quite possibly we could have included the crown's movement in Clause 3 in this chain. The third chain, which contains '*crown*' and '*Queen*' is another semantically related similarity chain.

To sum up

By examining sequential and cumulative patterns of Theme, we can often discover the degree to which:

- the messages mesh with an overarching purpose or concern
- the text exhibits a transparent design
- the speaker/writer anticipates the needs of the addressees (that is the hearer/reader should not be surprised by the choice of Theme as this would indicate that the progress or drift of the text is not well constructed).

It is easy to apply the ideas of thematic progression and thematic drift to uncover any of the writer's points of departure for a text, but there are other benefits from this simple technique, especially when constructing our own texts. We can use the technique to ensure that topical Themes progress in an orderly, and even predictable, way – either by repeating the Theme or thematic pattern over several clauses or by incorporating the Rheme from one clause into the Theme of the next. We can also use textual Themes to make the connection between clauses clear. The resources are there in English for staying with a Theme or for bringing elements in or out of psychological focus.

Exercises

1   Construct three clauses, the first with Circumstance as topical Theme, the second with Process, the third with a post-modified nominal group.

2   Add a textual and interpersonal Theme to each of the three clauses you have just constructed.

3   Divide each of the following clauses into Theme and Rheme. If there are multiple Themes, make further subdivision into textual, interpersonal and topical.
    a. Are you going to Scarborough Fair?
    b. Probably we're going tomorrow afternoon
    c. Remember me to one who lives there
    d. Because she was once a true love of mine

4   Divide the following paragraph into clauses and identify the Themes. From an examination of the thematic choices and the Theme-Rheme patterns, make an assessment of the purpose and/or type of the text.

During this summer of 1846, while her literary hopes were waning, an anxiety of another kind was increasing. Her father's eyesight had become seriously impaired by the progress of the cataract which was forming. He was nearly blind. He could grope his way about, and recognise the figures of those he knew well when they were placed against a strong light; but he could no longer see to read, and thus his eager appetite for knowledge and information of all kinds was severely balked. He continued to preach.

Elizabeth Gaskell *Cranford* (1857)

Implications for language teaching

Textual meanings organise the richness of experiential meanings and the fluidity of interpersonal meanings into coherent, comprehensible language. This chapter uses the metaphor of signposting to describe the work of textual meanings in the grammar of English. Many language teachers are already familiar with the notion of signposts. The information in this chapter allows us to build on this notion in several ways. This chapter also introduces us to resources that contribute to a text's cohesion. We will consider cohesion from the perspective of language teaching in the section on texture in Chapter 9.

How is knowledge of the textual grammar of the message useful to language teachers and learners?

A focus on textual meanings can have startling and immediate results in the language classroom, particularly in the teaching of literacy. When students' texts are difficult to follow and it is hard to pinpoint exactly what they are talking or writing about, the problem often originates in the choice of Themes and the expression of Rhemes.

In this chapter we are shown how organising meanings in English involves laying down language elements one after the other like railway tracks from the beginning to the end of the journey. In the clause, the Theme (the beginning of the journey) orients the reader to the experiential and interpersonal meanings in the text. It establishes what the meanings in the clause are concerned with and acts like a signpost to show where the meanings have come from and where they are going. Towards the end of the clause's journey, in the Rheme, is the 'point' of the clause (the destination of the journey) where the meanings have been heading. The beginning-end organisation of clause complexes, paragraphs and texts mirrors and draws on the beginning-end organisation of the clauses they contain. (A subtle Theme-Rheme organisation can also be glimpsed in groups and phrases.)

Theme can also be thought of as an anchor that secures the clause to what has gone before so it is not set adrift aimlessly in the text. Thus, at the beginning of a clause, students must learn to orient listeners and readers both by introducing what the clause is concerned with and by making a link back into the context or the preceeding text to anchor the clause into the text. Similarly, in written texts, they must learn to use the topic sentence of a paragraph to anchor the paragraph to the introduction of the text.

Once the Theme has oriented the listener or reader effectively, New information introduced in the Rheme is more likely to make sense. In written texts information introduced towards the end of the clause often 'flows' into the beginning of the next clause. When we draft long texts, for example spoken presentations or essays, it is important to organise the information so that it flows thematically through the whole text in such a way that the audience can follow the meaning from beginning to end.

Once language learners understand how the ordering of language elements works in English to orient the audience and to signpost and organise meanings, they have gained a powerful tool for managing the meanings of texts which are just beyond their current level of language proficiency. In other words, an understanding of Theme can increase the comprehensible input accessible to students, especially when they work with written language.

How can knowledge of the textual grammar of the message enhance language teaching programs?

For language learners to organise meanings effectively into clauses, clause complexes, paragraphs and text, they need to make the beginning and the end of all units of language organisational focal points. They also need to know how to order words, clause constituents, clauses and paragraphs within texts.

When student writers struggling with basic clause structure write texts made of clauses which do not have an effective progression of *topical Themes*, the reader is not given any orientation to what the text is about nor any signposts to show where the information has come from and where it is going. When student writers introduce too many topical Themes unrelated to the thematic progression of the text, the reader easily loses the thread. The quality of writing in workplace, business and academic English can be improved dramatically if attention is given to the thematic progression of information in texts. If teachers use model texts to illustrate the basic patterns of thematic progression, students can apply these patterns to their own writing.

Student writers also need to be able to control the use of *textual Themes*; that is, conjunctions and other connecting words and phrases. It is textual Themes that language teachers have traditionally called signposts because of the work they do in shaping and structuring texts. This work makes their use critical to the organisation of texts which achieve their purpose effectively.

Learning how to manage *interpersonal Themes* is important for those learning how to manage spoken interaction. What comes first in the Mood Block signals the type of clause chosen to exchange meanings. For this reason, learning to manage the relationship between Mood and Theme is central to effective participation in spoken interactions, whether the student is joining in the interaction or sustaining it. Teachers can use their knowledge of Mood and Theme to prepare skeleton exchange outlines for students to use in guided practice activities and structured role plays.

This chapter introduces the idea of *markedness* – a notion that is particularly useful in language education. Students usually focus at first on unmarked language patterns; that is, on the expected way of structuring meaning in a particular clause. There is a point in their development, however, when students need to consider how to make elements of a clause stand out from the background, or deviate from the unremarkable pattern when this is necessary for their text to achieve its purpose.

In genres organised by time, such as story genres, using sequencing conjunctions as textual Themes (eg *and, and then, when, as, after, next*) is the unmarked way of signposting the unfolding of events. Once students have mastered these unmarked signposts, they can learn to use marked topical Themes such as Circumstances and dependent clauses (eg *After lunch ..., When I had finished with him ...*) to highlight particular points of time in the unfolding of events.

Similarly, in texts which instruct, explain or persuade, using sequencing conjunctions as textual Themes (eg *first, second, next, finally*) is the unmarked way of signposting the move from step to step, phase to phase, or argument to argument. But students also need to learn how to highlight salient points in a process or argument by using Circumstances and dependent clauses as topical Themes (eg *Slowly ..., If the ice melts ..., For this reason ...*). Marked Themes are the resource speakers and writers use to foreground, for example, manner, condition or cause. Careful and precise, even exact, use of marked Themes is often essential if a text is to achieve its purpose effectively, for example, a recipe, a scientific explanation or a legal argument.

When they are being introduced to a new genre, student writers can be guided with skeleton texts based on the structural pattern of the genre. Teachers prepare skeleton texts by writing the first paragraph of the text followed by a topic sentence and a series of clause Themes for each subsequent paragraph. The clause Themes include marked Themes as needed to achieve the purpose of the text. The students then draft a text of their own around this organisational skeleton.

The notion of Theme is particularly valuable in the teaching of reading, especially when student readers are working with information-rich texts in the subject areas of formal education. Students' attention can be drawn to each layer of Theme development one by one. Using a coloured highlighter, underlining, or a similar technique, students can uncover the way information is organised in the text by highlighting:

- the first paragraph
- the topic sentence of each paragraph
- the Themes of the clauses.

The first paragraph orients the reader to the text. The topic sentences orient the reader to each paragraph. The topical Themes of clauses signal what the text is concerned with (the gist of the text). Textual Themes and marked Themes signal structure and structural shifts as the text unfolds. Interpersonal Themes signal the kind of interaction taking place and the point of view of those interacting.

Following a study of Themes in a text, students can look through the remainder of the paragraphs and clause Rhemes to discover the 'point' of the text; that is, where the text is heading. These meanings usually accumulate until they are drawn together in the final paragraph in order to conclude the text's purpose effectively. Students can use a different colour, font or underline style to uncover the way information accumulates and is drawn together as the text unfolds.

The textual grammar of the message and text structure

We have already seen how textual grammar is used to signpost the structure of different types of texts. In fact, the textual metafunction is often called the ENABLING metafunction because it enables experiential and interpersonal meanings to be organised so that they can be realised in whole texts that make sense to listeners and readers. There are several ways that students can explore the interplay between the textual grammar of the message and text structure. They can undertake activities that explore the way interpersonal meanings are organised in order to structure spoken interactions using their knowledge of the word order that constructs declarative, interrogative and imperative clauses. During these activities students can practise using intonation patterns to highlight the textual grammar of the message, for example, the New information in the Rhemes of their clauses.

If learners undertake activities that explore the way Theme and Rheme are used to organise experiential and interpersonal meanings in structuring written texts, they will notice that often a choice of Theme or a shift in thematic progression signals that a text has moved into the next stage. For example, in narratives, students might look:

- in the Orientation for
  - Circumstances of time and place as marked Themes or in the Rheme in order to set the story in a time and place.
- in the Complication for
  - time and sequence conjunctions as textual Themes to signpost unfolding events in a temporal sequence
  - Circumstances of time as marked Themes to highlight an event in a temporal sequence
  - a contrast conjunction (such as *but*) as textual Theme to signal the complication or crisis point of the story
  - an interpersonal Theme (such as *unfortunately*) to signal the way the writer is evaluating the events of the Complication
- in the Resolution for
  - a consequence conjunction (such as *so*) as textual Theme to signal a return to normality.

Notice how the name given to the first stage of the narrative pattern, *Orientation*, reflects the thematic work that is done with language at the beginning of stories written in this pattern.

If students have explored how patterns of Theme and Rheme enable the organisation of different types of texts, they can consciously and strategically draw on this knowledge to organise their own texts more effectively. An understanding of thematic progression can be very useful for both study and work where students need to read and write longer texts such as textbooks, essays or reports. Patterns of thematic progression recur at every level of longer texts. Just as Theme, or the beginning of a clause, orients the reader to the message in the clause, the same pattern can be seen in paragraphs and whole texts, even in sections and chapters of books.

Generally a topic sentence orients a reader to what a paragraph will be about and is usually the first sentence in the paragraph. It tends to predict the Themes of the sentences in the paragraph. The last sentence in the paragraph 'sums up' what the paragraph is about. This is the concluding sentence. Similarly, the introductory paragraph of a whole text orients the reader to what the text will be about and predicts the topic sentences of each paragraph of the text, while the concluding paragraph sums up the point of the whole text. In this way information flows in 'waves' at each level of the whole text. In longer texts the same wave pattern moves on into the headings and conclusions of each section and into the introductory and concluding chapters.

Being able to control the expression of mode through thematic progression greatly enhances students' ability to read and construct longer texts. The thematic pattern across a text is very useful for *readers* of texts because it can guide note-taking and summarising. A quick way to find out what a lengthy text is about before deciding whether to read it in detail, is to read the first paragraph, the headings, the topic sentences and the concluding paragraph. For *writers*, knowing how to organise information into wave patterns which flow through the text is a useful tool for planning and drafting texts.

The textual grammar of the message and mode

The mode of a context of situation relates to the distance in time and space between people who are communicating and how this influences the way they manage that communication. For example, if people are communicating at the same time and in the same place, they are probably face-to-face and using spoken language. If people are communicating at the same time but from different places, they might use the telephone or perhaps interactive electronic chat. If people want to capture their communication so someone can use it at a later time, they will put it into written language.

The distance between the communication and the activity it is communicating about determines how much work the language has to do. If two people are sharing the same activity, there is a lot of contextual information which they can assume the other person is aware of and so they do not have to put it into language. In addition, they can supplement what they are saying with intonation, gesture and facial expression. If the person listening does not understand something or loses track of what is being talked about, they can ask for clarification or repetition immediately. When we play sport, for example, we might use language to direct the ball or show our excitement at a goal, but there is no need to organise a description of the place or the people, a list of the rules or a recount of the game.

When people are communicating about an activity at a distance, that is, in a different place or at a later time, the language will have to do a lot more work in order to reconstitute that activity for the audience. For example, if we are talking or writing about a sporting match that happened yesterday for people who were not there, we have to orient our audience to the time the game took place, the venue, the players, the spectators and the game so they are able to understand what we are telling them. As the distance in time and place between events and communication about them increases, the language has to do even more work. For someone learning a language this can be quite challenging.

Many people will have had the experience of a small child suddenly starting to talk about something without orienting the listener to their topic or their purpose. In this situation most adults automatically ask questions which guide the child to supply the missing meanings. For example, the adult might ask *Who did this happen to?* that is, they are asking for a Participant in Theme position. If they ask *When did this happen?* they are asking for a Circumstance of time as marked Theme. Language teachers can guide students in the classroom in similar ways.

Many problems in student writing occur because students either leave out or do not organise effectively the information the reader needs in order to reconstitute meaning at a distance. This meaning might be to do with a context which the reader does not share with the writer or it might relate to what is going on inside the writer's head as they reflect on an aspect of experience.

One of the most effective ways to help student writers make meanings that bridge the distance between writer and reader is to give students opportunities to prepare a spoken language presentation of their material before they draft the written text. For example, if students are preparing to write a recount about a class excursion, the interim step would be for them to tell a group of people who did not go on the excursion what happened. This task will necessarily involve the students in organising their meanings so that the excursion is reconstituted through language for those who were not there.

Being able to control the expression of mode through textual grammar greatly enhances students' ability to organise language to bridge the distance between themselves and their audience effectively, adjusting their language to manage, for example:

- the difference between face-to-face spoken interaction and spoken interaction on the telephone
- the difference between interactive spoken language in a shared context and written language for an audience who cannot provide any feedback and who have not shared the context or the activity.

In fact, being able to control the expression of mode through textual grammar is critical to the development of the higher level literacies students need if they are to be successful in education and employment.

Using the textual grammar of the message to build a critical response to text

Knowledge of textual grammar and thematic progression helps student readers and writers to develop the critical skills they need to evaluate the 'readability' of a written text – both their own texts and those of others.

Checking for effective thematic progression and drift in their own texts can be one of the earliest editing skills student writers are taught. Classroom activities can be designed in which students working in pairs and groups can use the metalanguage of Theme and thematic progression to discuss how to improve the organisation of their texts in order to improve signposting and information flow. Students can evaluate the thematic progression of a text, deciding whether:

- the Themes have provided an effective orientation for the reader in terms of topic and structure
- the accumulation of meanings at the end of clauses and paragraphs has culminated effectively in the final paragraph to give the text a clear point.

In addition, when students encounter a text they find difficult to read, looking for Theme patterns will reveal:

- whether the difficulty lies in the signposting and information flow of the text itself
- how to navigate the text in order to manage its meanings more easily.

Students might also explore how text organisation differs when we use different channels of communication, for example, face-to-face, telephone, email, electronic chat, letters, radio, television, newspaper or books. On the basis of their findings they might consider:

- the effect of different technologies on the way we organise our meanings
- the impact of new technologies on the meanings different groups of people are able to make
- how new technologies can be exploited most effectively and equitably.

Further reading

You can read more about cohesion and information units in Chapters 8 and 9 of *An introduction to functional grammar: 2nd edition* (Halliday 1994)) and in *Language, context and text: Aspects of language in a social semiotic perspective* (Halliday and Hasan 1985).

For a more detailed account of Theme read 'The structuring of information in written English text' (Fries 1992).

For a detailed account of text progression, see Martin (1992, Chapter 6).

For an account of how to use spoken language as an interim step to literacy for ESL learners see Gibbons (1991, 1998).

For more detail on how teachers can use knowledge about the expression of mode in language to support literacy development see Hammond (1990a).

For ideas about how to use intonation patterns to highlight the textual grammar of the message in effective ways, see Zawadzki (1994).

Exercises for language teachers

1 Identify a good example of a type of text you would like your students to be able to use effectively. The text might be spoken or written. If you wish, you may choose one of the texts in Chapter 1.
   a. Look for patterns of textual grammar and thematic progression which:
       •   contribute to the structure and purpose of the whole text
       •   build the mode of the immediate situation.
   b. Relate what you have discovered about the textual grammar and thematic progression of the text to your students' learning needs and goals.

2 Use what you have discovered about the textual grammar of the text to design activities that support your students' progress towards their learning goals. These activities might draw your students' attention to:
   •   the purpose and structure of the text as revealed in textual grammar and thematic progression
   •   the nature of the mode (eg What is the distance in time and space between those communicating? Is the language part of a shared activity or does it have to reconstitute the activity for people who were not there?)
   •   how the mode is represented in the word order and markedness of the grammar of the text
   •   how well the meanings in the text have been organised.

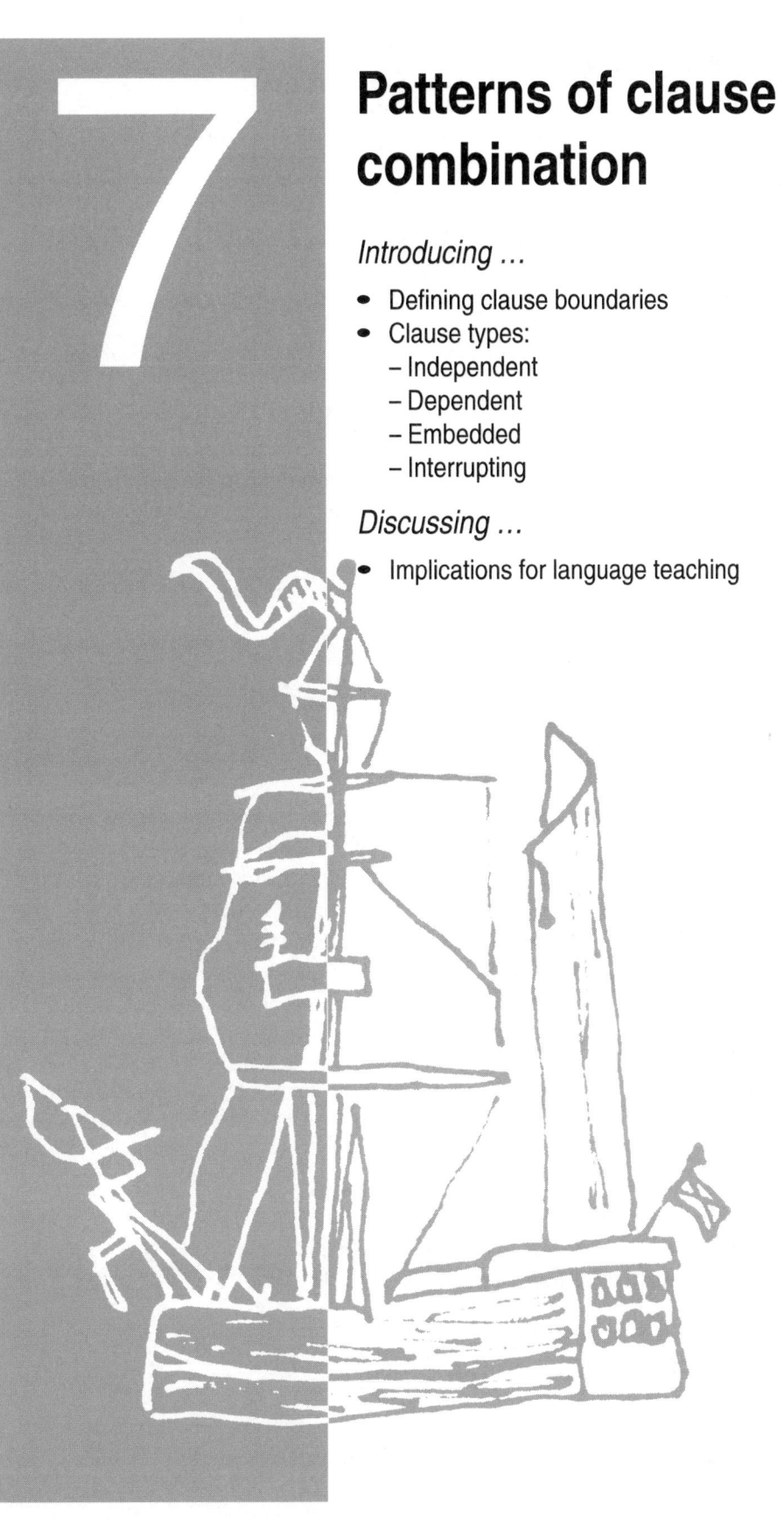

7

Patterns of clause combination

Introducing ...

- Defining clause boundaries
- Clause types:
  - Independent
  - Dependent
  - Embedded
  - Interrupting

Discussing ...

- Implications for language teaching

From Chapter 2: The rank scale
From Chapter 3: The experiential function – Processes
From Chapters 4 and 5: The interpersonal function – Subject/Finite
From Chapter 6: The textual function – Theme/Rheme

In Chapter 2 we introduced the notion of rank scale where each grammatical rank is made up of one or more elements from the rank below: one or more morphemes to a word, one or more words to a group or phrase, one or more groups or phrases to a clause, one or more clauses to a clause complex.

	clause complex
	clause
RANK SCALE	group or phrase
	word
	morpheme

In Chapters 3, 4, 5 and 6 we looked at the internal patterns within a clause – where groups and phrases create experiential meanings, where the interpersonal meanings arise from the relationship of Subject to Finite and where organisational aspects of the message are signalled through Theme/Rheme choices. In this chapter we explore the top level of the rank scale, looking at the elaborate and intricate possibilities of combining messages into the clusters of clauses we call clause complexes. As at every other rank, the clause complex is made up of one or more of the rank below, in this case one or more clauses.

The notation convention for the analysis is to separate clauses by two parallel lines ‖ and to put three parallel lines ‖‖ at the end of a clause complex, as shown in the following examples of clause complexes:

a. Let's go down to the Tourist Office ‖ and ask for directions ‖‖
b. Before diving into water, ‖ always check the depth ‖‖
c. The concert was cancelled ‖ because the lead singer was ill ‖‖
d. The minister said ‖ that he had been quoted out of context ‖‖

Defining the clause boundaries

Just as in biology one finds intricate patterns – in spiders' webs, in bees' hives, in forms of crystalline structure – so too we can think of the interconnection of clauses as constituting a type of subtle human architecture. In creating their own particular designs, speakers and writers select from the various possibilities in order to make their experience accessible to others.

Steps in a clause complex analysis

When we want to unravel the creator's design, the first step in a clause complex analysis is to define the clause boundaries and draw in the double lines. We need to use many of the grammatical concepts already presented in this book to describe where each clause begins and ends. Here is a useful procedure to follow:

1 Underline all verbal groups.
2 Check that they are all functioning as Process in a clause.
3 Look for the internal patterns of the clause in the experiential function: Participants, Process, Circumstances.
4 Look for the internal patterns of the clause in the interpersonal function: the Subject/Finite relationship.
5 Try to identify the function of each clause in the clause complex.

We will use Text 1, 'My Aunt', to walk you through these steps. The clause complex boundaries coincide with sentence boundaries as is the case with most written texts. The clause complex division appears under the text itself.

Text 1: My Aunt

I can clearly remember we used to visit an elderly aunt in Surry Hills. She lived in a tiny bed-sit and was not at all well off, but she entertained her guests in style. Corner stores in those days would sell their broken biscuits for a fraction of the price of whole ones, and she always had a tin of broken Arnotts milk arrowroot biscuits in the pantry. On her tiny two-ringed stove there was always a kettle boiling its head off. Unlocking her china cabinet, she would invite the one of us who was currently most in her favour to carry her precious china cups, saucer and plate settings to the table. I am still not sure whether I was more anxious in case I dropped one when she chose me, or was more jealous of my brother or sister when she didn't.

Clause complexes in Text 1

1 I can clearly remember we used to visit an elderly aunt in Surry Hills.
2 She lived in a tiny bed-sit and was not at all well off, but she entertained her guests in style.
3 Corner stores in those days would sell their broken biscuits for a fraction of the price of whole ones, and she always had a tin of broken Arnotts milk arrowroot biscuits in the pantry.
4 On her tiny two-ringed stove there was always a kettle boiling its head off.

5   Unlocking her china cabinet, she would invite the one of us who was currently most in her favour to carry her precious cup, saucer and plate settings to the table.

6   I am still not sure whether I was more anxious in case I dropped one when she chose me, or was more jealous of my brother or sister when she didn't.

Step 1. Underline all verbal groups

It is best to take a wide view of the possibilities and then cast out any that on closer inspection seem not to be functioning as Process in a clause pattern:

> I <u>can</u> clearly <u>remember</u> we <u>used to visit</u> an elderly aunt in Surry Hills. She <u>lived</u> in a tiny bed-sit and <u>was</u> not at all well off, but she <u>entertained</u> her guests in style. Corner stores in those days <u>would sell</u> their <u>broken</u> biscuits for a fraction of the price of whole ones, and she always <u>had</u> a tin of <u>broken</u> Arnotts milk arrowroot biscuits in the pantry. On her tiny two-ringed stove there <u>was</u> always a kettle <u>boiling</u> its head off. <u>Unlocking</u> her china cabinet, she <u>would invite</u> the one of us who <u>was</u> currently most in her favour <u>to carry</u> her precious china cups, saucer and plate settings to the table. I <u>am</u> still not sure whether I <u>was</u> more anxious in case I <u>dropped</u> one when she <u>chose</u> me, or <u>was</u> more jealous of my brother or sister when she <u>didn't</u>.

Step 2. Check that the underlined words are all functioning as Process in a clause structure

In this step we need to look at the environment of the underlined words to make sure that they are functioning as Process in a clause. In fact, one word is not: *broken* is twice functioning as Epithet in a nominal group, *broken biscuits* and *broken Arnotts milk arrowroot biscuits*. Once *broken* has been dropped we are left with nineteen verbal groups functioning as Processes in clause patterns. Note that *can remember* is one verbal group even though the two parts of the group are separated by *clearly*.

Step 3. Look for the internal patterns of the clause in the experiential function

Given that we appear to have nineteen Processes, we can hypothesise that we will find nineteen clauses. So our third step in defining the clause boundaries is to look for the experiential patterning of these nineteen clauses. As we need to look for the Participant and Circumstance patterns that surround each Process, we need to look closely at the nominal groups, the prepositional phrases and the adverbial groups and ask the kinds of questions about clause consituency that we asked in Chapter 3. It could be a help to write out the clauses on separate lines, or at least to pencil in tentative boundaries. To help you we do both:

1   I <u>can</u> clearly <u>remember</u>
2   we <u>used to visit</u> an elderly aunt in Surry Hills.
3   She <u>lived</u> in a tiny bed-sit
4   and <u>was</u> not at all well off
5   but <u>entertained</u> her guests in style.
6   Corner stores in those days <u>would sell</u> their broken biscuits for a fraction of the price of whole ones
7   and she always <u>had</u> a tin of broken Arnotts milk arrowroot biscuits in the pantry.

8	On her tiny two-ringed stove there <u>was</u> always a kettle
9	<u>boiling</u> its head off.
10	<u>Unlocking</u> her china cabinet
11	she <u>would invite</u> the one of us
12	who <u>was</u> currently most in her favour
13	<u>to carry</u> her precious cup, saucer and plate settings to the table.
14	I <u>am</u> still not sure
15	whether I <u>was</u> more anxious
16	in case I <u>dropped</u> one
17	when she <u>chose</u> me
18	or <u>was</u> more jealous of my brother or sister
19	when she <u>didn't</u>.

I <u>can</u> clearly <u>remember</u> || we <u>used to visit</u> an elderly aunt in Surry Hills. ||| She <u>lived</u> in a tiny bed-sit || and <u>was</u> not at all well off, || but she <u>entertained</u> her guests in style. ||| Corner stores in those days <u>would sell</u> their broken biscuits for a fraction of the price of whole ones, || and she always <u>had</u> a tin of broken Arnotts milk arrowroot biscuits in the pantry. ||| On her tiny two-ringed stove there <u>was</u> always a kettle || <u>boiling</u> its head off. ||| <u>Unlocking</u> her china cabinet, || she <u>would invite</u> the one of us || who <u>was</u> currently most in her favour || <u>to carry</u> her precious china cups, saucer and plate settings to the table. ||| I <u>am</u> still not sure, || whether I <u>was</u> more anxious || in case I <u>dropped</u> one || when she <u>chose</u> me, || or <u>was</u> more jealous of my brother or sister || when she <u>didn't</u>. |||

At first glance this analysis may look reasonable, but a closer examination of nominal group structures in Clauses 8 and 11 indicates that it is not good enough. In Clause 8 the nominal group *a kettle* does not stop at the Thing (*kettle*) but is further defined by post-modification in the form of an embedded clause (*boiling its head off*). In the same way, *the one of us* in Clause 11 is further defined by the embedded clause, *who was currently most in her favour*.

At this point we need to think back to the discussion about nominal group Qualifiers in Chapter 3 and remind ourselves that such embedded clauses are said to be rank shifted. Although they *are* certainly patterned as clauses, they do not operate at the clause rank on the rank scale, but have been rank shifted to do service within a nominal group (as Qualifier). As we saw in Chapter 3, embedded clauses can also function as Postmodifiers in adverbial groups (see pages 70–71). There is another type of embedded or rank shifted clause, one that functions as nominal element in its own right. We will discuss this later in the chapter.

Remember from Chapter 3 that the convention for marking out embedded clauses is a pair of double square brackets. When we combine this convention with our double and triple parallel lines, our passage will look like this:

I <u>can</u> clearly <u>remember</u> || we <u>used to visit</u> an elderly aunt in Surry Hills. |||She <u>lived</u> in a tiny bed-sit and <u>was</u> not at all well off, || but she <u>entertained</u> her guests in style. ||| Corner stores in those days <u>would sell</u> their broken biscuits for a fraction of the price of whole ones, || and she always <u>had</u> a tin of broken Arnotts milk arrowroot biscuits in the pantry. ||| On her tiny two-ringed stove there <u>was</u>

always a kettle [[boiling its head off.]] ||| Unlocking her china cabinet, || she would invite the one of us [[who was currently most in her favour]] || to carry her precious china cups, saucer and plate settings to the table. ||| I am still not sure,|| whether I was more anxious || in case I dropped one || when she chose me, || or was more jealous of my brother or sister || when she didn't. |||

We are thus left with seventeen clauses functioning at the clause rank.

1　I can clearly remember
2　we used to visit an elderly aunt in Surry Hills.
3　She lived in a tiny bed-sit
4　and was not at all well off
5　but entertained her guests in style.
6　Corner stores in those days would sell their broken biscuits for a fraction of the price of whole ones
7　and she always had a tin of broken Arnotts milk arrowroot biscuits in the pantry.
8　On her tiny two-ringed stove there was always a kettle [[boiling its head off]].
9　Unlocking her china cabinet
10　she would invite the one of us [[who was currently most in her favour]]
11　to carry her precious cup, saucer and plate settings to the table.
12　I am still not sure
13　whether I was more anxious
14　in case I dropped one
15　when she chose me
16　or was more jealous of my brother or sister
17　when she didn't.

Step 4. Look for the internal patterns of the clause in the interpersonal function

In this step we look for the Subject/Finite relationship in each of our clauses. This will help to confirm the pattern recognition of the previous step and will also tell us which clauses are finite and which are non-finite. In the clauses set out below, the Subject is in italics and the Finite is in bold type. (Note: If the Finite is mapped onto the head of the verbal group in a one word verbal group, the whole word is bold).

1　*I* **can** clearly remember
2　*we* **used** to visit an elderly aunt in Surry Hills.
3　*She* **lived** in a tiny bed-sit
4　and **was** not at all well off
5　but **entertained** her guests in style.
6　*Corner stores* in those days **would** sell their broken biscuits for a fraction of the price of whole ones
7　and *she* always **had** a tin of broken Arnotts milk arrowroot biscuits in the pantry.
8　On her tiny two-ringed stove *there* **was** always a kettle boiling its head off.
9　Unlocking her china cabinet
10　*she* **would** invite the one of us who was currently most in her favour
11　to carry her precious cup, saucer and plate settings to the table.
12　*I* **am** still not sure

13   whether *I* **was** more anxious
14   in case *I* **dropped** one
15   when *she* **chose** me
16   or **was** more jealous of my brother or sister
17   when *she* **didn't**.

Clauses 9 and 11 do not have a either a Subject or a Finite, while Clauses 4, 5 and 16 each have a Finite but appear to have no Subject. Clauses 9 and 11 are non-finite clauses. In Clauses 4 and 5 the Subject is *she* which can be retrieved from Clause 3, English allowing the leaving out, or *ellipsis*, of the Subject element (and sometimes also the Finite element) under certain circumstances. Clause 16 is a similar case; here the subject *I* can be retrieved from Clause 13. When we can retrieve an ellipsed part of the clause from a previous clause, it is a good idea to put the ellipsed part back into the clause as we divide and number the clauses of the text. At the same time we should have a numbering system that identifies the separate clause complexes as well as the individual clauses.

Following such a system, and putting the ellipsed text into bold block capitals preceded by a ^, we would then have a picture of the text that looked like this:

Cl. C. I   cl. 1   I can clearly remember

        cl. 2   we used to visit an elderly aunt in Surry Hills.

Cl. C. II   cl. 3   She lived in a tiny bed-sit

        cl. 4   and ^**SHE** was not at all well off

        cl. 5   but ^**SHE** entertained her guests in style.

Cl. C. III   cl. 6   Corner stores in those days would sell broken biscuits for a fraction of the price of whole ones

        cl. 7   and she always had a tin of broken Arnotts milk arrowroot biscuits in the pantry.

Cl. C. IV   cl. 8   On her tiny two-ringed stove there was always a kettle boiling its head off.

Cl. C. V   cl. 9   Unlocking her china cabinet

        cl. 10   she would invite the one of us who was currently most in her favour

        cl. 11   to carry her precious cup, saucer and plate settings to the table.

Cl. C. VI   cl. 12   I am still not sure

        cl. 13   whether I was more anxious

        cl. 14   in case I dropped one

        cl. 15   when she chose me

        cl. 16   or ^**WHETHER** I was more jealous of my brother or sister

        cl. 17   when she didn't.

Step 5. Try to identify the function of each clause in its clause complex

With the text now conveniently set out into clause complexes and clauses within the complexes, we can start to ask some questions about the ways in which the clauses relate to each other within their particular clause complex.

Clauses 1, 3, 4, 5, 6, 7, 8, 10 and 12 appear to be messages giving fairly straightforward information and in each case could stand alone as complete messages (allowing for retrieval of Subject where necessary). Clause 2 also looks to be a complete message in its own right, but in fact there is another common piece of English ellipsis here – the first sentence could also have been written *I can clearly remember **that** we used to visit…* *Remember* is a verb like *say, know, think, tell, believe* and allows us to project messages. Here the projection is reported (or indirect) speech as opposed to direct speech (see Chapter 3). Clauses 9 and 11 offer circumstantial support for Clause 10.

Clauses 13, 14, 15, 16 and 17 all seem to be tied in some way to Clause 12 (*I am still not sure*). In fact what we have here are two parallel *projected* messages (*I am not sure* is very like *I don't know* which is a projecting process) comprising Clauses 13, 14, 15 as one group, and 16 and 17 as the second. Within the first group, Clause 14 offers circumstantial support for 13 while 15 offers circumstantial support for 14. In the second group, Clause 17 offers circumstantial support for Clause 16. Thus, Clauses 2, 9, 11, 13, 14, 15, 16 and 17 cannot stand alone to make independent messages; they are all tied in some kind of dependency pattern to other clauses.

Clauses that can stand alone are known as INDEPENDENT CLAUSES, and clauses which function as supporters of other clauses are called DEPENDENT CLAUSES.

So for our text we have:

independent clauses: 1, 3, 4, 5, 6, 7, 8, 10, 12
dependent clauses: 2, 9, 11, 13, 14, 15, 16.

Clause types

Independent clauses

In earlier forays into the world of grammar you may have learnt to use the labels *principal* or *main* for what we will call INDEPENDENT clauses. As noted above, independent clauses are clauses that can stand alone, or function independently of other messages.

An independent clause is always Finite; that is, it contains a Subject and a verbal group with a Finite element (except where the Mood of the verb is imperative – see Chapter 4). It may be linked in a clause complex with other independent clauses or with dependent clauses, or with various combinations of both, but if the clause complex contains just one clause, that clause is usually an independent clause. In the following examples of clause complexes, the independent clauses are in bold type:

1 **Linguistics can be a fascinating pursuit**
   (Clause complex containing one clause)

2 **He fumbled with the speargun ‖ and slid with it into the water**
   (Clause complex with two clauses, both independent,
   ellipsis of Subject in 2nd clause)

3 **Night fell, ‖ the silence deepened ‖ and the child huddled closer to the tree trunk for comfort**
   (Clause complex containing three clauses, all independent)

4 As she looked down into it ‖ **the auditorium seemed bigger than ever**
   (Clause complex containing two clauses, the first dependent,
   the second independent)

5 While they listened ‖ **the bird song changed** ‖ moving suddenly into calls of alarm
   (Clause complex containing three clauses: dependent, independent,
   dependent)

Notice in example 2 that there is no Participant structure functioning as Subject of the finite verbal group *slid*. It is a feature of English usage that the Subject and the Finite can be left out in subsequent clauses under certain conditions. Ellipsis of this type can occur when:

- the clauses are of the same type; that is, both (all) independent or both (all) dependent; and
- the Subject is the same for each clause.

In such cases the Subjectless, and perhaps Finiteless, subsequent clauses are considered to be finite clauses, the receiver of the message being easily able to retrieve the Subject and Finite from the first clause. There are several examples of this grammatical phenomenon in the 'My Aunt' text (Text 1).

Dependent clauses

If you have been used to the term principal clause for an independent clause, then you will probably remember the term subordinate clause as a label for the majority of clauses we call DEPENDENT clauses. Dependent clauses cannot stand alone but function to provide some kind of supportive information for other clauses. In this book we will look specifically at the dependent clauses which provide *circumstantial* information about other clauses and those which are *projections* from verbal and mental processes.

Dependent clauses of the first type perform a very similar role in the clause complex to that performed by Circumstances in the clause itself. They can support the meaning of another clause by offering a condition, suggesting a cause, telling how, or by locating it in time or place. Dependent clauses of the second type are the kinds of messages that are full clause projections from projecting processes realised by verbal groups that express saying, thinking, reporting, believing and so on (see Chapter 3). The examples below are all circumstantial dependent clauses; the issue of projection in clause complexes is explored later in the chapter.

In the following clause complexes, the dependent clauses are in bold type:

1   The revellers scattered ‖ **when the bull charged across the field**
    (Clause complex containing two clauses: one independent, one dependent)

2   **When the whales return** ‖ the spirits of our ancestors will return also
    (Clause complex with two clauses: one dependent, one independent)

3   **Shaken at last out of his complacency,** ‖ Richard watched warily ‖ **as Sally eased herself into the opening of the cave**
    (Clause complex with three clauses: dependent, independent, dependent)

4   James won't be home tomorrow ‖ **because the ABC called** ‖ **and offered him a job interview tomorrow morning**
    (Clause complex with three clauses: independent + two dependent linked by *and*, with ellipsis of Subject in second dependent clause)

5   Sometimes, << **if the nights are very warm,** >> we like to sleep outside
    (Clause complex with two clauses: an independent interrupted by dependent)

Remember that dependent clauses can be finite, as in the majority of the examples above, or non-finite, as in the first clause in example (3).

Embedded clauses

Embedded clauses do not have the same status; that is, they are not at the same rank as independent or dependent clauses. Because they are doing service within a group, they are described as embedded. Look at the examples below:

		Post-modification (Qualifier)
NOMINAL GROUP	The pistol shot	[[that started the First World War]]

		Post-modification
ADVERBIAL GROUP	so quickly	[[that he could not catch them]]

A third type of embedded clause, which has not been mentioned so far, is a clause that is actually functioning as if it is a Thing in its own right, rather than as merely part of a thing structure (nominal group) as above. When this happens the embedded clause functions as Participant in the clause structure or as the nominal group constituent of a prepositional phrase, as in the following examples:

[[**When you see the wind gusting at 120 km/h**]] is the time to panic
(Embedded clause as participant)

The level of our dams are considerably below [[**where we would like them to be**]]
(Embedded clause as nominal group constituent of a prepositional phrase)

In these next examples, embedded clauses functioning as Participant are in bold type. Notice how many are popular sayings or catch-cries:

1	[[**What I really want**]]	is	a glass of water
	Participant	Process	Participant
2	[[**What you see**]]	is	[[**what you get**]]
	Participant	Process	Participant
3	I	am trying to do	[[**what you asked**]]
	Participant	Process	Participant
4	The last thing [[**we needed**]]	was	[[**for you to wake the baby**]]
	Participant	Process	Participant
5	[[**Seeing**]]	is	[[**believing**]]
	Participant	Process	Participant
6	[[**What the committee had in mind for the next function**]]	was made	plain
	Participant	Process	Participant
7	Annie	knows	[[**what she wants**]]
	Participant	Process	Participant

Notice that embedded clauses of this type, like any other type, can be finite (as in example 1, 2, 3 and 6); or non-finite (as in examples clause in 4 and 5).

Interrupting clauses

We should look just briefly at something else some clauses do inside a clause complex. Sometimes a writer or speaker will begin a clause and then interrupt the flow of that clause to insert another clause – usually one with a close relationship to the interrupted clause – returning to complete the original clause in due course. For example:

> After three days, when all hope of reaching a settlement had had to be abandoned, the negotiators were packing their bags for home.

> She told them that, even if they had lodged the application on time, it would not have been successful.

Let's look at a clause division of these clause complexes. Now, instead of our straight parallel lines to show the clause boundaries, or the double square brackets for an embedded clause, we use double chevrons << ... >> to enclose the interrupting clause.

Example 1

> After three days, <<when all hope of reaching a settlement had had to be abandoned>>, the negotiators were packing their bags for home.

Cl. 1   After three days << cl. 2 >> the negotiators were packing their bags for home

Cl. 2   when all hope of reaching a settlement had had to be abandoned

Example 2

> She told them ‖ that, << even if they had lodged the application on time >>, it would not have been successful.

Cl. 1   She told them

Cl. 2   that << cl.3 >> it would not have been successful

Cl. 3   even if they had lodged the application on time

Differences between embedded clauses and interrupting clauses

Embedded clause

An embedded clause is an intrinsic part of another clause because it is either part of a group constituent of a clause (perhaps a Qualifier in a nominal group) or functioning as a group itself (see the examples above where a clause functions as a whole Participant in its own right). An embedded clause is not a ranked clause in a clause complex, but is shifted down a rank – whence 'rank shifted', the other label commonly applied to such clauses.

Interrupting clause

An interrupting clause, on the other hand, is a ranked clause; that is, a clause functioning at clause rank on our rank scale. As such it is a full partner in the clause complex, although it will usually be a dependent clause in the pattern of clause complex relationships.

Thus in the first example above, the interrupting clause gives time-related circumstantial support for the independent clause that it interrupts. In the second example, Clause 3, the interrupting clause, gives conditional circumstantial evidence in support of Clause 2 (which it interrupts). Of course Clause 2 itself is actually a dependent clause, being an indirect speech projection from Clause 1 – the only independent clause in this clause complex.

Independence and dependence in projected clauses

Earlier in this chapter we looked at some examples of message expansion by way of dependent clauses that provide some kind of circumstantial support for an independent clause (or sometimes for another dependent clause). The same relationship of independence and dependence can be carried into an examination of projection (see Chapter 3 for projecting processes). The following examples give some idea of the range of possibilities:

He	said	a lot of nonsense
Sayer	Process: verbal	Verbiage
independent clause		

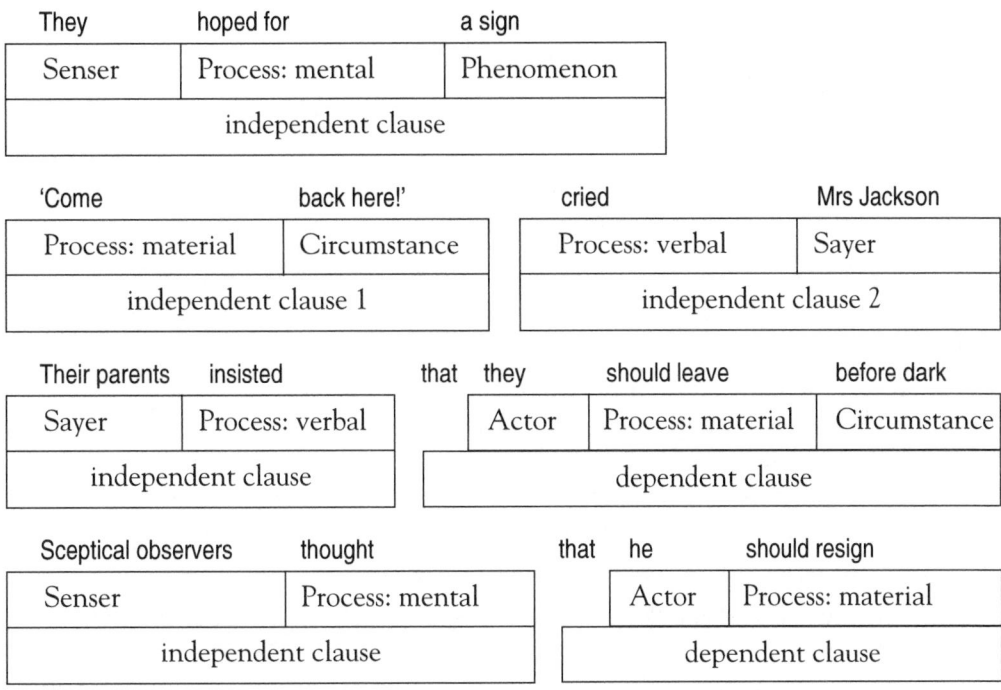

The first two examples are one-clause clause complexes, each made up of one independent clause. In each case the projection is completed by a nominal group within the clause. In the other examples the projection is by way of a separate clause. Notice that in the third example (*Come back here! cried Mrs Jackson*) the projected message is by way of direct speech. Here the direct speech clause is an independent clause; that is it has equal status with the clause that projected it.

The situation is quite different in the fourth and fifth examples, however. Here the projected messages are reported (indirect) speech or thought and the resulting clauses are in a relationship of dependency with their projecting clauses.

Ways of binding clauses

One of the most common ways clauses are bound to each other is through the use of CONJUNCTIONS. In Chapter 2, where we talked briefly about word classes, a conjunction was defined as a joining word. The function of a conjunction in joining clauses predicts the relationship between those clauses. *And*, *but* and *or*, for instance, join like with like so these conjunctions can join either independent or dependent clauses in a relationship that is called coordination:

The door was unlocked ‖ and he opened it ‖ and walked in quietly in his bare feet

The first clause here is independent, so the other clauses joined by *and* are also independent.

In the following example, the conjunction *because* begins three dependent clauses of cause joined by *or*. *Because* belongs to each of the three clauses but does not need to be expressed each time:

... because everyone is listening to music, || or sleeping || or trying to sleep

In this next clause complex, two clauses joined by *and* function as Qualifier in a nominal group; they are thus both embedded clauses:

... a lovely place [[where children and pets can play happily || and parents can relax]]

Other conjunctions, known as subordinating conjunctions, function to link a subordinate (dependent) with a dominant clause which may be either independent or dependent. The choice of subordinating conjunction predicts the logical relationship between the two messages. For instance, *if* and *although* are conditional, *when* is temporal, and *because* introduces a reason. Subordinating conjunctions join clauses in relationships that we call SUBORDINATION. In the following examples the subordinate (dependent) clauses are in bold type and their logical function is shown in brackets:

1   We will all set out together || **when everybody has arrived** (temporal)

2   **Where you find a twisted old oak tree standing alone**, (place) || there you will bury your lord with all honour

3   **As the river flows endlessly towards the sea** (manner) || so my love for you goes on and on

4   They had to run for their lives || **because the fire had almost completely surrounded their position** (cause)

5   They thought || **that they still had plenty of time** (projection)

Coordinating and subordinating conjunctions make the relationship between clauses explicit. Where there is no conjunction the meaning is usually clear, although guess work is sometimes required. For instance we could see:

I'm tired: you took the car

as two independent clauses, each making a simple statement, but some contextual information could lead us to see the second clause as giving an implicit reason for the tiredness of the speaker, suggesting a relationship of subordination between the two clauses.

A closer look at clause relationships

To close this chapter, we will show how relationships among clauses can be explored in a little more detail. We have seen how the meaning of a single clause can grow by expansion or projection with the increase taking the form of either an equal clause or a subordinate clause. But you may have felt that in the example of coordination that we used before, in the clause complex:

The door was unlocked || and he opened it || and walked in quietly with his bare feet

the second and third clauses were not entirely equal with the first. Here it helps to think of the first clause as the *initiating* clause and the others as the *sequent* or following clauses. In spite of this we regard them as three independent clauses with equal status in the clause complex.

On the other hand, it is easy to see that in the clause complex:

They had to run for their lives || because the fire had almost completely surrounded their position

the first clause is dominant (in this case independent) and the second subordinate (dependent). The second clause would still be subordinate even if the order of the clauses were reversed and it became the first clause:

Because the fire had almost completely surrounded their position, || they had to run for their lives

Like the Circumstance consituents of a clause, the circumstantial dependent clauses in a clause complex are fairly mobile. Whether a speaker or writer begins a message of the kind above with the independent clause or the dependent clause (or perhaps even allows the dependent clause to interrupt the flow of an independent clause) may reflect idiosyncratic elements of style, or may involve conscious manipulation of the Theme/Rheme structure of the clause complex. Questions of how best to move ideas through a text, that is, questions of thematic progression, will often motivate the choices made here (see Chapter 6).

A final point to remember is that a dependent clause can be subordinate to an independent clause or to another dependent clause. In the latter case the dominant clause in the sequence of two clauses is a dependent rather than an independent clause. It, in turn, is likely to be subordinate to a dominant independent clause:

[1]We can't make it this trip || [2]because we have to be home || [3]before the wet season begins

In the above example Clause 2 is subordinate to the dominant and independent Clause 1. Clause 3, on the other hand, is subordinate to Clause 2 (a dependent clause), which is thus dominant in the sequence Clause 2, Clause 3.

To sum up

At the top of the rank scale is the language structure we have called a clause complex. In most cases the sentences of written language equate with clause complexes. Clause complexes are made up of one or more clauses which relate to each other in various patterns of independence and dependence. Many dependent clauses function in their clause complex in similar ways to Circumstances in clause patterns; others will be projections arising from verbal and mental processes.

Embedded clauses, on the other hand, do not take their place as full constituent partners in the clause complex structure. Embedded clauses are rankshifted in that they are functioning at the next rank down, not as clause but either as part of a group constituent structure of a clause (Qualifier in a nominal group; Postmodifier in an adverbial group), or as a constituent of the clause in their own right (embedded clause as Participant).

For a fuller discussion of the kinds of relationships involved in the binding of clauses into clause complexes see Halliday (1994: Chapter 7).

Exercises

1 Construct three examples of an independent clause containing an embedded clause.

2 Construct a clause complex of each of the following shapes:
   a. dependent clause + independent clause + independent clause
   b. independent clause + dependent clause + dependent clause
   c. non-finite dependent clause + independent clause + dependent clause.

3 Write a brief text of four or five independent clauses. Now try to rewrite the text using subordinating conjunctions and embedding so that all the clauses are bound together into one clause complex.

4 From the following passages make a list of:
   a. the independent clauses
   b. the dependent clauses
   c. the embedded clauses.

   1 As you come into town, you will see a big service station on the right. Just beyond it is an old factory that's now being converted into an industrial museum. If you drive round the back of the factory, you'll find a kind of open shed that looks like an aircraft hangar.

   2 Droughts are extreme water shortages that last for a long time. Rain falls at different rates in different areas of Australia. Droughts occur when the average rainfall drops below what is expected for that area, and stays there for an extended time. What would be normal rainfall in Alice Springs would be drought in Sydney. There are more droughts in the interior areas of Australia than in the coastal areas. The inland areas have more dramatic changes in rainfall. Droughts from the past can be seen in the rings made on trees as they grow wood each year. In wet years the layer of wood is thick, in dry years the layer of wood is thin. No-one can predict when droughts will occur in the future.

   3 Traumatic inflammation of the stomach results from the presence of a foreign body. This condition is not rare in cattle, because these animals have the habit of swallowing their feed without careful chewing, and so nails, screws, hairpins, ends of wire, and other metal objects may be swallowed unconsciously. Such objects gravitate to the second stomach where they may be caught in the folds of the lining mucous membrane, and in some instances the wall of this organ is perforated. From this accident, chronic indigestion results. The symptoms include pain when getting up or lying down, pain when moving suddenly, and coughing.

   4 Until recent times, the political power to dispose of land in disregard of native title was exercised so as to expand the Crown's 'radical' title to absolute and exclusive ownership. But where that has not occurred, there is no reason to deny the law's protection to indigenous citizens who can establish their entitlement to rights and interests which survived the Crown's acquisition of sovereignty. Those rights and interests may now claim the protection of section 10(1) of the *Racial Discrimination Act* 1975, which gives traditional native title holders the same immunity from legislative interference with their human right to own and inherit property as it gives to others in the community.
   (Butt and Eagleson, 1993, *Mabo: What the High Court said*, Federation Press.)

Implications for language teaching

In this chapter we are given an overview of clause combining in English. In Chapter 6 we explored the work of conjunctions as textual Themes. In this chapter we explore the role of conjunction in clause combining.

How is knowledge of clause combining useful to language teachers and learners?

Combining clauses in English is challenging for language learners. Learners must, however, acquire the knowledge they need to combine clauses effectively if they are to be able to connect their messages and ideas in complex ways. For example, speakers of English combine clauses in order to express sequences in time, to explain, to indicate causes and consequences, to provide evidence in support of an argument, to compare or contrast. This chapter sets out the knowledge learners need if they are to master this key aspect of English grammar. In summary learners need to be able to:

- recognise clause boundaries
- understand the difference between the following types of clauses:
  - independent (with or without ellipsis)
  - dependent (both finite and non-finite)
  - interrupting
  - embedded (as a Post-modifier in a group or as a Participant in a clause)
- use a clause to expand another clause, for example, by adding circumstantial information
- add a projected clause to a projecting clause
- bind clauses with
  - coordinating and subordinating conjunctions
  - explicit and implicit conjunction.

Although this chapter is about joining clauses structurally, the focus remains on meaning. The structural patterns for combining clauses in English are revealed and explained through the understandings about function developed over the previous chapters. Using this approach, teachers can explain clause combining and related structural features (for example, ellipsis, embedding, non-finite clauses or projection) in terms of function and meaning in whole texts.

Teachers can draw students' attention to the different patterns of clause combination used in the varieties of language, or registers, relevant to their learning needs and goals. Differences in patterns of clause combination are particularly noticeable between spoken and written varieties of language. In spoken language English speakers are more likely to link chains of independent clauses together using the conjunctions *and, then, so* and *but*.

The following example is a spoken recount:

Orientation	There's this girl in my class … |||
Record of events	she tried to do a backward roll || **and** she um like her neck clicked or something || **and** um she was taken to hospital in an ambulance ||
Re-orientation	**and** I had to write down [[what happened]] || **because** I was in her group. |||
Coda	I've done that before || **and** it doesn't hurt that much. ||| I think || she's over-reacting just a bit.

A recount retells events in a time sequence. Notice how the time sequence in this spoken recount is framed by the conjunction *and* adding the events together one after the other. This is the dominant, but not the only, clause combination pattern used in the text. The clause combinations that do not fit the dominant pattern are found towards the end of the text. In the re-orientation an embedded clause is a Participant (Verbiage) in an independent clause and a dependent clause adds a cause to an independent clause using the conjunction *because*. At the end of the recount, in the coda, the speaker projects her own thoughts about the incident.

When the speaker writes down her recount for her teacher, however, she uses different patterns of clause combination. Notice how the clause combinations in the written version below introduce more complexity into the retelling of how the events unfolded:

Orientation	The teacher told our class || to put our sports uniforms on || **and** go to the gym for a gym class. |||
Record of events	**When** we were all dressed and settled, || she told us || to make a series of stretches and different things [[that had to do with gymnastics]]. |||
	Next we got into groups of four || **and** had to make a sequence of rolls and tumbles. ||| The teacher told us specifically || not to push ourselves to the limit. |||
	As we thought and tried out ideas, || I suggested backward rolls. ||| I also demonstrated it. |||
	As Megan tried to do it, || **instead of** rolling on her shoulder, || she rolled on her neck || **and** clicked it somehow. |||
	Megan couldn't stand up or bend down || **so** she sat with her back straight. |||
	The teacher told her || to breathe in and out.||| She helped her **as much** [[as she could.]] |||
Re-orientation	**After** this happened, || Megan was taken to hospital || **and** the rest of our class got changed.

In the written recount traces of spoken language chains remain where the conjunctions *and* and *so* are used to add independent clauses together. In this version, however, the incident is not retold as one event added on to the next. The relationship between events is expressed in a more complex way. The writer achieves this by combining clauses so that some events are revealed as dependent on other events, either in terms of circumstance or in terms of projection.

Most of the circumstantial dependent clauses locate events in time (*When we were all dressed and settled; As we thought and tried out ideas; As Megan tried to do it; After this happened*). These clauses are placed in the Theme position of their clause complexes, and thus they help frame the pattern through which a recount achieves its generic purpose of retelling a sequence of events. The dependent non-finite clause expressing contrast (*instead of rolling on her shoulder*) is not placed in Theme position where it would disrupt this pattern.

The four non-finite dependent projections report what the teacher said (*to put our sports uniforms on and go to the gym for a gym class; to make a series of stretches and different things that had to do with gymnastics; not to push ourselves to the limit; to breathe in and out*). The writer uses this pattern of dependent projection to report how, as events unfolded, the teacher fulfilled her professional responsibilities. This clearly was why the writer was asked to retell, in writing, what happened.

Knowing how to recombine the rambling chains of independent clauses in spoken language into the more crafted clause combinations of written language is essential for students developing skills in English literacy. This is not enough, however, if students are to manage the specialised, formal and abstract texts of higher education and skilled employment. As written texts become more specialised, formal and abstract, some clause combinations give way to increasingly compact constructions in which complex meanings are packaged into noun groups.

Notice how, in this formal report about the accident in the gymnasium written for the school authorities the meanings have been packed into noun groups to create a very compact text:

Orientation	At 10:15 am on Friday 23rd March there was an incident [[in which a student sustained a minor injury]]. |||
Record of events	The student was participating in a gymnastics class [[involving a series of floor exercises.]] ||| During an attempt at backward rolls the student strained her neck slightly. |||
Re-orientation	Following assessment of the injury by the supervising teacher || the student was taken to hospital, || where the injury was diagnosed as minor neck strain. |||
	The medical officer on duty advised the student || that she would be fit [[to return to school the next day]]. |||

The packaging of meanings into noun groups is achieved in two ways:

- *embedding,* in which clauses are used as Post-modifiers in noun groups

    an incident [[in which a student sustained a minor injury;]]
    a gymnastics class [[involving a series of floor exercises;]]
    fit [[to return to school the next day]]

- *nominalisation*, which shifts the expression of events from verbs to nouns so they can be packaged into noun groups:

as Megan tried to do it	→	an attempt at backward rolls
she helped her as much as she could	→	assessment of the injury

Notice how, in these shifted expressions, the person involved in each event is no longer in the language.

Students studying English for Academic Purposes or English for skilled or professional employment will need to learn how to package meanings into written language of this kind.

How can our knowledge of clause combining enhance language teaching programs?

Learners can explore clause combining from the perspective of a whole text in a number of ways. First students need to be able to recognise clause boundaries. The five steps for defining clause boundaries at the beginning of the chapter can be used as a basis for activities in which students explore clause boundaries. The steps would need to be adapted to the students' language level.

To explore clause combining effectively, students will also need to learn how to use different types of conjunction (such as addition, sequence, cause, comparison) across different contexts of situation (spoken and written language, formal and informal language, everyday and specialised language and so on) for different social purposes (to tell stories, to instruct, to explain, to persuade etc). They will need to recognise how clauses are combined into different clause complex patterns of expansion and projection. This needs to be followed with opportunities for experimentation and practice.

When teaching spoken language, the intonation patterns that map on to combined clauses also need to be introduced and practised. When teaching written language, punctuation associated with clause combining needs to be introduced and practised. This includes, for example, commas and quotation marks.

There are many examples of clause combining exercises in English language teaching materials. It is always preferable to adapt these exercises to include clauses which relate to contexts of language use relevant to the students. Students also need opportunities to explore the patterns of clause combination in the texts types and contexts of situation relevant to their learning needs and goals.

Figure 7.1 is a clause combining recognition exercise adapted from a secondary school writing textbook (de Silva Joyce and Feez, 2000: 90). This exercise was one of an extended series of exercises designed to develop students' ability to write literary descriptions.

Combining clauses

Work out how the clauses have been combined in each of these examples.

1   Clause 1:   *The branches dipped elegantly.*
     Clause 2:   *The branches sighed knowingly.*
     Clause 3:   *The branches brushed delicately against the trunk.*
     Combined clause: *The branches dipped and sighed elegantly, knowingly, brushing delicately against the trunk.*

2   Clause 1:   *The tree was strong.*
     Clause 2:   *The tree was a gentle guardian.*
     Clause 3:   *The tree waited like an elder from another time.*
     Combined clause: *The tree was a strong but gentle guardian, waiting like an elder from another time.*

3   Clause 1:   *The tree waited.*
     Clause 2:   *The tree watched.*
     Clause 3:   *The tree whispered its secrets to the breeze.*
     Combined clause: *The tree waited, watched, and whispered its secrets to the breeze.*

4   Clause 1:   *The tree waited.*
     Clause 2:   *The tree watched.*
     Clause 3:   *The tree whispered its secrets to the breeze.*
     Combined clause: *While the tree waited and watched, it whispered its secrets to the breeze.*

5   Clause 1:   *The tree waited.*
     Clause 2:   *The tree watched.*
     Clause 3:   *The tree whispered its secrets to the breeze.*
     Combined clause: *Waiting and watching, the tree whispered its secrets to the breeze.*

Figure 7.1 Clause combining recognition exercise

Further reading

For more information on clause combining read Bloor and Bloor (1995: Chapters 8–10).

A classroom teacher describes how she applied a functional understanding of conjunction to a dictagloss activity in Lukin (1995: 53–55).

Exercises for language teachers

1   Identify a good example of a type of text you would like your students to be able to use effectively. The text might be spoken or written. If you wish, you may choose one of the texts in Chapter 1.

2   Undertake a clause complex analysis using the five steps in Chapter 7.

3   Use your analysis to look for patterns of clause combination across the text.

4   What patterns of combination tend to be used the most (eg independent, dependent, embedded, expansion, projection)?

5   How does the use of these patterns contribute to the text achieving its purpose?

6   What do these patterns reveal to you about:
    • the text's structure and purpose
    • experiential meanings in the text
    • interpersonal meanings in the text
    • textual meanings in the text?

7   Relate what you have discovered about the clause combination in this text to your students' learning needs and goals.

8   What do you think your students need to learn about clause combination in order to be able to use this text effectively?

9   Use what you have discovered about clause combination in the text to design activities that support your students' progress towards their learning goals. These activities might draw your students' attention to:
    • the purpose and structure of the text as revealed in the way the clauses are combined at different stages of the text
    • clause boundaries
    • different types of clause (eg independent with or without ellipsis; dependent, both finite and non-finite; interrupting; embedded)
    • using a clause to expand the meanings of another clause, for example, by adding circumstantial information
    • using a clause to project another clause
    • binding clauses with coordinating and subordinating conjunctions or explicit and implicit conjunction.

Exploring context

Introducing ...

- A fuller description of contextual features
  based on lexicogrammatical patterns

Discussing ...

- Implications for language teaching

This chapter returns us to two fundamental questions about any text:

- What's going on in the world outside language (the extralinguistic level) to make this text as it is?
- What can we tell about the world outside language by exploring this text?

In this chapter we move from the patterns of lexicogrammar and semantics that have been the focus of earlier chapters towards a concern with interpreting the overall patterns of a text in order to see what they reveal about its context. To make this exciting step, we need to be comfortable with everything we have done so far. Appendices A and B provide two complementary charts that summarise the main issues in the previous chapters and lead us to the next step in our discussion of context. Appendix A summarises the metalanguage for each part of our metafunctional analysis while Appendix B summarises the overall meaning patterns uncovered by our analysis.

As we explore the relation between text and context, we will discover that the questions at the top of this chapter are essentially not two questions, but opposite sides of the same question. The relation between context and meanings is dynamic and reversible, with contexts being realised in texts and texts revealing contexts. This means that knowledge of the context allows us to make predictions about the lexicogrammar of a text. Conversely, grammatical analysis of the type we have been doing allows us to understand the context of a text's production because the sum of the meanings encoded in the lexicogrammar becomes the sign of the context.

Of course, this is what we have been implying from the first time we introduced the now familiar diagram: Levels of language (Figure 8.1).

Metalanguage for exploring the relation between text and context

The metalanguage needed for our discussion was introduced in Chapter 1 where we said that context of situation motivates the meanings of texts in three main areas:

The metalanguage of context

Field of discourse
Tenor of discourse
Mode of discourse

- the field of human experience encompassed by the text and its purpose in encompassing it (*field of discourse*)

- the social relationship between the speaker or writer and the addressee (*tenor of discourse*)

- the nature of the text itself and the role that language plays in it (*mode of discourse*).

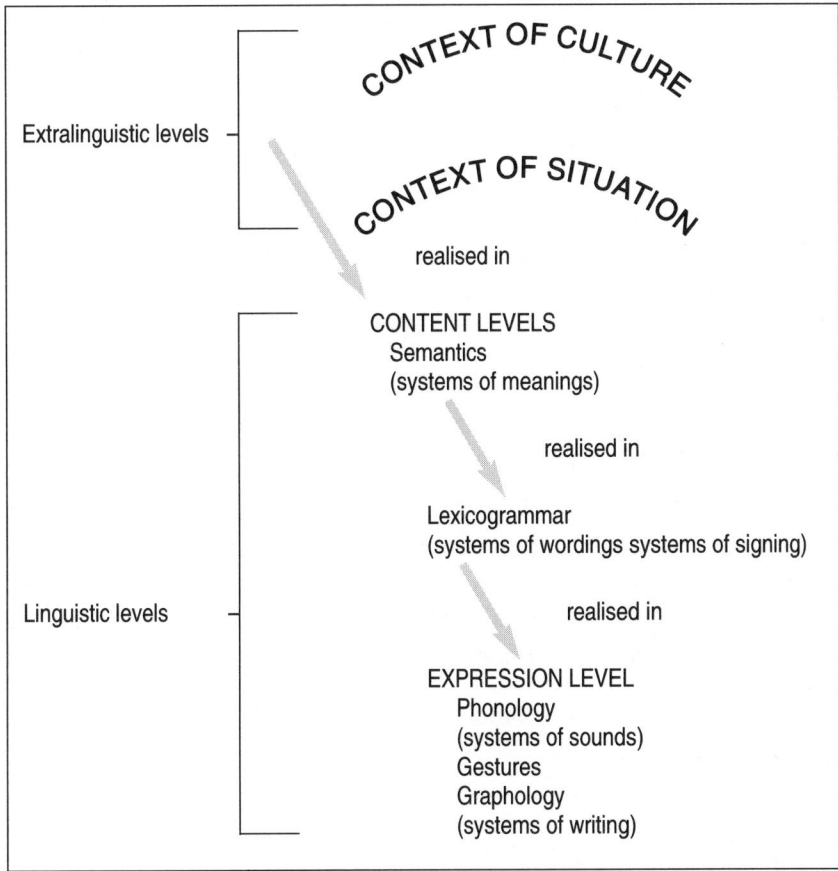

Figure 8.1: Levels of language

From context to text: From text to context

Imagine that you are constructing three texts in which the field of discourse – the description of the finals of an international tennis tournament in which you participated – is constant.

In the first text, you write a letter about the game to your closest friend, and, in the second, you phone him to discuss it. In these two, the *tenor* of discourse is also constant but the *mode* of discourse is different – the first text would be a written monologue and the second a spoken dialogue. We would expect that this vital difference would be reflected in the shape and lexicogrammatical choices of the two texts.

In a third text, you have written a description of the match for your local, suburban newspaper. The *field* of discourse would be the same description of the tennis match and, like the first text, the *mode* would be written and monologic. But in this third text the *tenor* of discourse (the statuses and roles of the participants) would be different and the difference would be reflected in your description.

Now imagine the reverse situation, where instead of creating the texts you are the reader or addressee. The lexicogrammar of the texts provides you with clues about their context of situation.

It almost goes without saying that it would be virtually impossible for you to produce or interpret the texts if you were not familiar with tennis matches, letter writing, telephones or suburban newspapers. Yet for many people in the world these situations would indeed be unfamiliar and the construction and interpretation of the three texts would be most unlikely. This kind of constraint means that contexts of situation always occur within the context of culture which encompasses the total of all the contexts of situation within that culture.

Interpreting context

Our concern with the underlying motivations of a text should not sound daunting; after all, we use our knowledge of context with every text we write or speak or hear or read. We can test our ability to do so using Text 1 and its accompanying questions. As you read it, bear in mind these transcription conventions: the clauses are numbered, extra information is given in upper case, and each dot in a series represents a pause of a few seconds.

Text 1: A simple ball game

1	OK, Go over
2	And get the ball …
3	Now sit down there …
4	Sit down over there …
5	Now roll it
6	Roll it over to Tiffany
7	And then she'll push it back to you
8	There you go (LAUGHTER)
9	And back again (LAUGHTER)
10	And back again (LAUGHTER)
11	Oh not too hard (WARNING)
12	You'll hurt her
13	There you go (LAUGHTER)
14	Oh! O.K., pick it up
15	And throw it … like that
16	Oh (DISMAY) Go
17	And get it

Questions about context

- What activity is taking place?
- *What in the text tells us this?*
- Who is speaking?
- *What in the text tells us this?*
- Who is being spoken to?
- What sort of social distance is there between them?
- Is the relationship between them equal or unequal?
- *What in the text tells us this?*
- Are any items in the text positively or negatively appraised?
- What are the appraised motifs?
- *Again, how do we know?*
- Do we know precisely where the activity is taking place?
- How significant is this?
- Is the text interactive or not (is it a monologue or a dialogue)?
- Was this text originally spoken or written?
- *How do we know this?*
- How could we summarise the main tone or thrust of the text?
- Does language constitute the whole of the activity or is it helping some other activity along?

Although the language of the text is all we have to work with, it provides enough information for us to answer all but one of the questions with some degree of certainty. If we then ask ourselves why this should be so, the answer is that we learn language in contexts and we can compare texts to our previous language experiences. Because we have heard language like this text many times before, we can slot it into our experience and come up with a fairly accurate assessment of what is being talked about, the purpose of the talk, the relationship between the participants, and the role of language in the interaction.

The only unanswerable question is the precise location of the activity and, for this text, this is not really relevant. The exact location of the discourse in time and space is known as the MATERIAL SITUATIONAL SETTING and, except where it actually enters the text in some significant way, we generally keep it quite separate from the more important contextual features which we have been calling the *context of situation*.

If you think the speaker is a kindergarten teacher, you may think that the material situational setting is a pre-school and that Tiffany is another child of the same age – but you may be wondering why all the speech is addressed to the unnamed child. If you think the speaker is a mother, you probably think that the material situational setting is a park or garden or a room at home and that Tiffany, propped up to participate in the game, is the younger sibling of the addressee. Whether it was a room or garden, whether the day was fine or wet, what the children were wearing, are all irrelevant to the text. What we are really interested in here are the contextual features from the extralinguistic world that make the text what it is.

We can define CONTEXT OF SITUATION as an abstraction made up of the sum of the motivating features of the text's construction which make it what it is, what Hasan calls the 'motivational relevancies' (Hasan 1996a). Let's look more closely at the short text.

Investigating field

The main questions concern the experiential domain.

- What activity is taking place?
- What in the text tells us this?

The experiential meanings of Processes, Participants and Circumstances provide the answer. Here are the major patterns uncovered by our analysis.

Processes

Material processes are in bold type.

1	OK, **Go** over
2	And **get** the ball …
3	Now **sit** down there …
4	**Sit** down over there …
5	Now **roll** it
6	**Roll** it over to Tiffany
7	And then she'll **push** it back to you
8	There you **go** (*LAUGHTER*)
9	And back again (*LAUGHTER*)
10	And back again (*LAUGHTER*)
11	Oh not too hard (*WARNING*)
12	You'll **hurt** her
13	There you **go** (*LAUGHTER*)
14	Oh! O.K., **pick** it up
15	And **throw** it … like that
16	Oh (*DISMAY*) **Go**
17	And **get** it

Summary of Processes

Most processes are material. This pattern is so strong that it does not matter that we have not recovered *roll* or *push* in Clauses 9 and 10.

Participants

Actor is shown in bold and *Goal* in italics.

1   OK, Go over
2   And get *the ball* ...
3   Now sit down there ...
4   Sit down over there ...
5   Now roll *it*
6   Roll *it* over to Tiffany
7   And then **she'll** push *it* back to you
8   There **you** go (*LAUGHTER*)
9   And back again (*LAUGHTER*)
10   And back again (*LAUGHTER*)
11   Oh not too hard (*WARNING*)
12   **You'll** hurt *her*
13   There **you** go (*LAUGHTER*)
14   Oh! O.K., pick *it* up
15   And throw *it* ... like that
16   Oh (*DISMAY*) Go
17   And get *it*

Summary of Participants

The most common Actor is not shown in the clause. It is the addressee who is to perform the action, although Tiffany is also Actor in Clause 7. The most common Goal is the ball.

Circumstances

Place is underlined and **Manner** is in bold type.

1   OK, Go <u>over</u>
2   And get the ball ...
3   Now sit down <u>there</u> ...
4   Sit down <u>over</u> <u>there</u> ...
5   Now roll it
6   Roll it <u>over</u> to Tiffany
7   And then she'll push it <u>back</u> to you
8   There you go (*LAUGHTER*)
9   And <u>back</u> again (*LAUGHTER*)
10   And <u>back</u> again (*LAUGHTER*)
11   Oh not **too hard** (*WARNING*)
12   You'll hurt her
13   There you go (*LAUGHTER*)
14   Oh! O.K., pick it <u>up</u>
15   And throw it ... **like that**
16   Oh (*DISMAY*) Go
17   And get it

Summary of Circumstances

Most Circumstances answer the question *Where?* either about rolling the ball or directing the movements of the child. The Circumstances of manner refer to the child's actions.

Summarising field

We would have made an accurate assessment of the activity if we had said that the text concerns a simple ball game. To a large extent we gleaned this information about the field of discourse from the transitivity system of the clauses – the participants are largely concerned with positioning themselves and rolling and pushing and getting a ball. In other words, the experiential meanings combine as signs of the field of discourse.

Investigating tenor

This set of questions concerns the relationship between the speakers.

- Who is speaking?
- What in the text tells us this?
- Who is being spoken to?
- What sort of social distance is there between them?
- Is the relationship between them equal or unequal?
- What in the text tells us this?
- Are any items in the text positively or negatively appraised?
- What are the appraisal motifs?
- Again, how do we know?

The interpersonal meanings in the text provide the answers. Here are the major patterns uncovered by our analysis.

Mood

In this text, declarative mood is underlined and **imperative mood** is in bold type.

1	OK, Go over
2	And **get** the ball ...
3	Now **sit** down there ...
4	**Sit** down over there ...
5	Now **roll** it
6	**Roll** it over to Tiffany
7	And then she'll push it back to you
8	There you go (*LAUGHTER*)
9	And back again (*LAUGHTER*)
10	And back again (*LAUGHTER*)

11   Oh not too hard (*WARNING*)
12   You'll <u>hurt</u> her
13   There you <u>go</u> (*LAUGHTER*)
14   Oh! O.K., **pick** it up
15   And **throw** it ... like that
16   Oh (*DISMAY*) **Go**
17   And **get** it

Summary of mood

Almost all the clauses in this text are imperative mood. Even the declarative clauses (7 and 12) contain some modality. The speaker demands goods and services and the other participants apparently comply, so the relationship is quite unequal. If we add this information to our conclusions about the field of discourse and our past experiences of similar activities, we can expect that a young child is being taught a simple ball game by a mother or teacher. The adult does all the talking and the children accept her instructions so the power and status is unequal. The adult also appraises the child's actions:

There you go!   (positive appraisal)
Oh, not too hard!   (negative appraisal)

The adult even appraises a possible action to warn the child, though we could only be really sure about the adult's appraisal if we could see the accompanying facial expressions and gestures:

You'll hurt her

The relationship of adult and child seems very close and many things are taken for granted – the speech is familiar and elliptical – so the social distance between them is minimal. A summation of the roles of the participants and their relation to each other is known as the TENOR OF DISCOURSE and, to a large extent, comes from the inter-personal system of the clauses. In other words, the interpersonal meanings of the Mood system combine as signs of the tenor of discourse.

Investigating mode

The next set of questions concerns the role of language in the text.

- Is the text interactive or not, that is, is it a monologue or a dialogue?
- Was this text originally spoken or written?
- How do we know this?
- Do the overall grammatical patterns of the text reveal a structural pattern that conforms to a recognisable text type?
- How could we summarise the main tone or thrust of the text?
- Does language constitute the whole of the activity or is it helping some other activity along?

The textual meanings, which organise our experiential and interpersonal meanings into a linear and coherent whole, provide some of the answers to these questions. Here are the major patterns uncovered by our analysis:

Themes

In this text, <u>topical</u> themes are underlined and **textual** themes are in bold type.

1   OK, <u>Go</u> over
2   **And** <u>get</u> the ball ...
3   **Now** <u>sit</u> down there ...
4   <u>Sit</u> down over there ...
5   **Now** <u>roll</u> it
6   <u>Roll</u> it over to Tiffany
7   **And then** <u>she</u>'ll push it back to you
8   **There** <u>you</u> go (*LAUGHTER*)
9   **And** back again (*LAUGHTER*)
10 **And** back again (*LAUGHTER*)
11 Oh not too hard (*WARNING*)
12 <u>You</u>'ll hurt her
13 **There** <u>you</u> go (*LAUGHTER*)
14 **Oh! O.K.**, <u>pick</u> it up
15 **And** <u>throw</u> it ... like that
16 **Oh** (*DISMAY*) <u>Go</u>
17 **And** <u>get</u> it

Summary of Theme
Most of the topical Themes are the Predicator in imperative clauses and *she* and *you* in the declaratives. Many of the clauses are Rheme only. The Predicator Themes reflect the procedural nature of the text.

Cohesion

In this text the pronouns are replaced by the nouns they reference and lexical sets of Participants and Processes in the ball game are underlined. Notice also, the repetition in Clauses 3 and 4, 5 and 6, 9 and 10, and that 1 and 2 are repeated in 16 and 17.

1   OK, <u>Go</u> over
2   And <u>get the ball</u> ...
3   Now <u>sit</u> down there ...
4   <u>Sit</u> down over there ...
5   Now <u>roll the ball</u>
6   <u>Roll the ball</u> to <u>Tiffany</u>
7   And then <u>Tiffany</u> will <u>push the ball</u> back to <u>you</u>
8   There <u>you</u> go (*LAUGHTER*)
9   And <u>back again</u> (*LAUGHTER*)
10 And <u>back again</u> (*LAUGHTER*)
11 Oh not *too hard* (*WARNING*)

12   You'll *hurt* Tiffany
13   There <u>you</u> go (*LAUGHTER*)
14   Oh! OK, <u>pick the ball</u> up
15   And <u>throw the ball</u> ... like that
16   Oh (*DISMAY*) <u>Go</u>
17   and <u>get the ball</u>

Summary of Cohesion

This is a highly cohesive text about a ball game. Notice the small italicised lexical set *too hard* and *hurt*, which realise negative Appraisal, and the repetition of *There you go*, which seems to realise positive Appraisal. The main conjunction *and* signals the sequential nature of the activity.

Other patterns

Text 1 is, in fact, taken from a tape-recording of a mother and child at play. Even if we were not told that the language was originally spoken, we could work it out from the simple language and the ellipsis. Of course, the text could have come from a novel or a play; that is, it could have been written to sound spoken, but in either of these cases there would be other clues.

We never know the identity of *you*, nor the exact location of *over there*, just that they refer to people and places in the setting of the text. This helps us to conclude that language is helping the game along rather than constituting the whole activity. Where the role of language is ancillary, the material situational setting intrudes into the context of situation in some way, as it does here with the ball, but otherwise it is unimportant to the description. We can contrast this ancillary role with a lecture where the language *does* constitute the activity and the other things that go on in lectures, for instance, the overheads and the note-taking, are incidental. These conclusions about the language of the text tell us about the MODE OF DISCOURSE. In other words, the textual signs can be added together as signs of the mode of discourse.

Writing up context of situation

The field, tenor and mode of discourse summarise the 'motivational relevancies' which drive the text and make up the context of situation. Our analytic description of context of situation will be set out under these three headings. As we have already discussed, the essentials of the analysis are found in meanings encoded in the lexicogrammar of the text, so we begin with the lexicogrammar and proceed towards our description of context of situation. Traditionally, the description is written in almost telegraphic notes. The challenge in writing it is to be delicate and particular enough to go from the description of context to a fair approximation of the text while at the same time being general and abstract enough to compare texts with similar contexts.

Further metalanguage for writing up the context of situation

Field

The metalanguage for the telegraphic description of field of discourse, whose scope is the field of human experience and activity in the text, appears in the box on the left below.

> **The metalanguage of Field of discourse**
>
> *experiential domain*
> *short term goal*
> *long term goal*

Experiential domain is what the text is all about – the Processes, Participants and Circumstances.

Short term goal refers to the immediate purpose of the text's production.

Long term goal is rather more abstract and refers to the text's place in the larger scheme of things.

Tenor

The metalanguage for the telegraphic description of tenor of discourse, whose scope is the relationship between the participants, their roles and status (both temporary and permanent) and their patterns of appraisal, appears in the box below.

> **The metalanguage of Tenor of discourse**
>
> *agentive or societal roles*
> *power and status*
> *social distance*
>
> *appraisal motifs*

Agentive or *societal roles* are roles of the speaker and the addressee – for example, mother/child, doctor/patient, teacher/pupil.

Some people prefer to separate *power* and *status* while others consider them together. What you do probably depends on the specific text; normally they can be conflated, but you'd want to separate them if a high status person appears powerless and/or the person assuming power is of lower status.

In some languages, pronominal and even lexical choices are determined by the relative status of speaker and addressee. Status and power may be equal or hierarchic and temporary or permanent. Some pointers to an identification of status and power are mood choices by the speakers – that is, who gives the orders, who asks the questions, who makes the offers, who gives information – and the responses of the addressees – that is, who remains silent, who agrees, contradicts, or refuses to participate.

Social distance measures how well the participants know each other: whether they speak familiarly or distantly. Maximal social distance is used by speakers who have never met before, and minimal by those who interact on a familiar and frequent basis. It may be indicated by the levels of formality and objectivity in a text. It can be stretched by exclusive *we* and minimised by inclusive *we*, and can be stretched by negative judgements and minimised by the solidarity of positive judgements.

Mode

The metalanguage for the telegraphic description of mode of discourse, whose scope is role of language in the text, appears in the box below.

> The metalanguage of
> Mode of discourse
>
> role of language
> type of interaction
> medium
> channel
> rhetorical thrust

Role of language is either *constitutive or ancillary*. If language is ancillary to the text, it helps some other activity. On the other hand, if language constitutes the text, it is the whole activity.

Type of interaction refers to whether the text is all spoken by one person (*monologic*) or whether others participate (*dialogic*).

Medium refers to whether the text was originally *spoken* or *written*, or even *signed*. Patterns of cohesion and nominalisation allow us to make finer distinctions. Thus, we can often say that a text sounds written although it was spoken (for instance, a sermon or lecture) or written to sound spoken (for instance a television script).

Channel refers to how the text was originally received and is either *phonic* or *graphic* or, in the case of a signed text, *visual*.

Rhetorical thrust refers to the overall feeling of the text; for example, instructional, persuasive, literary. The emergence of structural patterns as the text unfolds contributes to our decisions about rhetorical thrust.

In the film industry, when a script writer is given a scenario, it will be detailed enough to create the text envisaged by the director. It will say what the text is about, who the characters are, enough about their personalities and the overall thrust of the text for the director's ideas to be realised in language. A contextual description of a text bears a close resemblance to a film scenario, but while the scenario allows a text to be created, a contextual description should allow a text to be re-created. The information under the formal headings of the description should be delicate and detailed enough to re-create something very close to the original. This is why functional grammarians speak of the dialectic relation between meanings and context; that is, the meanings display the context and the context is realised in the meanings. There are, in fact, functional grammarians presently engaged in computerised text generation programs using their delicate knowledge of text and context.

From lexicogrammatical analysis to contextual description

With the grammatical analysis of the text on the previous pages and a set of contextual parameters which apply to any text, we are now in a position to write up the contextual description of this particular text, as you will see on the following pages.

Field of discourse

Lexicogrammatical analysis

Experiential meanings

process types
 mainly material –
  go, get, roll, pick up,
  throw, push, sit
 	
 participants
 Actor: *the addressee,*
  Tiffany
 Goal: *the ball*
 	
 Circumstances
 place: *over there*
 manner: *like that*

As a result of our analysis and knowledge of context of culture we can write up our description

Contextual description

FIELD OF DISCOURSE	Commentary
experiential domain two children learning to roll a ball back and forth **short-term goal** teaching how to play the game gently **long-term goal** teaching reciprocity of interaction maintenance of family roles	

Tenor of discourse

Lexicogrammatical analysis

Interpersonal meanings

Mood selections
 	
 mainly imperative –
  go, get, roll, pick
  up, throw, push, sit
 some declarative with probability/futurity –
  will push, will hurt
 	
 person selections
 2nd = child addressee
 3rd = other child, ball
 	
 appraisal
 + praise for child's capacity from mother *There you go*
 	
 – warning that *child's action* *'too hard'* and *could lead to* *'hurting'* sibling

As a result of our analysis and knowledge of context of culture we can write up our description

Contextual description

TENOR OF DISCOURSE	Commentary
agentive or societal roles mother and children **status** unequal **social distance** minimal	The mother is the only speaker. Almost all the clauses in this text are in imperative mood – the speaker demands action and the other participants apparently comply so the relationship between speakers is unequal. However, it does seem very close, and the speech is familiar and elliptical so the social distance is minimal.

Mode of discourse

Lexicogrammatical analysis

Textual meanings
Thematic choices
topical Themes –
I, she, you go, get, roll, pick up, throw, push, sit
textual Themes –
and, now, and then
Cohesion
lexical sets to do with 'ball game' repetition reference to ball and Tiffany
ellipsis: in Clauses 9, 10, and 11
Structural patterns
fit with procedure

As a result of our analysis and knowledge of context of culture we can write up our description

Contextual description

MODE OF DISCOURSE	Commentary
role of language ancillary	Nonverbal compliance gives this text some dialogic qualities.
type of interaction monologue	
medium spoken	Text now transcribed.
channel phonic	
rhetorical thrust procedural/rather bossy	

A second descriptive analysis of context of situation

In this section we go through the same steps for another, rather different, text. In contrast to the detailed analysis of the previous text, we have often simply summarised the major patterns revealed by our analysis.

Text 2: Rugby notes

Captain: P W Goth; Vice-captain: L P Ghenge
(see team photograph elsewhere in this issue)

The team was a powerful combination once it established its own pattern of play. It was unfortunate to play the top side, Mertons, first up. Although losing, the margin was small.

The next game, against St Cuthberts, proved to be a torrid encounter with our forward pack crumbling in the remaining few minutes. Against Luscombe Grammar, quick, clean ball play enabled our back line to dominate and run in numerous tries. St Spirit's also proved to be little opposition, though poor goal-kicking and numerous dropped balls cost us many points in this game.

After the term holidays the team played many of its remaining matches in windy, wet conditions. Against St Bedes, powerful running by the back line established an early superiority which was not to be lost. The following week we played a club side, Forrest Hill, and found it difficult to compete against a stronger, more mobile pack. Dry conditions against Seeton Grammar allowed our back line to play well again and dominate the game. Unfortunately, the final game against Geneva proved to be our worst for the season, with careless handling and concentration lapses costing us the game.

If there is one thing to be remembered by the 1st XV from this season, it is that the team played best when individual glory was sacrificed so that team achievement could be maximised. A champion team, not a team of champions, was the motivating spirit behind this School rugby team.

Investigating field in experiential meanings

Processes

In this text, relational processes are underlined, material processes are in bold type and mental processes are in italics.

The team <u>was</u> a powerful combination once it **established** its own pattern of play. It <u>was</u> unfortunate **to play** the top side, Mertons, first up. Although **losing**, the margin <u>was</u> small.

The next game, against St Cuthberts, <u>proved to be</u> a torrid encounter with our forward pack **crumbling** in the remaining few minutes. Against Luscombe Grammar, quick, clean ball play **enabled** our back line to **dominate** and **run** in numerous tries. St Spirit's also <u>proved to be</u> little opposition, though poor goal-kicking and numerous dropped balls **cost** us many points in this game.

After the term holidays the team **played** many of its remaining matches in windy, wet conditions. Against St Bedes, powerful running by the back line **established** an early superiority which <u>was</u> not **to be lost**. The following week we **played** a club side, Forrest Hill, and **found** it difficult **to compete** against a stronger, more mobile pack. Dry conditions against Seeton Grammar **allowed** our back line **to play** well again and **dominate** the game. Unfortunately, the final game against Geneva <u>proved to be</u> our worst for the season, with careless handling and concentration lapses **costing** us the game.

If there <u>is</u> one thing *to be remembered* by the 1st XV from this season, it <u>is</u> that the team **played** best when individual glory **was sacrificed** so that team achievement **could be maximised**. A champion team, not a team of champions, <u>was</u> the motivating spirit behind this School rugby team.

Summary of Processes

Many processes are relational (*was* many times, *proved to be* three times). The most frequent material processes are *played* and *cost*, but also notice the passive voice *was sacrificed* in the final paragraph. It is also in the last paragraph that we find the only projecting process, *remembered*. Something that is different from the rest of the text stands out, or is said to be foregrounded (Hasan 1985). When one part of the text is consistently foregrounded it becomes a focus of the text's meaning.

Participants

In this text, Actors are underlined, Carriers are in bold type and Tokens and Value are in italics.

The team was a powerful combination once <u>it</u> established its own pattern of play. **It** was unfortunate to play the top side, Mertons, first up. Although losing, **the margin** was small.

The next game, against St Cuthberts, proved to be a torrid encounter with <u>our forward pack</u> crumbling in the remaining few minutes. Against Luscombe Grammar, <u>quick, clean ball play</u> enabled <u>our back line</u> to dominate and run in numerous tries. **St Spirit's** also proved to be little opposition, though <u>poor goal-kicking and numerous dropped balls</u> cost us many points in this game.

After the term holidays <u>the team</u> played many of its remaining matches in windy, wet conditions. Against St Bedes, <u>powerful running by the back line</u> established an early superiority which was not to be lost. The following week <u>we</u> played a club side, Forrest Hill, and found it difficult to compete against a stronger, more mobile pack. <u>Dry conditions against Seeton Grammar</u> allowed <u>our back line</u> to play well again and dominate the game. Unfortunately, *the final game against Geneva* proved to be *our worst for the season*, with <u>careless handling and concentration lapses</u> costing us the game.

If there is one thing [[to be remembered by the 1st XV]] from this season, *it* is [[*that the team played best when individual glory was sacrificed so that team achievement could be maximised*]]. *A champion team, not a team of champions*, was *the motivating spirit behind this School rugby team*.

Summary of Participants

In the relational clauses the first participant is most often *the team* or *the game* but is sometimes another school. In the final paragraph there is embedding on each side of the relational process (*one thing to be remembered by the 1st XV from this season is that the team played best when individual glory was sacrificed so that team achievement could be maximised*). The mental process (*to be remembered*) within the embedded clause is in the passive voice so the Senser looks like an Agent. The Actor in almost all the material clauses is *the team* which *plays*, *dominates* and *competes against* other school teams. It is interesting that this material process pattern only occurs when the team wins or when it meets the club side of older players that it is not really expected to defeat.

There are not many nominalisations in this text; most of the action occurs congruently in the processes. So it is worth noting that all those events which are nominalised (*poor goal-kicking, numerous dropped balls, careless handling* and *concentration lapses*) allow the agency of the negatively appraised events to be ignored.

A final point worth mentioning here is the Agent-less passive material processes *was sacrificed*, and *could be maximised*. The message of this clause is that playing as a team is more praiseworthy than *individual glory*. In this last paragraph the only Actor/Agent is *the 1st XV team*.

Summary of Circumstances
The Circumstances are to do with the temporal order of the matches (*first up, after the term holidays, the following week* and so on) or time within the matches (such as *in the remaining few minutes*) or the opposing teams (such as *against St Bedes*).

Summary of time and modality
Most of the text uses simple past tense but once again the first clause complex in the final paragraph is foregrounded by the use of the simple present tense.

Investigating tenor in interpersonal meanings

Summary of mood
All Finite clauses are declarative, giving information.

Person selection
In this text, <u>first person</u> is underlined; all other nominal groups are third person.

The team was a powerful combination once it established its own pattern of play. It was unfortunate to play the top side, Mertons, first up. Although losing, the margin was small.

The next game, against St Cuthberts, proved to be a torrid encounter with <u>our</u> forward pack crumbling in the remaining few minutes. Against Luscombe Grammar, quick, clean ball play enabled <u>our</u> back line to dominate and run in numerous tries. St Spirit's also proved to be little opposition, though poor goal-kicking and numerous dropped balls cost <u>us</u> many points in this game.

After the term holidays the team played many of its remaining matches in windy, wet conditions. Against St Bedes, powerful running by the back line established an early superiority which was not to be lost. The following week <u>we</u> played a club side, Forrest Hill, and found it difficult to compete against a stronger, more mobile pack. Dry conditions against Seeton Grammar allowed <u>our</u> back line to play well again and dominate the game. Unfortunately, the final game against Geneva proved to be <u>our</u> worst for the season, with careless handling and concentration lapses costing <u>us</u> the game.

If there is one thing to be remembered by the 1st XV from this season, it is that the team played best when individual glory was sacrificed so that team achievement could be maximised. A champion team, not a team of champions, was the motivating spirit behind this School rugby team.

The first person pronominals *we, us* and *our*, whose referent is *the team*, turn this from objective reporting into something more subjective.

Summary of Appraisal

Like other writers of similar texts, this writer is concerned with how good the team was, how well they played and how much luck came into the outcomes of the season. Not surprisingly, the main appraisal motifs are social judgements about tenacity (*dominate, established its own pattern of play, crumbling* and so on) capacity (*quick, clean ball play, powerful running by the back line* and so on) and normality (*unfortunate, unfortunately*). Even the weather seems to fit here as *dry conditions* produce good results and *wet, windy conditions* are unlucky. In the last paragraph the motif switches to social sanction as the writer moralises about school spirit. To a lesser extent appraisal resources of engagement and graduation combine with judgement. Thus the margin is *small*, the encounter is *torrid*, bad play *costs us the game*, and a game is the *worst for the season*.

Investigating mode in textual meanings

Themes

In this text, <u>unmarked</u> topical Themes are underlined, **marked** topical Themes are in bold type and *interpersonal* Themes are in italics.

<u>The team</u> was a powerful combination once <u>it</u> established its own pattern of play. <u>It</u> was unfortunate to play the top side, Mertons, first up. **Although losing**, the margin was small.

<u>The next game</u>, against St Cuthberts, proved to be a torrid encounter with our forward pack crumbling in the remaining few minutes. **Against Luscombe Grammar**, quick, clean ball play enabled our back line to dominate and run in numerous tries. <u>St Spirit's</u> also proved to be little opposition, <u>though poor goal-kicking and numerous dropped balls</u> cost us many points in this game.

After the term holidays the team played many of its remaining matches in windy, wet conditions. **Against St Bedes**, powerful running by the back line established an early superiority which was not to be lost. **The following week** we played a club side, Forrest Hill, and found it difficult to compete against a stronger, more mobile pack. <u>Dry conditions against Seeton Grammar</u> allowed our back line to play well again and dominate the game. *Unfortunately*, <u>the final game against Geneva</u> proved to be our worst for the season, with careless handling and concentration lapses costing us the game.

If there is one thing to be remembered by the 1st XV from this season, it is that the team played best when individual glory was sacrificed so that team achievement could be maximised. A champion team, not a team of champions, was the motivating spirit behind this School rugby team.

Summary of Theme

The only interpersonal Theme (*unfortunately* in the third paragraph) reveals the partisanship of the writer. It allows us to contextualise this recount in a school magazine rather than a local newspaper. The unmarked Themes relate in some way to the team and their opponents, with the possible exception of *dry conditions against Seeton Grammar*. Some of the marked Themes place the games in time or in terms of the opposition. The whole conditional clause, which could be seen as the marked Theme of the last paragraph, is quite didactic and signposts the inspirational moral of the text.

Cohesion

A cohesion analysis provides information about how a text is constructed and where it changes direction. Although a complete analysis is part of the grammar beyond the scope of this book, we are already able to explore some of its techniques. One way of assessing cohesion is to look at the lexical sets of sense relations; that is, the words whose meanings are connected. Lexical sets to do with school are underlined, and **sets to do with rugby matches** are in bold type.

The team was a powerful combination once it established **its own pattern of play**. It was unfortunate **to play the top side**, Mertons, first up. Although **losing, the margin** was small.

The next game, against St Cuthberts, proved to be a torrid encounter with **our forward pack** crumbling in the remaining few minutes. Against Luscombe Grammar, **quick**, **clean ball play** enabled **our back line** to dominate and **run in numerous tries**. St Spirit's also proved to be little opposition, though **poor goal-kicking** and **numerous dropped balls** cost us **many points in this game**.

After the term holidays **the team played many of its remaining matches in** windy, wet conditions. Against St Bedes, **powerful running by the back line** established an early superiority which was not to be lost. The following week we played **a club side**, Forrest Hill, and found it difficult to compete against a **stronger, more mobile pack**. Dry conditions against Seeton Grammar allowed **our back line** to play well again and dominate **the game**. Unfortunately, **the final game against Geneva** proved to be our worst for **the season**, with **careless handling** and concentration lapses costing us **the game**.

If there is one thing to be remembered by the **1st XV** from this season, it is that **the team** played best when individual glory was sacrificed so that **team** achievement could be maximised. A champion **team**, not a **team** of champions, was the motivating spirit behind this **School rugby team**.

Summary of cohesion

From our analysis of the text, we can see that many of its meanings belong to a very few closely related sets to do with school and rugby. Words like *remembered, glory,* and *champion* do not appear until the last paragraph, once again foregrounding that part of the text.

Another point to be considered here is the ease of interpreting the pronominal references and, once again, we notice that *we* and *it* both refer to the school team.

From lexicogrammatical analysis to contextual description: Text 2

As we did with Text 1, we will now present the contextual description for the text 'Rugby notes'.

Field of discourse

Lexicogrammatical analysis   **Contextual description**

Experiential meanings	

process types
relational with Attributes;
relational identifying in last
paragraph material –
    play, dominate, run in, cost,
    compete	

participants *the forward pack, the team,* *poor goal kicking and* *numerous, dropped balls* (and so on); embedded clauses in last paragraph	
nominalisations avoid agency for mistakes	
Circumstances *first up, against St Cuthberts,* *in the remaining few minutes,* *against Luscombe Grammar,* *after the term holidays, in wet,* *windy conditions* *against St Bedes,* *the next week etc*	
time and modality* past until last paragraph	

As a result of our analysis and knowledge of context of culture we can write up our description

FIELD OF DISCOURSE	Commentary
experiential domain school rugby matches **short-term goal** recount of season's games, minimising losses and maximising victories **long-term goal** maintenance of team spirit and cooperative activity	The first clause of the last paragraph has been foregrounded by the mental process, the use of present tense and by complex embedding around an identifying relational process. This foregrounding underlines the importance of the long-term goal.

*   This is a very fuzzy area because it dissolves the boundary between experiential and interpersonal meanings. On the one hand, the primary tense and modality are an essential part of our interpersonal investigation into how speakers and writers take a position in their texts. On the other hand, the time when activities take place is an essential part of our experiential investigation. This double reading reminds us that although our analysis separates experiential, interpersonal and textual meanings, they are, in fact, interdependent and enmeshed, recombining to make one total meaning realising the context of situation.

Tenor of discourse

Lexicogrammatical analysis   **Contextual description**

Interpersonal meanings
Mood selections   declarative
person selection   *we, us, our*: This *we* seems exclusive, referring only to the players but it is also inclusive as the team represents the school.
appraisal motif   judgement of social esteem of team until last paragraph then social sanction of team spirit creates solidarity

As a result of our analysis and knowledge of context of culture we can write up our description

TENOR OF DISCOURSE	Commentary
agentive or societal roles captain or coach of team/members	In the last paragraph, the addressee appears to be the wider school community as well as the team.
status equal	The relative status also changes in the last paragraph from equal to hierarchic.
social distance minimal	

Mode of discourse

Lexicogrammatical analysis

Textual meanings
Thematic choices unmarked topical Themes – *the team, the games, the opponents* marked Themes – *time* and *opponents*
clause as Theme paragraph 1 – *although losing* paragraph 4: *if there is one thing to be remembered by the 1st XV from this season*
cohesion: lexical sets and reference to schools and rugby; tight but with new lexical items in the final paragraph.
structural patterns fit with recount until last paragraph

As a result of our analysis and knowledge of context of culture we can write up our description

Contextual description

TENOR OF DISCOURSE	Commentary
role of language constitutive **type of interaction** monologue **medium** written **channel** graphic **rhetorical thrust** recount then inspirational	The rhetorical mode changes in the last paragraph from a simple recount to something more inspirational. The cohesion analysis also showed that this paragraph differed from the rest of the text.

To sum up

Because texts with enough common features in the field, tenor and mode of discourse will also have meanings in common, they are said to belong to the same REGISTER. Register can be defined as the way meanings vary consistently with the context of situation or according to use. Thus, we might speak of a register of classroom teaching, a register of advertising or a register of baby talk since texts in each of these areas have things in common in field, tenor and mode of discourse. If we want to make our description more delicate, we can use field to distinguish between, for example, teaching science and teaching literature, or advertising patent medicines and advertising soft drinks. We can use field and tenor to differentiate between two advertisements for the same product in a medical journal and a popular women's magazine. We can even use field, tenor and mode to distinguish between advertisements for the same product in a variety of media, such as teenage magazines, radio and television.

At the same time, the metalanguage for describing context of situation heightens our consciousness of linguistic diversity and binds together many of the strands we have discussed in this book. The same tools that describe a context of situation can be used to describe a writer's style or the similarities between writers of the same school or period.

Experiential, interpersonal and textual meanings are realised in wordings that become accessible through phonology or writing. In our study of context we become aware of the dynamic relationship between the meanings we want to convey, the grammatical structures we use, and the context of situation that frames these meanings. Thus, when we know the field, tenor and mode of the context of situation of a text, we can predict the grammatical structure with a great deal of certainty and, conversely, we can go from the grammatical structures to the context of situation. This is what we mean by the dynamic relation between text and context of situation.

Whether we apply this dynamic to children's writing or creations of verbal art, we can still go behind the text to the meanings. By investigating the grammatical patterns in an objective way we can see how users of language create meanings and achieve intended effects. Our comparisons of the field, tenor and mode of discourse and of the patterns of experiential, interpersonal and textual signs which realise these meanings allow us to differentiate between movements, periods and ideologies as well as between genres and individual writers. Indeed, the patterns of patterns we discern in our analysis make the definition of style almost as simple as the description of a context of situation because both are artefacts of the functional diversity of language.

Exercises

1 List the attitudinal words in the Rugby text and discuss how they construct the point of view.

2 Write a contextual description of one or more of the following:
   a. Speaker 1: You know it's just not a constructive way to go about solving your problems. What are you? ... You're fifteen now?

   Speaker 2: Next December.

   Speaker 1: You'll be fifteen in December. It won't be long before you're ... Only be a couple of years before you'll be appearing before the adult courts. You don't get any mileage out of this sort of behaviour once that happens. It's malicious damage and off to prison after that. Do you understand that? ... You're the one who'll suffer ultimately for it even though you might go away and laugh about this because it doesn't ... er ... touch you. I urge you to think about it. Very good. Thank you, Bennie. You can go ... Thank you, Mr Jones.

   b. Mike's text which you will find on page 87
   c. The conversation between a mother and child on page 99
   d. Iain's text on page 138
   e. The Medea text on page 94.

Implications for language education

At the end of each chapter we have looked at the different types of grammar – experiential, interpersonal and textual – and discussed how a student's knowledge of these grammars allows them to control the related aspect of the context of situation. At the end of Chapter 3 we considered the kinds of meanings students are able to control once they can manage the expression of field through experiential grammar. At the end of Chapters 4 and 5 we considered the kinds of meanings students are able to control once they can manage the expression of tenor through interpersonal grammar. At the end of Chapter 6 we considered the kinds of meanings students are able to control once they can manage the expression of mode through textual grammar.

In this chapter we are shown what can be discovered about all three aspects of the context of situation when we use our knowledge of grammar and the metalanguage introduced in the book so far to explore the three metafunctions of a text simultaneously. This exploration generates a rich description of the way the context has motivated the text, its meanings and, therefore, its structural patterns. We are shown how 'the sum of meanings encoded in lexicogrammar become signs of the context'.

The ability to explore language in this way makes it possible for language educators to understand different contexts of language use on the basis of the meanings in different texts. It also makes it possible for them to consider the language patterns that are likely to emerge in texts realising a particular context of situation.

The reciprocal illumination of context and text allows language educators to target their teaching specifically to the particular needs of students by analysing the contexts of situation relevant to their students' needs and goals. Teaching language can thus become a much less hit-and-miss affair. In addition, students can be given portable knowledge about patterns of English they can apply strategically to a range of contexts of situation, rather than a set of arbitrary rules which may or may not be effective as contexts change.

In this chapter our attention is also drawn to the fact that, to produce and interpret texts in a particular language, we need to be familiar with the contexts of situation which occur within the culture in which the language is used – in other words we need to be familiar with:

- what people talk about in the culture, that is the topics, subject matter and social activities which make up the experience of people living in that culture
- the kinds of roles and relationships people build with each other in that culture
- how people communicate in that culture, whether in spoken or written language using channels of communication such as face-to-face communication, telephone, electronic and print media, letters, and so on.

If this information is incorporated systematically into language teaching programs, students build up language experience across a variety of contexts of situation, allowing them to produce and interpret an increasing repertoire of language varieties. The set of questions used to interpret context in this chapter provide teachers with a useful framework for guiding students' exploration of the way different contexts of language use are expressed in the meanings and structures of different texts.

Perhaps one of the most important distinctions made in this chapter is between context of situation and the material situational setting. Language educators have for a long time been used to establishing a material situational setting; that is a location in time and space, for the language they are teaching, for example *At the railway station, In the restaurant* or *On the weekend.* Some of the features of these material settings are significant for the texts that are used in these settings and some are not.

Context of situation, however, is a more precise way of determining what features of a context make the text 'what it is' because it reveals the three general aspects of the context (field, tenor and mode) which account for differences in lexicogrammatical patterns from text to text. Using these three general headings teachers and students can ask strategic questions about any context in which language is used in order to identify and categorise the extralinguistic features that motivate the patterns of the text and to ignore those extralinguistic features which have no impact on the text. Being able to account for the differences in language patterns from text to text within three general domains of context gives teachers a manageable yet comprehensive tool for:

- selecting what language patterns to teach, within which texts and in which contexts
- deciding how to present those language patterns and the texts they are part of in authentic contexts of language use
- selecting which aspects of the context to draw learners' attention to
- deciding which aspects of the context to alter in order to reveal to learners how language patterns change systematically as the context changes, for example:
  - changing the field so the subject matter changes
  - changing the tenor so a new role or relationship needs to be negotiated
  - changing the mode so the text is spoken rather than written.

Where language education is occurring across the curriculum, students need to build a solid knowledge of the subject matter (the field) and its expression in language. For example, if learners are working in the discipline of science they will need to have many experiences with the material they are learning about – including opportunities for hands-on exploration and guided discussion that reveal the language scientists use to talk about the phenomenon they are studying. It is through these experiences that they will build the field knowledge on which their language use in that discipline can be based.

This chapter provides full contextual descriptions of two texts – one spoken and one written. These descriptions are very detailed and reveal the overall drift of the meanings in each text. There would be few language teaching situations where it would be practical or effective to draw learners' attention to all these features. However, the descriptions do reveal the meanings that make the text what it is – whether a dialogue (mode) where one more skilled interactant is telling the other (tenor) how to play with a ball (field), or an article for a school newspaper (mode) that glorifies (tenor) a school rugby match (field). The challenging task for the teacher is to select from meaning-rich texts such as these the specific language features that match students' language development and that will trigger the next developmental step. We will return to this question in Chapter 10.

Exercises for language teachers

1 Identify a good example of a type of text you would like your students to be able to use effectively. The text might be spoken or written. If you wish, you may choose one of the texts you have already worked with in completing exercises in earlier chapters.

   a. Prepare a contextual description of the text.

   b. What did you learn about the text and its context which you had not noticed before completing this exercise?

   c. Use the description to select key features of context and language use that you believe are relevant to the students' learning needs and goals.

   d. How would you adapt the questions on pages 186, 188, and 189 to guide your students as they work with this text?

Exploring text

Elaborating …
- Texture and structure

Discussing …
- Implications for language teaching

From Chapter 1

This chapter returns to the two fundamental characteristics of texts – texture and structure.

- Texture weaves the meanings of the text together into one coherent whole.
- Text structure is the unifying structural shape that emerges from the configurations of meanings that make up the text.

What is important is that a text is a harmonious collection of meanings appropriate to its context. This unity of purpose gives a text both texture and structure. Texture comes from the way the meanings in the text fit coherently with each other – in much the same way as the threads of a piece of fabric or carpet are woven together to make a whole. Structure refers to the way that most pieces of language in use will contain certain obligatory structural elements appropriate to their purpose and context.

Texture

In Chapter 6 we began to explore some of the resources English speakers use to weave meanings together into cohesive, whole texts (pages 147–149). These resources give texts their TEXTURE. In this chapter we examine these resources more closely.

You may have noticed that some of the resources used to produce cohesive texts have been introduced incidentally in several of the chapters exploring lexicogrammar. This is because the language elements that tie the meanings of a text together turn up in clauses as words and grammatical structures. As well as doing lexicogrammatical work at the level of the clause, these elements also stretch their meanings out beyond the boundaries of the clause. Texture emerges because a text has language elements that:

- tie meanings together from one clause to the next to make strands of meaning that run right through the text
- tie the strands of meaning in the text to the social context.

Meanings in a text are tied together when, in order to make sense:

- a meaning in one clause depends on a meaning in another clause
- a meaning in the text depends on shared knowledge of the social context outside the text.

Here is an example in which meaning in one clause depends on meaning in an earlier clause. The meaning of the word *she* in Clauses 2, 3 and 4 depends on the nominal group *this girl* in Clause 1.

1　There's **this girl** in my class …
2　**she** tried to do a backward roll

3   and **she** um like her neck clicked or something

4   and um **she** was taken to hospital in an ambulance.

But in the following example meaning depends on shared knowledge.

Compare the use of the word *she* above with the use of the definite article *the* in the next example.

On Friday we went to **the** Blue Mountains.

This is the first clause in a text. In this case, the writer uses the definite article in the noun group *the Blue Mountains* because she presumes that the audience will share knowledge of the Blue Mountains she is referring to outside the text.

In summary a text can be thought of as a collection of meanings woven together to make a textured 'fabric'. The clauses of the text can be thought of as cross-threads held together by down-threads, that is, by the strands of meaning running through the text creating the texture which holds the text together. Texts are unified wholes because the meanings in the clauses which make up the text are interdependent and interwoven.

Texture is located on the map of levels of language (Figure 1.3 and 8.1) at the semantic, or meaning, level. This is because texture is concerned with the way meanings become text. In contrast the clause is located at the level of lexicogrammar.

Texture is what ties together the meanings of individual clauses into strands of meaning which span a text. It is through texture that individual clauses are unified into a text, that is, into a cohesive whole unit of meaning.

We have seen that there are three overall uses, or functions, of language; that is, we use language to make:

- ideational meanings, incorporating experiential and logical meanings
- interpersonal meanings
- textual meanings.

We have also seen that these three functions are systematically related to the context of situation. We can think about the strands of meaning that hold clauses together and that give a text texture in terms of these functions.

Strands of experiential meaning are expressed in LEXICAL CHAINS; that is, chains of words related by repetition, similar or opposite meanings, association, part/whole or composition relationships. The chain of words is in bold face in the following example:

1   Here's some advice for kids [who are just learning to **surf**].

2   Use a light, small fibreglass **board** with a **legrope**

3   and (use) a **wetsuit**

4   if it's **cold**.

5   Find a safe, uncrowded spot on the **beach**.

6   The **water** should be not too **choppy**

7   so that you will get a clean **ride**.

Strands of logical meaning link clauses through different types of CONJUNCTION, including additive conjunction, sequence conjunction of time or importance, cause and effect conjunction and conjunction which links in meanings that exemplify, elaborate, compare, contrast or run counter to our expectations. In the following text the conjunctions are in bold face:

1 she tried to do a backward roll
2 **and** she um like her neck clicked or something
3 **and** um she was taken to hospital in an ambulance
4 **and** I had to write down [[what happened]]
5 **because** I was in her group.

Strands of textual meaning keep track of people and things as the text unfolds using REFERENCE CHAINS of language elements such as pronouns, definite articles and demonstrative adjectives. Reference chains appear in bold in the following example:

1 There's **this girl** in my class ...
2 **she** tried to do a backward roll
3 and **she** um like her neck clicked or something
4 and um **she** was taken to hospital in an ambulance.

Textual meanings that contribute to texture include the resources English speakers use to avoid unnecessary repetition, including:

- substitution
- ellipsis.

SUBSTITUTION is used to replace an unnecessary item with a minimal placeholder or a bridging word. In the following example the verb *done* and the pronoun *that* substitute for the event described in the earlier clauses:

1 she tried to do a backward roll
2 and she um like her neck clicked or something
3 I've **done that** before.

ELLIPSIS is used in order to leave out unnecessary items. In the example below repeating the verb *use* is not necessary so it is ellipsed:

1 Use a light, small fibreglass board with a legrope
2 and (**use**) a wetsuit
3 if it's cold.

In the next example, it is not necessary to repeat the noun *hailstones*.

1 Hailstones the size of tennis balls smashed roofs,
2 (**hailstones**) battered cars,
3 and (**hailstones**) injured people across Sydney in a freak storm last night.

In Chapter 6 we have seen how patterns of THEME contribute to texture by giving texts a 'backbone' of textual meaning:

1   **Pelicans** are part of the Bird family.
2   **Pelicans** have a big bill with a pouch.
3   **Most pelicans** have white body features.
4   **All pelicans** have short legs.
5   **Most pelicans** have webbed feet.
6   **Most pelicans** live around the coast.
7   **Pelicans** eat crustaceans, crabs, fish and shrimps.
8   **Pelicans** fly with their head back.
9   **Pelicans** lay two, three or four white eggs.
10 **They** take thirty-five days to hatch.

Interpersonal meanings that contribute to texture include patterns of EXCHANGE STRUCTURE for organising speakers' turns into a cohesive and coherent conversation.

Question:	Where did you get that Mars Bar?
Answer:	Bill gave it to me at lunch time.
Response:	No, he didn't
Counter response:	Yes, he did.

As we saw in Chapter 5, APPRAISAL spreads interpersonal meaning across the text to express the speaker's point of view and to influence the audience's point of view. A speaker's point of view can be spread over a text in lots of ways. These include the choice and number of attitude adjectives, the choice of particular types of content, amplifying or reducing intensity or quantity, choosing words that are colourful or that have a non-neutral value, the choice of tense, modal words, repetition and even different typographical features. In the following example expressions of appraisal are in bold face:

CITY **BATTERED** BY **GIANT** HAILSTONES
1   Hailstones **the size of tennis balls smashed** roofs,
2   **battered** cars,
3   and **injured** people **across Sydney** in a **freak** storm last night.

A fuller explanation of cohesion can be found in Halliday and Hasan (1976 and 1985), Halliday (1994). A very useful introduction to the notion of texture is Eggins (1994: Chapter 4).

Text structure

In this section we will explore the way text structure emerges from the configurations of meanings making up the text. The meanings of a text are configured to give the text a unifying 'architecture' or shape through which the text achieves its purpose. We have seen that the emergence of a structural pattern as a text unfolds contributes to our decisions about the rhetorical thrust of the text (page 193). The emergence of a recognisable structural pattern also makes it possible to compare the text with other texts of the same type.

Texts of the same type, that is, texts constructed to achieve the same general social purpose, tend to share comparable structural patterns. Some elements of these patterns may be obligatory if the text is to achieve its purpose successfully. Other structural elements are optional extras which can be used to finetune the text in different ways.

In Chapter 1 we saw that comparable texts which achieve the same general social purpose, and which therefore draw on the same relatively stable structural pattern, are said to belong to the same GENRE. We are now going to discuss this idea in a little more detail.

In real life, each text is a unique expression of its particular context, that is, its context of culture and its context of situation – the subject matter, the roles and relationships of those communicating and the mode of communication. It would be impossible to communicate, however, if each time we constructed a text we had to start from scratch. Instead we start each time with a cultural blueprint; in doing so we draw on our knowledge of the conventional text structures used to configure the meanings of our language and culture into whole texts.

Some texts are more prototypical examples of the genre they belong to than others. If you are just beginning to use a particular text type, or if you want to achieve a very pragmatic purpose as efficiently as possible, it is more effective to stay close to the blueprint. Figure 1.4 in Chapter 1 lists the purposes for using language that a particular primary school syllabus document specified learners should be able to achieve in order to meet the stated outcomes of the school syllabus. These purposes are necessarily very general and teachers working within this syllabus environment will select examples of the text types to reflect the learning needs and goals of the particular students they are teaching.

Chapter 1 introduced us to a set of texts produced by young learners within this syllabus environment. The texts exemplify some of the purposes identified in the syllabus. These sample texts were collected from across all the schools using the syllabus. Students in these schools include those who speak English as a second language.

We are going to revisit the set of texts introduced in Chapter 1, this time combining what we now know about text structure, texture and lexicogrammar to describe the meanings in these texts. But, before we do this, we will reflect on some of the different perspectives on text types proposed by functional linguists.

Text types – a second look at register and genre

As first set out in Chapter 1, a central reason for developing a functional grammar is to be able to relate the meaning in patterns of wording to the purposes which motivate the structuring of whole texts. Once a functional exploration of the grammar of a text has revealed, for example, patterns in the selection of Theme/Rheme or Process/Participant, shifts in Mood or modality, stretches of non-finite clauses, and changes in the accumulation of independent or dependent clauses, we can see that all of these patterns have consequences for the overall meaning, or in other words, 'structure' of the text. In the discussion of context in Chapter 8 we saw how to set out these patterns of wording as a contextual description, highlighting the relationship of probability between text structure and the grammar. This relationship is based on the meanings which the grammatical choices contribute to the text. Functional grammar assists us, then, in relating what in the context is motivating these choices message by message to the global purpose of the text.

When linguists who study texts organise different types of texts into categories based on purpose and structure, they are said to be developing a 'theory' of genre. Functional linguists refer to differences in purpose and patterns of meaning between texts as variation in register, or functional variety. In this case 'functional' highlights the different place the text holds in the patterns of community behaviour. (Note: Functional linguists contrast register variation, that is, difference motivated by *use*, with dialect variation, which refers to different speech habits of *users*.)

Functional linguists have detailed a number of ways for managing variation in whole texts, that is, for managing the description of text types. (These are summarised in Matthiessen 1993, Register in the round.) Hasan's (1996b) characterisation of children's nursery tales is the most complete account of how one might argue for the elements which make up a text type. Her account shunts systematically between three levels of linguistic description:

- a description of generic text structure
- a description of semantic criteria
- a description of the most likely selections of words and grammar.

A fuller exploration of Hasan's account of nursery tale structure is included in Appendix I.

In educational contexts a widely applied functional model was developed in Sydney based on the work of Martin (1993) and Rothery (1996). Their approach is built around an additional level on the 'map' of language and context. They propose a higher, more abstract level of genre aligned to the context of culture and separate from the level of register which they align with the context of situation. Genres are conceived of as 'goal-directed, staged activities' which can be expressed by different texts and registers. This approach is designed to accommodate both text type (similarity) and text variation (difference). In other words, while individual texts vary from situation to situation, genre descriptions attempt to capture the general meaning potential we select from when we use a text to achieve a social purpose in our culture. Genre pedagogy aims to make this resource for meaning available to students.

Martin and Rothery's approach has proved very useful to teachers when it is tied to functional accounts of register and lexicogrammar. In the TESOL environment, for example, having distinct levels of genre and register makes cross-cultural comparisons possible. It is also possible to compare similar social purposes (genres) and, at the same time examine the distinctive ways these might be varied linguistically (registers) across communities within the culture.

Some very practical educational applications become possible when language variety (register) and purpose (genre) are considered separately, but there are also some problems with this model. If language and culture are conceived of separately, there is a danger that culture and purpose might appear to exist separately from the actual texts through which they are, in fact, realised. Texts and other symbolic behaviours *are* the culture. The evidence for a particular text's purpose is found in the accumulating choices dispersed across the patterning of the text. To avoid the problems inherent in the separation of register and genre, it may be useful to conceive of genre descriptions as working approximations of the text structures that are possible in the culture.

Using texts to achieve different social purposes

Despite the important theoretical issues raised by their model, Martin and Rothery's approach remains an adaptable framework for language teachers. Using this approach, Martin, Rothery and their colleagues have worked for many years with teachers to develop curriculum and materials in actual systems of education, for example, primary schools in NSW and the Adult Migrant English Program in Australia. This approach has helped make syllabus documents across a number of disciplines more explicit and organised. It remains important, however, for teachers to recognise that genre descriptions developed within this approach are working hypotheses about texts and language, not non-negotiable prescriptions or final statements.

Some teachers find it useful to provide students initially with model texts that represent prototypical examples of genre descriptions. Once students can control prototypical examples, they are provided with contexts in which the global text descriptions need to be adapted or challenged.

Martin and Rothery have used their model of genre to encapsulate text type and text difference to assist literacy teachers working in schools. They recognise the numerous and simultaneous functions that different texts achieve. For example, stories are used to chronicle the actions of heroes, reinforce community solidarity and values, give ancestral histories and explain religious concepts. Martin and Rothery, however, initiate their pedagogical model with an overarching distinction between *story* genres, which function to entertain, and *factual* texts. Rothery (1994: 84) describes this distinction in the following way:

> What the story genres have in common is a social purpose to entertain. They achieve this by dealing with particular or unique events in which specific characters are involved and through meanings which make these events noteworthy in some way. A most important feature, one which clearly distinguishes the story genres from factual ones, is that they highlight or foreground meanings which evaluate or give significance to the events depicted.

We will explore the way this global distinction has been elaborated for teachers by examining sets of texts taken from documents supporting a primary English syllabus derived from Rothery and Martin's approach. We will use our knowledge of lexico-grammar and texture to examine how the dispersal of patterns of meaning across these texts appear to coalesce into recognisable global text structures that reflect cultural purposes. As the *English K-6 syllabus* (Board of Studies NSW 1998: 66–7) reminds us, these '[t]ext types and their structures should not be seen as straitjackets but as starting points'. Once students have reached these starting points, they 'are in a better position to create and manipulate texts and combine elements in a purposeful way'.

An exploration of text types

First we will explore text types used at school to tell stories. Then we will explore text types used at school to present factual information. You have already met some of these texts in your journey through this book. As we progressively explore examples of different text types, we will pause occasionally to reflect on the way language varies from context to context within the conventions of the text types.

Telling stories

Following Rothery, we can use our knowledge of lexicogrammar and texture to explore how the language we use to tell stories about people and events is structured to be entertaining. Storytellers make their stories entertaining by evaluating the people and events in the story to show how they are significant. Different types of stories reveal the significance of people and events in different ways.

Overview of story genres

Recount	to tell what happened, to document a sequence of events and evaluate their significance in some way
Narrative	to construct a pattern of events with a problematic and/or unexpected outcome that entertains and instructs the reader or listener
News story	to chronicle a newsworthy event

Telling stories: Recount

A recount is a story genre which is used to tell what happened. When we tell recounts we reveal the significance of the people and events in the story by sharing our personal feelings about them. Text 1 is *spoken* using the recount pattern. A schoolgirl told her sister the following story after her sister asked her what happened at school that day.

Text 1

Structural elements	Textual features	Recount	Grammatical features
Orientation (obligatory) • provides information about *who*	reference out into context (*this, my*)	There's this girl in my class …	existential clause asserting the existence of a Participant
Record of events (obligatory) • in the order in which they occurred	additive conjunction (*and*) to sequence events in time reference chain (*she*) linking back to *this girl*	she tried to do a backward roll and she um like her neck clicked or something and um she was taken to hospital in an ambulance	past tense material processes chain of declarative clauses combined by coordination only *she* (ie the girl) is predominant Theme; passive voice (*was taken*) used to maintain Theme
Reorientation (optional) • rounds of the sequence of events	additive and causal conjunction (*and, because*) reference out into context (*I*)	and I had to write down what happened because I was in her group	past tense modal Finite (*had to*) embedded clause as Participant/Verbiage (*what happened*) past tense relational dependent clause
Coda (optional) • gives personal evaluation of the significance of the events	reference linking Participant and events to self (*I, that, it, she*)	I've done that before and it doesn't hurt that much. I think she's over-reacting just a bit.	different types of present tenses (*have done, doesn't hurt, think, is over-reacting*) mental processes (*think, over-reacting*) measuring words (*that much, just a bit*)

Text 2 is another story by a school student. This text is *written* using the recount pattern.

Text 2

Structural elements	Textual features	Recount	Grammatical features
Orientation ● provides information about *who, where, when*	reference – out to context (*we, the Blue Mountains*) – back to Participant introduced in previous clause (*David and Delia's house – it*)	**Our Trip to the Blue Mountains** On Friday we went to the Blue Mountains. We stayed at David and Delia's house. It has a big garden with lots of colourful flowers and a tennis court.	Circumstance as marked Theme (*On Friday*) to set the story in time Participants introduced in nominal groups (*we, the Blue Mountains, a big garden with lots of colourful flowers, a tennis court*) Circumstances to set the story in place (*to the Blue Mountains, at David and Delia's house*) relational clause to link the house (*it*) with its description
Record of events ● in the order in which they occurred	series of clauses in temporal sequence linked with additive and temporal conjunction (*and, then*) Blue Mountains lexical chain spans text (*Three Sisters, scenic railway, antique shops, Scenic Skyway, cockatoos*) reference chain (*we*) spans text progression of marked Themes to signpost text structure	On Saturday we saw the Three Sisters and went on the scenic railway. It was scary. Then Mummy and I went shopping with Delia. We went to some antique shops and I tried on some hats. On Sunday we went on the Scenic Skyway and it rocked. We saw cockatoos having a shower.	Circumstances as marked Themes to extend the setting in time (*On Saturday, On Sunday*) Circumstances to extend the setting in place (*on the scenic railway, to some antique shops, on the Scenic Skyway*) pairs of declarative clauses combined using coordination only past tense material processes (*went, tried on, rocked*) in a sequence of events

Text 2 (continued)

Structural elements	Textual features	Recount	Grammatical features
Record of events (continued)			past tense mental processes (*saw*) projecting Phenomenon in nominal groups (*the Three Sisters, cockatoos having a shower*) past tense relational process to evaluate an event and give it significance (*It was scary.*)
Reorientation • rounds off the sequence of events	Thematic progression culminates in marked Theme reference chain culminates in *we*	In the afternoon we went home.	Circumstance as marked Theme to bring the story full circle in time (*In the afternoon*) Circumstance to bring the story full circle in terms of place (*home*)

Text from *English K-6 modules* 1998: 109 © NSW Board of Studies NSW

Exploration of Texts 1 and 2

Both these texts have the same global structure. In other words they belong to the same genre.

- Use the metalanguage for talking about language use you have learned in this book to describe how these two texts are the same.
- Are both these texts successful recounts in their context of use? In what ways?
- How do the storytellers use language to give the events in their recounts significance?

Each of these texts, however, use distinct varieties of language. Text 1 is spoken and Text 2 is written.

- Use the metalanguage for talking about language use which you have learned in this book to describe how these two texts are different.
- If you were a teacher working with the writer of Text 2, what knowledge about language would you include in a teaching program to support this young writer's development?

The speaker of Text 1 and the writer of Text 2 stay very close to the recount prototype in constructing their texts. Often, however, the prototype is adapted to suit specialised contexts of use.

In Text 3 a learner has adapted the recount pattern in order to chronicle an historical event.

Text 3

Structural elements	Textual features	Recount	Grammatical features
Orientation • provides background information about *who, where, when*	presentation of and reference to main character (*Edward Hargraves, he*) clauses linked with cause conjunction (*because, to*) beginning of lexical chains to build field (*gold, goldfields*)	**The Discovery of Gold:** **Edward Hargraves** Edward Hargraves came to Australia directly from the Californian goldfields in 1850. He was sure that he could find gold in NSW because the land was so similar to the Sierra Nevada area in America. He went with John Lister to find gold near Bathurst. Lister had already found some before.	material processes (*came, went, found*) relational processes (*was*) mental process (*was sure*) clauses combined in different ways ie expansion and projection, finite and non-finite dependent use of past tenses including past with complete/perfect aspect (*had found*) Circumstances of time and place (*from the Californian goldfields, in 1850, in NSW, near Bathurst*)
Record of events • in the order in which they occurred	series of clauses in temporal sequence linked with additive and cause conjunction (*and, [in order] to*) lexical chains continue (*gold, reward, cradle instrument, gold nuggets*)	Hargraves panned a small amount of gold and set off to Sydney to collect a reward. Lister stayed behind and worked the site with a cradle instrument that Hargraves had seen in California. It separates gold nuggets from sand.	technical terms (*site, cradle instrument, gold nuggets*) postmodified nominal groups (*a small amount of gold, a cradle instrument that Hargraves had seen in California*) sequence of past tense material processes (*panned, set off, collect, stayed, worked*)

Text 3 (continued)

Structural elements	Textual features	Recount	Grammatical features
Statement of Significance • rounds off the sequence of events by evaluating their significance		When Hargraves discovered gold he said, 'This is a memorable day in the history of NSW. I shall be a baronet, you will be knighted and my old horse will be stuffed and put in a glass case and sent to the British Museum.'	past tense dependent time clause as marked Theme (*When Hargraves discovered gold*) past tense verbal process (*said*) projecting quoted speech present tense existential clause in quoted speech (*This is a memorable day in the history of NSW.*) future tense passive voice in quoted speech to maintain characters as Theme (*will be knighted, will be stuffed and put ... and sent ....*)

Text from *English K-6 modules* 1998: 199 © Board of Studies NSW

Exploration of Text 3

- Do you think the young writer has adapted the recount genre effectively to write about an historical event?
- How has the writer used language to give the events significance?
- If you were a teacher working with the writer of Text 3, what knowledge about language would you include in a teaching program which helps this young writer further refine and adapt the recount pattern to write about historical events?

The recount pattern is used in school Science to recount what happened in an experiment. It is also used when we report an accident or incident to an authority such as the police or an insurance company.

- How would you adapt the recount pattern in order to report what happened in these specialised contexts of language use?
- How would you use language to give the events significance in each of these contexts of use?

Telling stories: Narrative

A narrative is a special kind of story that is valued very highly in English-speaking cultures. Narratives are structured to be entertaining and to teach cultural values. In narratives normal events are disrupted and language is used to build up suspense around the disruption so it reaches a crisis point. The way the characters in the story confront and resolve the crisis teaches the audience about ways of behaving which are valued in the culture.

Text 4 is a narrative written by a young writer to capture the action of an after-school encounter.

Text 4

Structural elements	Textual features	Narrative	Grammatical features
Orientation (obligatory) • to set up what is to follow by introducing *who, where, when* ie setting and narrator (*I*)	reference – forward to foreshadow disruption to normal events (*it all*) – out into context (*I*) – time conjunction (*when*)	**The Fight** It all happened when I was walking home from school.	dependent time clause (*when I was walking home from school*) with Circumstances of place (*home from school*) to build setting past tenses with complete (*happened*) and incomplete (*was walking*) aspects
Complication (obligatory) • sequence of events disrupted creating a problem or crisis for for character/s • character/s evaluate problematic events to give them significance	reference – tracking main characters (*two twits – they; I – me; Kelly/Matthew – he*) – referring back to sections of text (*this*) conjunction – series of clauses in temporal sequence (implicit, *while, and, when*)	Two twits from my class decided to pick on me. They started yelling stupid names like spazzo, pigface etc. I didn't mind this. I also didn't mind Kelly punching me in the shoulder. What I did mind was that Kelly kept me occupied while Matthew (better known as Roberts) rode my bike around the cul de sac of the street. This was harmless.	clauses combined in different ways ie expansion, projection, non-finite and finite dependent, embedded clauses as Participants Participants (*two twits from my class, they, I*) predominant Theme sequence of past tense material processes (*rode, kicked, jumped, took off*)

Text 4 (continued)

Structural elements	Textual features	Narrative	Grammatical features
Complication (obligatory) (continued)	– signalling crisis point (*but*) appraisal – repetition to build up suspense (*I didn't mind*) – expressions of attitude (*stupid, harmless, sore*)	But, still riding, he kicked off my bag and jumped off the bike leaving it to fall. This made me sore. I gave in to my temper. When Matthew saw this he took off.	past tense verbal processes (*started yelling*) past tense mental processes (*decided to, didn't mind, made me sore, gave in to my temper, saw*) and past tense relational processes (*was*) to evaluate events, to slow down action and build up suspense
Resolution (obligatory) • problems/crisis resolved and normal events resume	conjunction – causal (*so*) signalling beginning of resolution of crisis – temporal sequence (*when, finally, and*)	So it was me and David Kelly to battle it out. I chased him around and around the street. When I finally caught up to him I threw punches galore. Most of them missed. Kelly managed to escape and run home.	sequence of past tense material processes in quick succession (*chased, caught up, threw, missed, managed to escape, run*)
Coda (optional) • shows how character/s have been changed by the events • evaluates whole incident	conjunction – counter expectancy (*but*)	I think I was the victor, but if I was, I don't think it was worth it.	mental processes projecting thoughts (*think*) relational processes to evaluate (*was*) expressions of attitude (*victor, worth it*)

Text from *English K-6 modules* 1998: 302 © Board of Studies NSW

Exploration of Text 4

- Do you think the young writer has written an effective narrative? Why?
- How are the characters and the setting described?
- How has the writer used language to give the events significance?
- What does this narrative 'teach' the reader? How does it do this?
- Compare Text 4 with Text 2.
  - Use the metalanguage for talking about language use which you have learned in this book to describe how these two texts are the same.
  - Use the metalanguage for talking about language use which you have learned in this book to describe how these two texts are different.
- If you were a teacher working with the writer of Text 4, what knowledge about language would you include in a teaching program to support this young writer to further develop skill in writing narrative?

The narrative pattern is used as the basis of stories in novels, plays, poems, comics, soap operas, movies, and even advertisements, in English-speaking cultures. We often value very highly those stories in which the narrative pattern is adapted, even subverted, in original and innovative ways.

- Think of some examples of stories in which the narrative pattern has been used in a prototypical way. What cultural values does each of these stories 'teach'?
- Think of some examples of stories in which the narrative pattern has been adapted in original and innovative ways. Here are some examples you might look for:
  - resolution or complication at the beginning
  - a series of temporary resolutions
  - more than one resolution
  - writing a comic narrative in which banal events are constructed as crisis events
  - narrative pattern with other text patterns.
- What cultural values does each of these stories (texts 1, 2, 3 and 4) 'teach'?

Telling stories: News story

News stories are told everyday in the mass media. Most people treat them as if they are objective reports about current events. For this reason they can be very influential. A close investigation of the language of news stories, however, reveals that, like all stories, the purpose of news stories is to entertain by showing how the events are significant. The way journalists show events are significant is by structuring stories so the events seem 'newsworthy'. To portray events as newsworthy, journalists structure their news stories to highlight how the events have disrupted the normal order of things.

In narratives suspense is created by slowing down the action and gradually building up to the point of greatest disruption, the crisis point. In contrast, a news story begins with the crisis point, that is, it begins with the events the journalist thinks are the most disruptive. Journalists call the events they place at the beginning of their story the 'angle' of their story.

Because the most disruptive events are placed first, events in a news story do not unfold in chronological order. Instead, the events selected as the most disruptive – the events in the Lead – become the nucleus of the story. The Lead is the centre of both the structure and the texture of a news story. A news story is structured by adding each new event to the story as if it were a satellite orbiting the main disruptive event. The staccato texture of a news story emerges because the cohesive ties in the satellites often link directly back to the nucleus without weaving through previous satellites.

Journalists do not write in paragraphs. Instead they write in what they call 'pars', which in news stories are usually one or two sentences long. The nucleus-satellite structure of a news story makes it very easy for newspaper sub-editors to delete and add pars as they edit stories to fit into the available space on the pages of a newspaper.

Text 5 is a news story about a natural disaster.

Text 5

Structural elements	Textual features	News story	Grammatical features
Lead (obligatory) [headline + lead par] • nucleus of story • crisis point/'angle'	core experiential meanings introduced (*hailstones, Sydney, storm*) concentration of amplified interpersonal meanings to highlight maximum disruption (*battered, giant hailstones, hailstones the size of tennis balls, smashed, injured, freak*)	CITY BATTERED BY GIANT HAILSTONES Hailstones the size of tennis balls smashed roofs, battered cars and injured people across Sydney in a freak storm last night.	truncated clause in headline two or more clauses combined to maximise information in Lead sentence past tense material processes Circumstances of time, place and manner
Lead Development (optional) • recycles nucleus more than once, restating crisis in different terms each time • each par like a 'satellite' orbiting the nucleus • satellites ordered according to significance not chronology	cohesive ties reach back to nucleus ie lexical and reference chains, conjunction amplified interpersonal meanings less concentrated (*stranded, hit, torn off, aftermath, pummelling, flat-out*) Satellites: 1 consequence of crisis	1 Thirty motorists were stranded in the Royal National Park at Sutherland and cars taking shelter in the Sydney airport tunnel caused major traffic problems. Some 30 sets of traffic lights went out after the hailstorm hit at 8pm.	two or more clauses combined in different ways to maximise information in each sentence many Participants are postmodified nominal groups to maximise information load (*the Royal National Park at Sutherland, cars taking shelter in the Sydney airport tunnel, the aftermath of the 20-minute pummelling, people with head injuries and severe lacerations from huge chunks of ice*) past tense material processes with complete and incomplete aspects shifts from passive to active voice to keep 'news' in Rheme position past tense verbal processes projecting reported and quoted speech

Text 5 (continued)

Structural elements	Textual features	News story	Grammatical features
Lead Development (optional) (continued)	2 description of crisis by authorities ie police	2 Roofs were torn off houses in Caringbah, in Sydney's south, roads were flooded in North Manly, and cars were 'floating away' in the eastern suburb of Edgecliff in the aftermath of the 20-minute pummelling, a police spokesperson said.	
	3 consequence of crisis for emergency services	3 Ambulance crews were flat-out attending to people with head injuries and severe lacerations from huge chunks of ice, and a driver was taken to Royal Prince Alfred Hospital after blinding hail caused him to swerve off the road and into a power pole at Marrickville, in Sydney's inner west.	
	4 consequence of crisis for urban infrastructure	4 The storm caused a power failure in Collaroy and along Oxford St, in the eastern suburb of Paddington. Many motorists sought refuge by parking under eaves on the footpath.	
	5 consequence of crisis for individual	5 Chris Chambers suffered mild concussion when he was hit by a giant hailstone while walking 12m from his car into a Paddington hotel. The front and back windscreens on his $65,000 new model Alfa Romeo were smashed.	

Text 5 (continued)

Structural elements	Textual features	News story	Grammatical features
Lead Development (optional) (continued)		6 'It was just huge' he said, blood pouring down his face as hotel staff provided medical treatment. Hundreds of people emptied restaurants and cafes to witness the hailstorm, many gathering giant samples from the streets and footpaths. 7 'It sounded like a plane was about to crash,' Robyn Bradfield said. 'Then stones the size of golf balls – no, cricket balls – started bouncing into the restaurant.'	
Wrap-up (optional) • returns to normality		8 Ms Bradfield's partner, a doctor, was busy treating the injured.	past tense material process with incomplete aspect

Georgina Safe and Matt Price, *The Australian*, April 15, 1999

Exploration of Text 5

In this text the journalists have used structure, texture and lexicogrammar to give the events in the story significance – that is to give the events in the story newsworthiness.

- Use the metalanguage for describing language which you have learned in this book to describe how the news story makes the events newsworthy.

Typically in news stories journalists include lots of measurements, exact titles and proper names. This is because they are indisputable facts which give the story its ring of 'truth' and reliability.

- Find all the measurements, exact titles and proper names in the news story. Describe the grammar of each, for example, a measurement might be a Numerative in a nominal group.

Journalists also quote authority figures, such as the police and eyewitnesses, to make their version of what happened appear reliable.

- Find the 'satellites' in which authorities and eyewitnesses are reported or quoted. Describe the grammar of these reports and quotes.
- Do you think these are the exact words spoken by these people at the time?

Like all stories, news stories 'teach' cultural values. Often they do this by making certain values seem 'natural'.

- What cultural values does the language of this news story 'teach'? Do you support those values?
- What information relating to the natural disaster is not revealed by this news story?

Language teachers often use news stories in their teaching programs. Learners rarely have to write news stories in real life, but they do need to learn how to read them.

- What language features in this news story might be challenging for student readers?

Writing activities can be based on the events in news stories.

- Try writing the following texts based on the news story about the hailstorm.
  - Pretend you are Chris Chambers and write a recount of your personal experience of the hailstorm
  - Explain how hail is formed.
- What knowledge about text structure, texture and lexicogrammar do you need to complete these writing tasks effectively?

The text structure and the amplified, colourful language of news stories influence the way we perceive current events. News stories lead us towards a particular point of view about these events which seems 'natural'. Exploring the structure, texture and lexico-grammar of news stories makes it possible for learners to become 'media literate' that is, to develop a critical orientation to the meanings which the mass media bombard us with every day.

A full analysis of this story can be found in Appendix H.

Presenting factual information

As well as exploring the language we use to tell stories, we can also use our knowledge of lexicogrammar and texture to explore how we use language to present factual information.

Factual texts enable people to take part in social life, for example, procedural texts show us how to do and make things. Factual texts play a particularly important role in formal education; for example, explanations reveal how and why things happen.

The following description of factual texts is from *English K-6 syllabus* (Board of Studies NSW 1998: 67) from which many of the texts in this chapter are taken.

> Factual texts are those that present information, ideas and issues in such a way as to inform, instruct, enlighten or persuade the reader or listener. [...]

> Whether written or spoken, factual texts present their content from a particular perspective. However, the perspective or point of view of the writer or speaker may not be overtly stated. Factual texts may suppress the point of view in an attempt to appear objective.

> Although factual texts may purport to present accurate, objective information, they are not simply objective representations of reality. Rather, they are constructions of reality, created by a writer or speaker.

Overview of factual genres

Procedure	to tell how to do something
Protocol	to set out the conditions for behaviour
Information report	to present information about something
Explanation	to tell how and why things occur
Exposition	to argue a case
Discussion	to look at more than one side of an issue; to explore various perspectives before coming to an informed decision

Giving instruction: Procedure

Procedures are very common factual texts. They take us through a sequence of steps which enable us to achieve a goal. Text 6 is a procedure that outlines the steps you take if you want to 'catch a wave'.

Text 6

Structural elements	Textual features	Procedure	Grammatical features
Goal • what is to be achieved	core experiential meanings introduced (*kids, learning, surf*)	**How to catch a wave** Here's some advice for kids who are just learning to surf.	– non-finite clause as Participant – relational clause to foreshadow what the text is bringing into existence (*Here's some advice …*) – clause as Qualifier in nominal group identifies audience (*kids who are just learning to surf*)
Materials	lexical chain builds on surf (*fibreglass board, legrope, wetsuit*)	Use a light, small, fibreglass board with a legrope and a wetsuit if it's cold.	– material process (*use*) in imperative clause – detailed nominal group with Qualifier – dependent clause to give condition (*if it's cold*)
Steps • in sequence	lexical chain continues (*beach, water, ride, surfed, wave, surfboard, paddling, kneeling, balance, falling off*)	Find a safe, uncrowded spot on the beach. The water should be not too choppy so that you will get a clean ride. Don't go out too far if you haven't surfed before.	– series of material processes in imperative clauses (*find, don't go, wait, lie, start, try kneeling*); processes usually Theme – modality used to make meanings stronger or weaker (*should, will, could*)

Text 6 (continued)

Structural elements	Textual features	Procedure	Grammatical features
Steps • in sequence (continued)	conjunction – series of clauses sequenced in order actions must be carried out – reason (*so that*) – condition (*if*) – time sequence (*until, then, when*) – consequence (*or else*) reference – out into the context (*you*)	Wait until you see a small wave then lie on your surfboard. When the wave is close, start paddling furiously. If you are more experienced, you could try kneeling on the board once you are on the wave. The most important thing is to keep your balance or else you will end up falling off the board!	– negative polarity (*not, don't, haven't*) – independent and dependent clauses combined to add precision to imperative clauses in terms of *reason, condition, time sequence and consequence* – Circumstance of manner expressed by adverb (*furiously*) – graded evaluation (*not too choppy, most important*) – Theme position used to focus reader's attention (unmarked: imperative clauses; marked: *When the wave …, If you …, The most important thing …*)

'How to catch a wave': *English K-6 modules* 1998: 312 © Board of Studies NSW

Giving instructions: Protocol

The writer of Text 6 takes on the role of expert, telling less expert readers how to catch a wave. The writer does this by writing a series of sequenced steps that have to be carried out in that order if the goal is to be reached. In many procedures the steps are numbered.

Sometimes, however, when the goal is a general state of affairs – for example, safety or quiet – we give instructions for conditions that are designed to remain in place simultaneously. We can think of these conditions as protocol governing our behaviour. Often such conditions turn up as sets of rules. Text 7 is a set of rules a class of Year 1 school children agreed upon in order to make their classroom a good place to work.

Text 7

Structural elements	Textual features	Protocol	Grammatical features
Goal		1M's rules	nominal group with possessive showing ownership of the rules
Conditions	Theme position used to focus reader's attention on processes Reference – refers out of text to children in the class (*you, your*) Conjunction – time (*when*) – reason (*to*) – adding an instruction (*and*)	• Be quiet when others are talking and writing. • Put your hand up to talk. • Sit in your seat and put your hand up.	series of processes as Theme in imperative clauses: – relational (*be*) – material (*put, sit*) dependent clauses combined with independent clauses to add precision in terms of time (*when*) and purpose (*to*) independent clause added to independent clause to add an instruction (*and*) continuous aspect used in verbal group to show incompleteness (*are talking and writing*)

Exploration of Texts 6 and 7

- Do you think the young writer of Text 6 has written an effective procedure? Why?
- Do you think the young writers of Text 7 have written an effective protocol? Why?
- Compare Text 6 with Text 7.
  - Use the metalanguage for talking about language use which you have learned in this book to describe how these two texts are the same.
  - Use the metalanguage for talking about language use which you have learned in this book to describe how these two texts are different.
- If you were a teacher working with the writers of Texts 6 and 7, what knowledge about language would you include in a teaching program to support these young writers as they further develop their skill in writing procedures and protocols?

Effective procedures and protocols are not easy to write. (How many people can follow the instructions for using a video cassette recorder? How many people feel put out by officious notices in public places even when they know keeping the rules benefits everybody?) The effectiveness of procedures and protocols depends on how the writer has:

- listed the materials and equipment
- sequenced the steps or arranged the conditions
- packaged information into nominal groups
- added precision in Circumstances and dependent clauses
- addressed the audience.

The expression of field in a procedure must be clear and exact for the text to be effective. The expression of tenor in a protocol must be acceptable to the audience for the text to be effective.

- Find some procedures and protocols and test them for their effectiveness. How would you redraft these texts to make them more effective?
- How is the language of the procedure and protocol patterns adjusted in different contexts of use? Here are some examples you might consider:
  - recipes
  - instructions for looking after animals
  - instructions for using potentially dangerous substances or equipment, for example, garden sprays or electric drills
  - instruction manuals for cars, computers, appliances and other technology
  - directions about how to get to particular locations (both spoken and written)
  - procedures used in different disciplines of formal education eg Science, Art and Craft
  - rules of different kinds of games
  - rules modifying people's behaviour.

Organising information: Information report

An information report is a factual text used to organise and store information, particularly information in the fields of science and technology. Students at school are often expected to write information reports to display what they have learned.

In Text 8 the young writer has gathered information about pelicans and organised it into a short text using the Information Report pattern.

Text 8

Structural elements	Textual features	Information report	Grammatical features
General Statement • to identify and classify topic	experiential meanings introduced (*pelicans, bird family*)	**Pelicans** Pelicans are part of the Bird family.	general noun, ie text is about *all* pelicans (**NB:** *a pelican or the pelican could also be used.*) present tense relational process to identify and classify topic (*are*)
Description • describing appearance	information organised in 'bundles'/subheadings chain of lexical items relating to pelicans spans text; reflecting information 'bundles' The word *pelicans* is repeated in the Theme.	Pelicans have a big bill with a pouch. Most Pelicans have white body feathers. All Pelicans have short legs. Most Pelicans have webbed feet.	nominal groups to build information about the topic; Epithets (*adjectives*) to add description (*big, white, short, webbed*); technical nouns (*crustaceans*)
• describing behaviour		Most Pelicans live around the coast. Pelicans eat crustaceans, crabs, fish and shrimps. Pelicans fly with their head back. Pelicans lay two, three or four white eggs. They take thirty-five days to hatch.	present tense relational processes to describe appearance (*have*) behavioural processes (*live, eat, fly, lay*) Circumstances of place (*around the coast*) to describe habitat and manner to describe behaviour (*with their head back*)

'Pelicans': *English K–6 modules* 1998: 135 © Board of Studies NSW

Explaining how and why: Explanation

Explanations are factual text types used to explain how and why things happen. They are often used in the fields of science and technology.

The writer of Text 9 has used the explanation pattern to explain how hail is formed.

Text 9

Structural elements	Textual features	Information report	Grammatical features
Identifying statement	experiential meanings introduced (*hail, rain, snow, frozen, round pellets*)	**How hail is formed** Hail is rain or snow which has frozen into round pellets.	present tense relational process identifying topic (*is*) detailed nominal group
Explanation sequence	lexical chains relating to *hail* span text reference – chains span text (*raindrops – the raindrops – they – they – they*) – refers to previous segment of text (*this* as Theme) conjunction – sequence (*when, as, to, and, until, then*) – Theme predominantly *raindrops, pellets* and related pronouns	Sometimes in storms strong air currents force raindrops upwards into clouds of freezing water. When the raindrops begin to freeze into round pellets, they become heavier and start to fall. As they fall back into the air currents, they are forced upwards again into the freezing clouds. This coats the pellets in another layer of ice. The pellets continue to bounce up into the freezing cloud to be coated in more layers of ice and down into the air current, until they become too heavy for the air current. They then fall to earth as hailstones.	– technical terms (*air currents*) – sequence of material processes (*force, freeze, fall, coats, bounce*) – phases expressed in verbal groups (*begin to freeze, become, continue to bounce*) – use of passive so Goal can be Theme – nominal groups build topic (*strong air currents, clouds of freezing water, round pellets*) – clauses combined to express sequence in time – dependent clauses as Theme focus reader's attention on sequence in time – Circumstances of place (*in storms, upwards, into the air currents, to earth*)

Exploration of Texts 8 and 9

- Do you think the young writer of Text 8 has written an effective information report? Why?

- Do you think the writer of Text 9 has written an effective explanation? Why?

- Compare Text 8 with Text 9.

  - Use the metalanguage for talking about language use which you have learned in this book to describe how these two texts are the same.

  - Use the metalanguage for talking about language use which you have learned in this book to describe how these two texts are different.

- When we tell stories, we talk about specific people and about events which happened at a specific time. When we write information reports and explanations, we write about general categories and the way things always are and always happen. Use the metalanguage for talking about language use which you have learned in this book to describe the differences between language we use to talk about specific people, things and events and the language we use to write about things in general.

- If you were a teacher working with the writers of Texts 8 and 9, what knowledge about language would you include in a teaching program to support these young writers as they further develop their skill in writing information reports and explanations? How would you help students gather and organise the information about the subject matter they need to write these texts?

- Information reports and explanations represent and construct the world in ways which are valued in science and technology. They are also written to appear accurate. How might you test the accuracy of Text 8 or Text 9? What other ways are there to represent our experience of pelicans and hailstorms in text? How would these be valued in the scientific community?

Persuading

When we write to persuade, we craft our text with all the linguistic resources we have at our disposal. The young writers of Texts 10 and 11 have exploited their textual and lexicogrammatical skills to the utmost to argue their case.

Persuading: Exposition

An exposition is a factual text that is used to persuade people to a particular point of view. First the writer states a position and then constructs a series of arguments to support that position. The point of each argument is introduced then elaborated with supporting evidence.

The young writer of Text 10 has used the exposition pattern to persuade the reader that cars should be banned from the city. The writer has gathered evidence to support a series of arguments.

Text 10

Structural elements	Exposition
Statement of position	**Cars should be banned in the city** Cars should be banned in the city. As we all know, cars create pollution, and cause a lot of road deaths and other accidents.
Preview of arguments	Firstly, cars, as we all know, contribute to most of the pollution in the world.
Argument 1 • makes point and elaborates argument	Cars emit a deadly gas that causes illnesses such as bronchitis, lung cancer, and 'triggers' off asthma. Some of these illnesses are so bad that people can die from them.
Argument 2 • makes point and elaborates argument	Secondly, the city is very busy. Pedestrians wander everywhere and cars commonly hit pedestrians in the city, which causes them to die. Cars today are our roads biggest killers.
Argument 3 • makes point and elaborates argument	Thirdly, cars are very noisy. If you live in the city, you may find it hard to sleep at night, or concentrate on your homework, and especially talk to someone.
Reinforcement of Statement of Position	In conclusion, cars should be banned from the city for the reasons listed.

'Cars should be banned in the city': *English K-6 modules* **1998**: 254 © Board of Studies NSW

Here are the textual and lexicogrammatical features which shape the structural pattern of Text 10. Reread the text noticing how the young writer has used the following textual and grammatical features to organise and shape the arguments.

Textual features

Core experiential meanings span the text in the following lexical chain (eg *cars, city, pollution, road deaths, accidents, deadly gas, hit, die, our roads, killers*). A related lexical chain is woven into Argument 1 (*illness, bronchitis, lung cancer, asthma, illnesses, bad, die*). Another related lexical chain (city) is woven into Argument 2 (*city, busy, pedestrians, cars, pedestrians, city, our roads*).

The word *car* is a repeated topical Theme throughout the text. In Argument 1 the word *cars* is Theme in the topic sentence. The Theme of the final sentence in Argument 1 (*Some of these illnesses*) flows on from Rheme of the previous sentence. In Argument 2 the Theme of the topic sentence (*city*) links back to the Statement of Position. The Theme of the second sentence in Argument 2 (*pedestrian*) flows on from the topic sentence. The Theme of the concluding sentence returns to cars.

Reference is used to express solidarity (*we*), to refer out of the text to people in general (*you*) and to refer back to a whole section of text (*the reasons listed*).

Conjunction is used to sequence arguments (*firstly, secondly, thirdly, in conclusion*), add information (*and, or*) and give a condition (*if*). Cause conjunction is found in verbal groups (*create, causes, triggers off*).

Appraisal is used to position the reader in agreement with the writer (*as we all know*) and to amplify meanings spread across text (*banned, a lot of, most of, deadly, so bad that ...*, *very, everywhere, biggest*).

Grammatical features

General nouns show that the text is about cars and car accidents in general (*cars, road, deaths, accidents*). The writer uses technical terms (*gas, bronchitis, lung cancer, asthma, pedestrians*) and nominalisations (*pollution, deaths*). A modal Finite expresses obligation (*should*). The writer exploits the full range of processes, including relational (*create, causes, triggers off, contribute, are, is*), behavioural (*die, live*), material (*emit, wander, hit*) and projecting (*know, concentrate, talk*).

Information is packaged into nominal groups with detailed Qualifiers expressed as relative clauses (*a deadly gas that causes illnesses such as bronchitis, lung cancer and 'triggers' off asthma, so bad that people can die from them*).

The writer combines two independent clauses and uses a dependent clause to add circumstantial information to an independent clause.

Reflection

In this text the young writer is just beginning to use the reference system to refer back to whole sections of text (eg *the reasons listed*). In Argument 2 the writer uses the relative pronoun *which* to do this work (*which causes them to die*). In written English it is more effective to use the word *this* at the beginning of a new sentence to refer back to a section of text (eg *This causes them to die.*). The young writer is clearly ready to be given this grammatical information. What other grammatical information is this young writer ready for?

Persuading: Discussion

A discussion is a factual text that explores different sides of an issue in order to reach an informed judgement or recommendation. A discussion shares many of the language features of an exposition. Like an exposition, a discussion has arguments, but the arguments are balanced for and against the issue.

The young writer of Text 11 has used the discussion pattern to explore the arguments for and against doing homework. The writer has not yet learnt how to weigh up the for and against arguments in order to reach a final judgement or recommendation.

Text 11

Structural elements	Exposition
Issue	**Homework** I think we should have homework because it helps us to learn and revise our work.
Arguments for	Homework helps people who aren't very smart to remember what they have learned. Homework is really good because it helps with our education.
Arguments against	I think we shouldn't have homework because I like to go out after school to a restaurant or the movies. Sometimes homework is boring and not important. I think homework is bad because I like to play and discuss things with my family.

'Homework': *English K-6 modules* 1998: 151 © Board of Studies NSW

Here are the textual and lexicogrammatical features which shape the structural pattern of Text 11. Reread the text noticing how the young writer has used the following textual and grammatical features to organise and shape her arguments.

Textual features
Core experiential meanings span the text in the following lexical chain (eg *homework, learn, revise, work, remember, education, school*).

The predominant topical Theme is *homework*. The interpersonal Theme *I think* is used three times to project the writer's opinion.

Reference is used to express solidarity with reader (*we, us, our*) and to refer back to homework (*it*).

The conjunction *because* is used to express cause.

Appraisal spreads amplified meanings across the text (*not very smart, really good, boring and not important, bad*).

Grammatical features
The writer uses general nouns (*homework, people, a restaurant, movies*) and abstract nouns (*education*).

Mental processes (*I think*) project the writer's opinions. Modal Finites (*should, shouldn't*) in the projected opinions express obligation. Negative polarity is added to the modal Finite in the clause complex which introduces the Arguments against.

The writer uses relational processes (*have, aren't, is*), mental processes (*learn and revise, remember, learned, like*) and material processes (*helps, go, play*).

Information is packaged into a nominal group with Qualifiers expressed as a relative clause (*people who aren't very smart*).

The writer uses dependent clause to add circumstantial information to independent clauses. The writer also uses projection.

Reflection
What further grammatical information do you think this young writer is ready for in order to write this type of text even more effectively?

Exploration of Texts 10 and 11

- Do you think the young writer of Text 10 has written an effective exposition? Why?
- Do you think the young writer of Text 11 has written an effective discussion? Why?
- Compare Text 10 with Text 11.
  - Use the metalanguage for talking about language use which you have learned in this book to describe how these two texts are the same.
  - Use the metalanguage for talking about language use which you have learned in this book to describe how these two texts are different.
- Use the metalanguage for talking about language use which you have learned in this book to describe how writers employ the textual resources of the language to construct arguments and insert evidence into persuasive texts.

- If you were a teacher working with the writers of Texts 10 and 11, what knowledge about language would you include in a teaching program to support these young writers as they further develop their skill in writing expositions and discussions? How would you help students gather and organise the evidence they need to write these texts effectively?

- Expositions and discussions select and present arguments and evidence in ways which set up the reader to accept the position of the writer. How would you help your students to check the accuracy of evidence they read in expositions and discussions? For example, are there other perspectives on cars and homework, with supporting evidence, these young writers could have included in their texts? How might these young writers have presented their arguments to influence more effectively those in power in the school or community?

Combining generic structural patterns in texts

Most of the texts we have explored in this book were produced by young children. We have already noted that the reasons for using these texts are that:

- children's texts are short and less complicated so they are more manageable for people working with functional grammar for the first time
- children's texts reveal the foundations on which adult language use is built.

As texts become longer and language use becomes more sophisticated in order to meet the demands of adult life in the community, higher education or employment, language users often combine structural patterns in order to achieve specialised and customised purposes. Often two or more structural patterns are combined in one text to modify or refine the purpose of the text. Here are two ways of combining structural patterns.

Different structural patterns might be added together in the same text. For example, a recipe, while based on the genre of procedures, might begin with a *description* of what a completed dish looks and tastes like. A recipe for a soufflé or sponge cake might include an *explanation* of the rising process.

Alternatively the structural pattern of one genre might be embedded inside a structural element of a text which uses a different genre pattern. For example, the evidence inside an argument of an exposition or discussion can be presented as a recount or short information report.

Reflection

The journalists who wrote the news story about the Sydney hailstorm added the following satellite to their story. This satellite is structured as a recount. In other words, a recount structure was added to a news story:

> Weather Bureau spokesman Evan Bathe said the thunderstorm hit Nowra and Wollongong, on the NSW south coast, and was expected to drift out to sea, but came inland, hitting Bundeena.

> The storm then moved up to Sutherland Shire, in Sydney's south, wreaking extensive damage, and on through Sydney's inner west and across the eastern suburbs, before heading to the northern beaches.

- Describe the language features of this extract which make it a recount.
- Describe the language features of this extract which reveal that it is part of a news story.
- Find or think of other examples of texts in which different structural patterns have been combined in different ways.

Implications for language education

How does teaching about texts benefit language learners?

This chapter describes patterns of meaning in texts belonging to different genres. It demonstrates how we can combine our knowledge of grammar, texture and text structure to reveal the conventional language patterns that effective users of English apply to the texts they construct. These descriptions can be very useful tools for language learners as they investigate the meanings in texts and learn to control and manipulate texts in order to achieve different purposes with language.

However, these descriptions are not rules about language use. They are more like blueprints or prototypes which are useful starting points for exploring and constructing texts. Teachers are able to use these blueprints to:

- talk to students explicitly about language and its use
- show students how to reflect on and investigate language use.

In the past language teaching has at times involved students in learning rules about isolated and disconnected words and structures unrelated to the language used in real life. Students were left to integrate on their own these isolated fragments into whole units of meaningful language use.

If language teachers understand how whole texts make meaning in context, they are able to design language teaching programs aligned to the language that students need to use in real life. Language programs can be planned in terms of language 'wholes', or texts, and the micro-elements of language, such as words and grammatical structures, can be taught in relation to these wholes.

Many students, of course, are unable to work on their own with whole stretches of language. All they can manage are small fragments. For this reason an approach to language teaching has been developed which allows students to work with the fragments of language they are able to manage while the teacher completes the picture of how these fragments are incorporated in a whole text in the context of its use. This approach has been called a genre-based or text-based methodology.

What is a text-based methodology?

Using a text-based approach, teachers collaborate with and support students as they gain increasing control over different types of texts. As cycles of teaching and learning unfold, teachers and students adopt a variety of roles.

Initially teachers and students explore together the context in which language is to be used. For example, they might look at pictures, brainstorm ideas, go on excursions, do experiments or undertake research in order to build shared knowledge about this context as a basis for future learning. It is this phase of the cycle that gives students something to talk or write about.

Then the teacher adopts the role of expert who apprentices students into the use of a particular type of text. Teachers design a series of structured teaching and learning activities to support students as they develop increasingly effective and independent skills with that type of text within the shared field. In these activities students work with model texts which exemplify effective use of the text type they are learning to control.

In collaboration with the teacher and their peers, students use what they have learned to engage with and/or produce texts of the type they are studying. This phase of the cycle might begin with more activities to build up a new or related field of shared knowledge. Gradually, as learners demonstrate they can use texts of this type successfully on their own, the teacher withdraws support and the learners work more and more independently.

Mastering the use of different types of text in this way provides students with a repertoire that lays the foundation for successful language use in more specialised contexts, for example outside the classroom or within specific subject areas. (We will revisit this approach to language teaching in Chapter 10.)

Using functional grammar to teach about whole texts in context makes it possible to:

- talk explicitly and systematically about the different elements of language and context and the meanings they make
- locate elements of language and context relative to each other on a 'map' of the whole system of language
- present language elements in a way that reveals how the elements relate to and depend on each other in the construction of whole texts in context
- show students how to make conscious choices from the language system in order to construct texts effectively
- show students how to examine the language of texts in order to be aware of the value-laden meanings they make
- assess students' texts against principled and explicit assessment criteria.

Once students have mastered the basic text-type patterns, they can be encouraged to exploit these patterns in innovative and creative ways. In some genres, for example narrative, certain kinds of innovation and creativity are highly valued and will lead to greater success. At other times combining more than one pattern in a text is effective. For example, scientists and science students may be required to draw on procedure, recount and explanation patterns to write a laboratory report.

A more detailed introduction to a genre-based approach to literacy teaching can be found in Rothery (1996).

How can language learners explore tense in whole texts?

Managing tense in English verbal groups can be a significant challenge for language students. One useful way of exploring English verbal groups is through our knowledge of text structure and the language patterns that frame that structure.

In Chapter 3 we discussed processes and the verbal groups that encode Processes. We saw that the English verbal group is always based on a central word class verb – the Event. Sometimes the Event stands alone in the verbal group and sometimes it is preceded by other words.

We saw how the elements we use in the verbal group depend on four aspects of the event itself. These are:

- its location in time relative to the time of speaking (*tense*)
- its completeness or continuousness (*aspect*)
- the speaker's judgement of the certainty of the event (*modality*)
- the use of active or passive *voice*.

There are three *tenses* that we can encode in an English verbal group:

- *past* (before the time of speaking)
- *present* (at the time of speaking)
- *future* (after the time of speaking).

There are two *aspects* that we can encode in an English verbal group:

- *perfect* (complete)
- *continuous* (incomplete, continuing).

Sometimes we use a *simple* tense, where neither of these two aspects is used. At other times these aspects are combined for an even more subtle effect. Some verbal groups with a modal verb can also include a second tense as well as aspect. In spoken English especially, combinations of modality, tense and aspect can be expressed in some quite complicated verbal group forms. For example:

They **might have been going to finish walking** before we arrived.

Most patterns of text structure, or genres, have a default tense; that is, a tense which is predominant in texts of that type. For example, the default tense for stories is the past simple tense (*walked*). Sometimes storytellers want to include events that were not completed at the time an event in the story took place. They will then use the past continuous (*was walking*). At other times they will want to tell us that the event was completed before an event in the story. They will then use the past perfect (*had walked*). Sometimes storytellers use the present tense or future tense to create particular effects or to foreground particular events.

When students are first learning to tell stories in spoken or written language, they can begin by learning to use the default past simple tense. Then, as they read and listen to the stories of others, their attention can be drawn to the way storytellers use different types of past tense, or even present or future tenses. For example, when we use spoken language to tell stories about what we have experienced, we often begin the Orientation with the present perfect (eg *I've visited* ...) to show that the events were completed at some unspecified time before the time of speaking. Then we continue to tell the story using past tenses to locate the events more specifically in time.

The default tense of many of the genres of factual writing is the present simple, a tense we use when we want to talk about habitual events, that is, the way things always are or usually happen. This tense is sometimes called the universal, or timeless, present (eg *Most Pelicans live around the coast.*). The imperative clauses of procedures, however, have no tense because they have no Finite in the clause.

A more detailed discussion of tense in context can be found in Mathiessen (1996).

Reflection
- Review the stories we have explored in this chapter. Notice whenever the storyteller does not use the default past simple tense. For each case think about why the storyteller moved away from the default at that stage of the story.
- When might a storyteller use the present tense or future tense in a story?
- Review each of the factual text types presented in this chapter. Find examples where the writers chose a tense other than the default. For each example think about why the writer moved away from the default at that stage of the text.
- How might an understanding of the default tense of genres help language learners use English verbs more effectively in their texts?

How might students develop a critical orientation to text structure?

Earlier in the chapter we foreshadowed problems that might emerge when generalised patterns of text structure and cultural purpose are described separately from the language varieties used in individual texts. To address these problems, educators have emphasised the importance of developing in students a critical orientation to the patterns of text structure they are learning. For example, some educators have been concerned that students might be using genre descriptions as fixed rules, following them uncritically even when the texts of that genre make meanings which reinforce questionable ways of doing things. These educators point out that different types of texts make some meanings seem more 'natural' or valued than others. According to Hasan (1996c: 404–5) the problem is:

> whether in learning discursive ability through genre-based pedagogy, one is also learning the ability to analyse and to challenge the desirability of the prevalent ways of being, doing and saying.

Hasan's concern with text-based pedagogy is that it may lead to 'a respect for convention which is not required to be tempered by analytical reflection' (1996c: 405). The challenge to language educators is to develop ways of incorporating 'reflection, enquiry and analysis' into teaching about the structural patterns of texts.

A critical orientation encourages students to explore how the meanings in texts influence both themselves and others. Understanding how texts position their audience and promote, or make invisible, particular points of view enables students to evaluate the texts of others and to experiment with revealing and challenging different meanings and world views in their own texts.

Knowledge about the stable patterns of texts used in formal education and dominant social institutions – including the variations on the patterns which are possible in these contexts – is a kind of 'cultural capital'. Not all students have equal access to this capital and those with reduced access are less likely to achieve successful educational and social outcomes. Often reduced access is a consequence of coming from a cultural background that does not match the dominant culture, for example, a non-English speaking background or a lower socio-economic background. Explicit teaching of text types is one way of increasing the cultural capital of all students regardless of background. Once these text patterns are made explicit, and their functions and purposes revealed, teachers and students are able to reflect consciously on the kinds of meanings and values which are expressed in these patterns. They are then in a position to choose whether they wish to conform to or change these meanings and, if so, how and in what contexts. In addition teachers and students can monitor how these patterns evolve as society evolves. As Cranny-Francis and Martin (1995: 17) put it:

> ... the genres used in society need to be taught explicitly and comprehensively, so that students have access to their meanings, to their possible recombinations, and to their evolution, and so that students can themselves recognise the deficiencies within mainstream genres; for example, in terms of the meanings they do not make and the voices they do not raise.

Text structure and new literacies

As society evolves and new social activities and technologies emerge, we develop new language varieties to respond to the changing context of language use. Advances in technology, for example, have allowed us to construct and engage with texts through an increasing array of communication channels. This has resulted in forms of communication that have revolutionised our understanding of the *mode* of discourse. Where once we could only use the telephone if we wanted to interact immediately with someone who is distant geographically, we can now also use electronic communication modes such as email and interactive chat. As those who have begun to use these technologies in recent years know, each new channel of communication generates new varieties of language. Electronic communication is also generating new varieties of *multi-modal* language.

We have always combined word-based language with other forms of meaning-making to create texts. For example:

- stories, in which visual images are an important element
- newspaper stories, which include headlines and photographs
- television news stories, which contain both vision and words
- theatre and cinema, which tell stories by combining words, actors, sets, costumes, movement, sound effects and music
- many of the procedures and protocols around us, for example, road signs, instructions on automatic teller and ticket machines, which combine symbols and words
- billboard advertisements, which use pictures, colours, shapes, layout and words to make meaning.

In this book we have been exploring how to apply the functional model of language to the analysis of word-based language. The functional model is now also being developed to enable us to describe how multi-modal texts are constructed to make meaning.

Today, technology makes it possible to combine previously incompatible modes of meaning-making into whole multi-modal texts. Recently the presenter of a radio program was heard to tell listeners that the roar of an endangered species of wolf could be found 'on a page'. This would have been a puzzling remark just a few years ago, but nowadays we know that the presenter was referring to a webpage which includes an audiorecording of the wolf's roar as part of an information report about this species of wolf. Increasingly, technology is making it possible for people to interweave words, visual images, video, animation, hot links and sound into dynamic texts that seem to break all the conventions.

Students can use their knowledge of text structure to analyse just how multi-modal texts make use of the conventional patterns of, for example, information reports, stories or procedures. They can use their knowledge of lexicogrammar, texture and text structure to explore questions such as:

- Do the new electronically-designed multi-modal texts really modify and reshape the conventional patterns of text structure or are they just reproducing conventional – even banal – meanings in forms which so dazzle us that we lose our critical orientation?

- What are the most effective ways of using multi-modal texts to make meaning?
- Are we exploiting the full potential of multi-modal texts to make meaning?

An ability to analyse all forms of meaning-making functionally will become very valuable to teachers as new technologies rapidly expand what is possible in the construction of texts and push at the boundaries of our definition of literacy. Access to knowledge about multi-modal text construction will be critical for all students of all backgrounds as, already, it is becoming evident that the literacies embodied in these texts are the valued cultural capital of the future.

A more detailed account of the grammar of visual design can be found in Kress and van Leeuwen (1996). An introduction to multimodal text construction can be found in Iedema and Stenglin (2000), while another useful approach to the analysis of multimodal texts is O'Toole (1989).

Exercises for language teachers

1 Identify a text that is a good example of a type of text you would like your students to be able to use effectively. The text might be spoken or written. If you wish, you may choose one of the texts you have already worked with to complete exercises in earlier chapters.
   a. Analyse the lexicogrammar and texture of the text to reveal how these resources give the text an architecture, or underlying structure.
   b. Does this text conform to one of the conventional patterns of text structure outlined in this chapter?
   c. Does the text adjust or modify one of these patterns, or does it combine two or more patterns? How does it do this?
   d. Is the text structured effectively? What could be done to the text structure for the text to achieve its purpose more effectively?

2 Use what you have discovered about text structure to design activities which support your students' progress towards their learning goals. These activities might explore:
   - the purpose and structure of the text as revealed in texture and lexicogrammar
   - the register of the text as revealed in expressions of field, tenor and mode
   - the way the text has conformed to or adjusted conventions of text structure
   - ways the text might be edited for it to achieve its purpose more effectively
   - the construction of other texts which use the same pattern
   - the construction of texts which adapt the pattern, or even break the conventions of the pattern.

3 You might like to repeat exercises 1 and 2 with a multimodal text which relates to your students' learning needs and goals.

10

Functional grammar and language education

Reviewing ...
- Implications for language teachers

Discussing ...
- Language learning
- Language teaching

From Chapter 1

... those linguists who take a functional view of language are supremely interested in what makes one piece of language different from another.

... functional grammar is not a set of rules but a set of resources for describing, interpreting and making meaning.

At the end of Chapter 1 we said:

> People sometimes think that 'learning a language' is a simple matter of learning vocabulary and grammar, but anyone who has visited a country where an unfamiliar language is spoken can tell you this is only part of the story. Our everyday lives are conducted in situations that are part of our context of culture and, to a large extent, these situations are familiar – which is partly how we recognise and understand other people's meanings – because we share the same cultural knowledge. Whenever we speak or write, we make selections from the entire lexical and grammatical system of English to produce appropriate meanings for the field, tenor and mode of a context of situation. When we first operate in a second language we may know the words but not the appropriate contexts; we really only understand other speakers when we share, not only words and grammar but also *which* words and *which* grammatical choices are appropriate for a situation.

Language as a resource for making meaning

Throughout this book we have been exploring language in terms of the meanings we make with it. We have explored how the meanings we make with language are:

- encoded in lexicogrammar (*wordings*)
- unified into whole units of meaning (*texts*)
- motivated by what is going on in the world outside the text (*context*).

The map we have been using to guide our exploration (Figure 1.3 and 8.1) gives us a bird's-eye view of language as a resource for making meaning. As we look down on this map from above, we see this meaning-making resource, language, laid out before us as a series of levels, each level finding shape, or realisation, in the next.

Context	What is going on in the world outside a text, *the context*, has two levels: • a *general* level of **culture** • an *immediate* level of **situation**.

Language	What is going on inside the language of the text also has two levels:
	• a level of **content**
	   *The layers of context shape the **meanings** in a text (semantics).*
	   *A text's meanings are encoded in **wordings** (lexicogrammar).*
	• a level of **expression**
	   *Wordings are expressed as **sounds**.*

The map of language levels gives language teachers an overview of the terrain students are entering and coming to know as they learn a language. It also reveals how different parts of the terrain relate to each other.

From the overview, it is possible to zoom in closer to explore the potential of any layer of the terrain on the map in more detail. This book has zoomed in to explore the content layer of *lexicogrammar* in considerable detail but, because lexicogrammar encodes meaning, it has also sketched in the meaning, or *semantic*, layer of content. And, because the extralinguistic layers of *context* shape meaning, these layers have also received attention too.

Unfortunately exploring the concrete layer of language, *expression*, has largely been beyond the scope of this book, although we have touched on it incidentally whenever we pointed out the alignment between grammar patterns and intonation patterns.

Let's now review the ideas our exploration of functional grammar has offered language education so far.

Review of chapters

Chapter 1: Ideas and philosophy underpinning this book
- Learning language is learning how to make meaning by shaping it into whole unified texts in context.
- Context generates the meanings in texts in systematic ways. The meanings in texts illuminate the context. An understanding of the relationship between text and context helps teachers design courses in terms of the contexts in which their students need and want to use the language.
- A specialised language, or metalanguage, for describing how different elements of language make meaning helps teachers to explore and discuss language and language development with colleagues and students.

Chapter 2: Towards a functional grammar
- A functional grammar encourages teachers to think about teaching grammar in terms of the functional patterns of the clause, how these are expressed and their potential for making meaning in whole texts. This is in contrast, for example, to some approaches in which students learn idealised rules and fixed grammatical forms isolated from their context of use.

Chapter 2: Towards a functional grammar (continued)

- The rank scale makes it possible for teachers and students to explore clause structure at different levels.
- Teachers can reveal to students the full meaning potential of the clause by showing them how the clause encodes three kinds of meaning people make with language.

Chapter 3: How speakers represent the world: Exploring experiential meanings

- When students explore experiential meanings in clauses they are learning how to put their experience of the world into the clause. At the same time, they learn about clause structure in a meaningful and functional way.

Chapter 4: How speakers interact with language: Exploring interpersonal meanings

- When students explore the Mood Block in clauses, they are learning about how to take turns in an exchange in order to build fluent and effective dialogues with others.
- As students work with the Mood Block of the clause, many of the grammar patterns which are challenging for students in terms of structural accuracy can be addressed from the perspective of meaning and function.

Chapter 5: How speakers take a position: Exploring interpersonal meanings further

- When students explore tense and modality in the Mood Block, they are learning how to express their personal perspective on the world and their experience in it.
- While interpersonal meaning converges on the Mood Block of the clause, expressions of attitude are spread out across whole texts. Students can learn systematically how to manage these resources in order to take a position effectively.

Chapter 6: How speakers organise their message: Exploring textual meanings

- Learning how patterns of Theme and Rheme are used to signpost texts for listeners or readers can greatly benefit language development, especially in the area of literacy.

Chapter 7: Patterns of clause combination

- Students can learn how to combine English clauses effectively by understanding how the structural patterns for clause combining relate to meaning.

Chapter 8: Exploring context

- The patterns of interlocking meanings expressed in lexicogrammar realise the context in text. Understanding the way the context of language use is systematically related to the variety of language used provides teachers with a valuable tool for planning language teaching programs which meet the needs of particular groups of students in a precise and comprehensive way.

Chapter 9: Exploring text

- Understanding the way texts are textured and structured to be meaningful in their context of use provides teachers with a tool for exploring systematically and explicitly with students how the levels of meaning and lexicogrammar work together in the creation of effective texts.

Now let's explore further how these ideas might influence language learning and teaching.

'Learning how to mean'

Making meaning in social contexts

Throughout this book we have been exploring language as a resource which we use to make meanings in order do things. The words and structures we choose to make meanings are motivated by the context in which we are using language. The exact location in time and space of language use (the material situational setting) is not the context which interests us because the *material* context is not the motivating force generating the language we use. What motivates and shapes our language use is the *social* context, that is, the experience of *human beings* (field), the relationships *between human beings* (tenor) and the role given to language *by human beings* (mode). In summary, through our exploration of functional grammar we have discovered that using a language is about making meaning in *social* contexts.

Those of us who are teachers (or parents or students or anyone else concerned with education) are now in a position to think about how this discovery might influence the way we think about language learning (and, in fact, the way we think about learning in general). Let's begin by applying what we have discovered about language to language learning. If using a language is about making meaning in social contexts, then learning to use a language necessarily involves learning how to make meaning in that language in social contexts.

In the next section we are going to explore this idea further before we consider its practical implications.

Meaning, learning and language development

Functional approaches to linguistics are often contrasted with linguistic theories which view language as a complex set of abstract rules. If you think of language as a system of rules, then you will think of language learning as a process of acquiring these rules. As you observe an individual's acquisition of the complex rules of language, you will think that this must be the result of an internal mental process related to the individual's cognitive capacity.

Systemic functional linguistics, the linguistic theory which underpins this book, is part of a wider field of functional linguistics. All functional linguists are interested in what human beings *do* with language. But, Halliday, the architect of systemic functional linguistics, is not only interested in what human beings do with language. He also argues that language is organised the way it is *because* of what human beings do with it; or, in other words, *because* of the meanings they make with it. As a result, systemic functional linguists are concerned with language, not so much as a psychological activity, but more as a *social* activity which varies according to the different uses people have for it.

Learning language

If you think of language as something human beings use to make meaning in order to do things in social contexts, you will think of language learning less as an internal psychological process and more as a process of learning how to make meaning in social contexts. As you observe an individual learning a language, you will be interested in social phenomena such as:

- the meanings the learner is trying to make with the language
- what the learner wants or needs to do with the language
- the social contexts in which the learner is using, or wants to use, the language.

Making meaning and doing things with language in social contexts are all about interacting with other people. Halliday (1980) defines meaning as 'an interactive process, not something you do on your own'. Research by Halliday and his colleagues has revealed that it is precisely the process of interacting with others in order to organise experience into meanings which constitutes learning. The meanings which learners are able to make increase as their social experience widens.

'Learning how to mean' is how Halliday (1975) characterises the process a human child goes through to learn language. His research into his own child's language development is supported by subsequent research, for example, Painter (1984), and Oldenburg (1987). This research shows that a child's first meanings are a 'protolanguage' of sounds, gestures and words which are meaningful in interactions with immediate caregivers in shared contexts. In their responses to the protolanguage, caregivers intervene in the child's meaning-making by reformulating their language into adult language. Accumulated experiences of 'successful' meaning-making and contextualised intervention in shared contexts guide the child over time into the full adult language system. Researchers in this field continue to build our understanding of the ways children learn language, for example, Cloran (1989), Hasan (1989 and 1996d), Painter (1996) and Williams (1994).

Halliday (1992: 19) describes all learning, not just language learning, as 'learning to mean and to expand one's meaning potential'. Furthermore, he describes language as 'the main instrument we have for interpreting and organizing our experience' and hence, 'the main instrument, or tool, for learning' (Halliday 1980).

In recent decades educational psychology has at times focused its attention on learning as a 'natural' internal process. Some approaches to language teaching suggest that it is enough to place students in a rich environment and then to allow natural internal learning processes to operate without being impeded or distorted by intervention from the teacher. If students are unsuccessful in these rich environments, it appears to be because of limited cognitive capacity.

Language teachers working within the framework of systemic functional linguistics are unlikely to think about language learning as a 'natural' internal process. Instead they see language learning as expanding the potential to make meaning and so they actively work to set up the optimum social conditions for achieving this. As they set up these conditions, they are mindful of the way that accumulated experiences of 'successful' meaning making combine with contextualised intervention to drive first language development.

First language development is an informal process in which child and caregivers are interacting throughout the day and in all facets of the child's life. Teachers who are preparing formal learning environments, on the other hand, are working consciously and strategically to focus students' attention during class time on salient features of language use in order to widen their experience with language and to expand the meanings they can make with it in a systematic and comprehensive way. The goal of social interactions in formal learning environments is to guide language learners via developmentally appropriate steps towards, for example, control of a new variety of the first language (such as the written language children encounter when they enter school) or the learning of a second or foreign language.

To understand more about learning as social interaction, many educators – for example, the well-known American educator, Jerome Bruner (1986: Chapter 5) – have turned to the work of Vygotsky, a psychologist who worked in Russia in the 1920s and 1930s. Systemic functional linguists have found Vygotsky's work particularly helpful because it is also concerned with learning as a *social* process constructed through different kinds of *social* interaction and it foregrounds the role language plays in learning.

At the time Vygotsky was developing his ideas about learning, behavioural psychology was suggesting that human beings learn by responding directly to environmental stimuli. Vygotsky rejected this idea. He argued that the way human beings experience the environment is 'mediated' through cultural and psychological 'tools'. Using these tools, we construct knowledge collaboratively with others in the same social context. Vygotsky identified language as the most important of these tools. Initially in the learning process, the 'tools' need to be outside us in the physical and social environment. In collaboration with 'more capable others' we progress through *zones of proximal development* to more abstract and complex use of such tools. As we gain control of these tools, we can use them independently as part of our own thinking and reflection. We may even reach the stage where we develop new tools for mediating experience and for contributing to what human beings know and understand (Vygotsky 1978).

For teachers, two key ideas emerging from Vygotsky's theory, as interpreted for us by Bruner and others, are:
- *collaboration* – in which the teacher and the learner share responsibility for functioning until the learner has the knowledge and skills to perform independently and with sole responsibility

- *scaffolding* – in which the teacher contributes explicitly what learners are not yet able to do or don't yet know, adjusting their contribution as learners become increasingly independent.

Through collaboration and scaffolding, learners experience what it is like to participate in the 'whole' of what is being learnt – contributing what they can while the teacher takes responsibility for the rest. Through interaction with the teacher, learners have the opportunity to function, with support and guided practice, at a level beyond what they are able to do on their own. The teacher gradually withdraws support as the learners demonstrate that they are able to function independently.

Much research into language and learning by systemic functional linguists has supported and expanded on Vygotsky's ideas (for example, Halliday, 1975; Painter, 1985 and 1996; Hasan, 1992b and 1995; Williams, 1995; Gibbons 1998).

Principles for selecting and sequencing language teaching content

We are now going to think about how we can use the ideas we have introduced so far about language and learning to plan teaching programs in language education.

Halliday describes educational learning as an organised process in which learning to mean and the expansion of meaning potential take place systematically:

> Education, I take it, means enabling people to learn; not just to learn in the natural, commonsense ways in which we learn in our daily lives, but to learn in an organised, progressive and systematic manner according to some generally accepted principles about what people ought to know. (Halliday 1992: 1)

Our exploration of functional grammar has spread out for us a whole map of language. It has also given us a set of principles and a metalanguage for thinking and talking about the different aspects of language and its use. Teachers can select from this array the content they wish to include in a teaching program.

We have argued that learning a language is about learning how to mean in that language; we have identified the units of meaning in language as whole texts. This suggests that the content of a language program might usefully be organised around the teaching of whole texts in context. Which texts and contexts to include in a teaching program will be determined after analysing what students need or want to do with the language they are learning.

In our brief discussion of language and learning we have argued that at the same time as we learn to use language, language is also our most important learning 'tool'. In our detailed exploration of language in this book we have argued that studying the nature of language itself can also contribute greatly to our ability to use it effectively. Halliday (1980) summarises what is involved in language learning by proposing that students are simultaneously:

- learning language
- learning *through* language
- learning *about* language.

If we combine Halliday's summary of what is involved in language learning with Vygotsky's ideas about learning as a collaborative and scaffolded social activity, we have a set of principles for incorporating the elements of a language program into a principled sequence of language teaching activities. These activities will be social interactions designed to guide students towards increasing control and independent use of the texts around which the course content is organised.

In Chapter 9 we briefly introduced an approach to language teaching and learning based on the use of whole texts in context. This approach is designed to enable teachers to work collaboratively with students, supporting – or scaffolding – their use of whole texts while guiding them towards increasing independence and control. We are going to look at this approach below in more detail, but before we do, we will review the notion of metalanguage from the perspective of the language teacher.

A language for talking about language

In our exploration of functional grammar in this book we have encountered a large number of technical terms. This rich metalanguage provides teachers with both a valuable resource and a practical problem. If teachers are to use this metalanguage to guide their teaching, they first need to learn it, and this takes time. Teachers also have to decide how much of this metalanguage it is useful and helpful to share with students. The response to these challenges will vary from teacher to teacher and from class to class and will depend on the resources (including time) available to the teacher, the previous learning experiences of the students, as well as their age and developmental stage.

A shared language for talking about language makes it possible for teachers and students to build collaboratively a systematic and comprehensive body of knowledge which can be applied to the study of language and its use. This shared language makes it possible for teachers to make clear and explicit statements about what students are expected to learn and what aspects of their language learning will be assessed to what standard at the end of a teaching program. This takes the guesswork out of assessment and eliminates the 'hidden' curriculum. In addition explicit statements about what is required of students are open to critique, review and renegotiation.

A metalanguage shared by teachers is also a valuable tool for professional exchange and professional development. A functional approach can still be applied, even where teachers are required to use traditional grammatical terms to talk about language. Derewianka (1998) provides teachers with a systematic and functional description of English grammar using traditional terms. A useful discussion of the teaching of grammar in language and literacy programs can also be found in de Silva Joyce and Burns (1999). For a discussion of using grammar in child literacy development, see Williams (1999b).

A text-based approach to language teaching

Over the last few decades language teaching has been organised at different times around, for example, grammar structures or lexical items, material settings or topics, functions or notions. Ur (1996: 178) has noted that increasingly these elements are combined into mixed syllabuses in order to be 'maximally comprehensive and helpful to teachers and learners'.

A language teaching program organised around whole texts in context is really a type of 'mixed syllabus'. As we have seen, texts are whole units of meaning. The following elements of a language teaching program can be taught in relation to these wholes:

- elements at the level of context of culture: the purposes people in this culture achieve with language, the meanings people make with the language, how people achieve these purposes and make these meanings, how this aligns with other cultures

- elements at the level of context of situation:

  field – working with everyday and general knowledge topics and the topics people talk about in casual conversation, researching the subject matter of educational disciplines or the workplace, strategies such as recognising gist and identifying topic shift

  tenor – strategies for managing different roles and relationships, including being polite, adjusting interpersonal distance and emotional intensity; classroom routines for monitoring student behaviour and guiding learning

  mode – strategies for managing different channels of communication, such as communicating face-to-face, using the telephone, writing letters and essays

- macro-elements of text at the level of semantics:

  texture – the strands of meaning woven through texts to make them cohesive

  text structure – the structure of individual texts in terms of general text patterns; text stages or phases which achieve particular functions within whole texts, such as greeting, explaining and describing

- micro-elements of text at the level of lexicogrammar (morphemes, words, phrases, groups and clauses) and how they are patterned within whole texts in context

- elements at the level of expression:

  spoken – segmental (articulation of sounds), prosodic (patterns of stress, rhythm and intonation), paralinguistic (gesture, posture and facial expression) *written* – spelling and punctuation, handwriting and keyboard skills, layout and presentation.

Students work with language elements in relation to the whole texts of which the elements are a part. Where students are not yet able to manage the whole text, the teacher fills in what the student is not yet able to do. In this way the students experience what it is like to participate in the use of a whole unit of meaning in anticipation of the time they will be able to do it on their own.

A methodology has been developed which enables teachers to address all these language elements in a cycle of teaching and learning. As the cycle unfolds, the teacher (in the role of expert), collaborates, interacts with and guides the student (in the role of apprentice) within a frame of experience they both share.

Cycles of language teaching and learning

At the end of Chapter 2 we noted that most teachers want their students to be both accurate and fluent language users. In other words, teachers want their students to reach an accepted and valued standard of language use but at the same time they want them to communicate with ease and fluency. We suggested that teachers can, therefore, find themselves in the middle of an educational paradox.

If learning activities focus only on 'correct' language use, there is the risk of limiting the language varieties students use. In addition, students' actual progress may be obscured. In activities concerned with accuracy students are often restricted to minimal responses. If learning activities focus only on communication without the teacher intervening to reveal patterns of structure and form, students may never learn effective use of the language varieties they need in order to achieve their learning goals. In communicative activities students can find themselves communicating only with other students, that is, with other novices, and thus they do not have the opportunity to work with models of effective or standard language use.

One way of addressing this paradox is to design cycles of teaching and learning around the use of whole texts in context. These cycles take students through a range of learning activities which address both accurate and fluent language use.

Through these activities teachers will:
1 provide social contexts and language learning activities in which learners use language for meaningful communication
2 intervene strategically so learners build their knowledge and skills explicitly, systematically and comprehensively.

This cycle will include opportunities for students to work with models of effective language use. Interaction will be between teacher and students as well as between the students themselves.

Such a cycle of teaching and learning has been designed by language educators as a 'means for giving all students the maximum opportunity to access the curriculum' (Rothery 1996: 99). The cycle comprises four different kinds of social interaction which support the learner's language development through a combination of:

- context exploration
- explicit instruction
- guided practice and joint construction
- independent application of newly acquired knowledge.

As learning progresses, the roles of teacher and students in the interaction shift between collaboration, direct teaching, strategic guidance and independent work. Here is a description of each of these four kinds of social interaction.

Using the cycle of teaching and learning

1 Context exploration

Students interact collaboratively with the teacher to build up a shared experience of the context of the texts they are learning to use. Activities might include hands-on experiences, research tasks, discovery learning and problem-solving activities, excursions and field trips. Through these activities students build four kinds of knowledge about the context of language use:

- relevant cultural knowledge, for example, about the text's purpose
- knowledge of the social activity and subject matter (field)
- knowledge about the roles and relationships of those communicating (tenor)
- knowledge about the means of communication and how it is used (mode).

2 Explicit instruction

During explicit instruction the teacher directs the social interaction in the classroom. Students are introduced to model texts of the type they are learning to use. At first they are often only able to work with fragments of the language of the text. The teacher's task is to fill in the whole picture so students experience using the whole text in its context.

The teacher focuses students' attention on the language of the text, explicitly and systematically showing learners how the meanings in the text are:

- shaped by the contexts in which they are used
- unified by texture and structure
- encoded in lexicogrammar

Learners are also shown how the meanings encoded in lexicogrammar are expressed in sound (articulation, stress, rhythm and intonation) or in the surface features of writing (spelling, punctuation, handwriting/typing, layout and presentation).

As students work with model texts, the teacher introduces a language for talking about language and how it works, in other words, a functional metalanguage. The terminology the teacher chooses to introduce will depend on the students' developmental stage and existing knowledge, as well as on the syllabus requirements of the teaching context.

3   Guided practice and joint construction

Using the metalanguage learned in the explicit instruction phase, the teacher guides whole groups of students in jointly constructing a text of the type just modelled. First the students are provided with research strategies to guide them as they build knowledge of the context of the text they plan to work with. Then, working from the basis of shared experience of the context and their knowledge of the language patterns of the text type, the students, with the teacher as guide, jointly construct the text, explicitly discussing and negotiating the meanings they are making as they go. For example, they might negotiate how much the text they are working with conforms to the patterns revealed in the model text and how much these patterns can be varied to customise this new text to its immediate context while still achieving its general purpose. The teacher intervenes as necessary, but begins to relinquish responsibility to the students as the students' own knowledge allows them to take over.

4   Independent application

The students are now ready to plan and undertake their own research, if required, and to construct their own text. The teacher is always available as a resource for consultation or advice, but equally students may consult and interact with their increasingly knowledgeable peers. At this stage the teacher only intervenes if needed.

Students can enter and move through the interaction phases according to need. As they move through the cycle, they gradually approximate control of the different facets of the text type they are learning to use, including text structure and texture, grammar and vocabulary, the pronunciation of spoken texts and the surface features of written texts.

Students are asked for direct contributions only when the teacher is sure they will be successful. Success is increased if the teacher and students are working together:

- on the basis of shared knowledge
- in an environment in which the routines are familiar
- over an extended period of time.

The teacher analyses student need and the demands of the curriculum to decide what texts the students will work with. The teacher also decides how students will progress through the phases of interaction by monitoring what they still need to learn in order to work with the text successfully. Often one complete cycle of interaction represents one unit of classroom work. Subsequent units of work build on what has already been learned.

Matching language learning activities to the cycle of teaching and learning

Each phase of social interaction in the cycle of teaching and learning is generated by different types of language learning activities.

Activities for exploring context include:

- structured and scaffolded research tasks, including guided note-taking, focus questions, task-based exploration, problem-solving, graphic organisers
- the use of reference sources such as libraries, dictionaries, the Internet, the media
- excursions, field trips, guest speakers and interviews with people in the community
- brainstorming, discussions and opportunities to reveal relevant personal experience and points of view
- vocabulary development
- discovery learning, experiential learning, problem-solving, exploration and experimentation
- working with concrete and visual representations of subject matter such as models, pictures, drama, mime, video, concept maps, diagrams.

Teaching strategies for explicit instruction include:

- establishing social contexts which generate a genuine need to use a text of the type being studied
- reading a model text out aloud or showing a video of a model spoken text, stopping at the end of each stage to ask students to predict what is going to happen next
- drawing students' attention strategically to language features in a model text which reveal the text's structure, texture, lexicogrammatical features and features of expression; or asking students to search or listen for these features
- providing activities at the level of meaning such as sorting texts, sequencing jumbled stages, using colours to highlight elements of text structure or texture, skeleton texts as the basis for guided text construction, drawing visual representations of text structure, paragraph-writing practice, dictogloss activities, barrier games/information gap activities, graphic organisers such as timelines, flow charts or matrix boxes to reveal how the meanings are shaped into the text's structure
- providing activities at the levels of lexicogrammar and expression, including sequencing jumbled words or groups, matching, colour-coding parts of clauses, learning the forms and structures of words and groups, vocabulary-building, pronunciation practice and spelling activities, cloze activities, multiple choice questions, grammar games, body grammar, fill-in-the-blank, substitution and transformation exercises, handwriting practice
- providing opportunities to evaluate the model text, to decide who the 'ideal' listener/reader is, to discuss how it might be improved or changed and to determine the effect of this text on readers or listeners
- giving learners opportunities to look for other examples of the text type to compare different choices made by writers/speakers when using the same text type

- designing activities in which learners investigate the function and structures of artwork and other visual material accompanying or incorporated into the text, for example, illustrations, diagrams, tables, icons, video clips, use of borders, breakers and white space, layout or presentation style.

Guided practice and joint construction activities include:

- activities which guide students' research as they investigate the context
- activities where the teacher acts as scribe while the whole class contributes to the construction of a text, discussing and negotiating the meanings as they go
- whole class reading of texts with accompanying guided exploration and discussion of context, meaning, lexicogrammar and expression
- problem-solving tasks in which different groups work on particular problems and return with suggestions to the joint construction activity
- discussing with learners whether a jointly constructed text exactly follows the structure of the model text or whether it departs from that structure to achieve a more specialised purpose
- conferencing activities to build drafting, editing and proof-reading skills for writing; or activities for building skills and strategies specific to reading, talking or listening as required
- when teaching writing, giving students opportunities to construct a similar text in spoken language first as a 'bridge' to literacy (Gibbons 1991: 30–34 and 1998).

Teaching strategies for generating independent work include:

- mentoring and peer support replacing teacher support
- role play activities
- structured and staged project work
- display, performance or presentation of work to other classes or guests
- preparation of class books, videos, formal correspondence etc
- self and peer evaluation, for example, using checklists, selecting material for portfolios, class discussions
- revision and review sessions prepared and presented by the learners
- building links to subsequent units of work
- setting up contexts in which it is more effective to innovate and experiment with the text type and its patterns including combining it with other text types.

Throughout the cycle of teaching and learning, the teacher monitors student progress. As necessary the teacher returns to more structured and supported activities until students are ready to undertake independent work again. When students are working independently, it is possible to assess what language learning they have achieved through participation in the cycle.

Language teachers will recognise many of the activities listed above. Many of them were first developed as part of other approaches to language teaching, for example, structural, situational, functional-notional, task-based or communicative approaches. Different activities are more effective for focusing student attention on different elements of language. Systematic knowledge about the way language is structured in terms of function makes it possible for teachers to incorporate the best elements of any language teaching approach into a principled sequence of teaching and learning.

If you want to find out more about this cycle of teaching and learning, read Rothery (1996), Gray (1987), Hammond et al (1992) and Feez with Joyce (1998). Derewianka (1990) provides examples of activities which can be used to teach about texts.

Analysing need, monitoring progress and assessing achievement

Language educators working with functional grammar have found it to be a valuable tool for analysing texts in order to:

- establish their relevance to specific groups of students
- assess student achievement in a comprehensive and systematic way.

Understanding functional grammar helps teachers develop explicit criteria for designing language courses and for assessing student achievement. The criteria can be shared with students so they are clear about what is expected of them in a course and clear about how their performance is being monitored by the teacher. Such criteria also make it possible for students to monitor their own performance and to plan for future learning.

Macken and Slade (1993: 205–6; 207) describe an effective approach to assessment in language education in the following terms:

> ... an effective language assessment program must be linguistically principled, explicit, criterion-referenced, and must inform different types of assessment ...

> ... Shared criteria based on a sound knowledge of language and its varieties will enable teachers to reflect on the strengths and to diagnose weaknesses in the texts produced by their students.

The texts and contexts teachers choose to include in language teaching programs depend on the needs and wants of students. Sometimes students need to meet the demands of a pre-determined syllabus; at other times teachers and students can negotiate their own teaching content. In both cases teachers analyse students' language learning needs prior to and at the beginning of the course of study in order to determine that the texts included in the course are appropriate and relevant. Diagnostic assessment determines the elements of language and context which will be the focus of the teaching program. These elements then become the basis for explicit assessment criteria. Teachers use the criteria to monitor student progress during a course and to assess student achievement at the end of the course.

Hood, Solomon and Burns (1996: 66–67) suggest the following steps as a basis for analysing written texts in order to establish their relevance and suitability for specific groups of learners. The steps are aligned to our map of language (Figure 1.3 and 8.1). Notice how the metalanguage of functional grammar has been modified to make these steps accessible to a wider audience.

1   Consider the purpose and the context.

What kind of text is it?

Who wrote it, for whom?

What is it about?

2   Look at the overall organisation of the text.

Can you identify stages in the text (eg a beginning, a middle and an end stage)?

Can you describe the function of each stage?

3   Consider how cohesive the text is and how cohesion is achieved.

Are conjunctions used?

Is cohesion achieved through reference backwards and forwards in the text by the use of pronouns?

Do the choices of vocabulary throughout the text help to tie the text together?

4   Consider the significant grammatical features in the text, for example:

Does the writer use mainly declaratives (statements), interrogatives (questions) or imperatives (commands)?

Does the writer use modal verbs like *could, would, may, must* etc?

Are there patterns in the use of types of verbs (ie action, mental, verbal, being or having verbs)?

Are there patterns in the choice of verb tenses?

What is the percentage of multiple clause sentences?

Are there patterns in theme, or what comes first in sentences or clauses?

Does the writer use long noun groups?

Does the writer use many prepositional phrases indicating the circumstances around events?

5   Consider the vocabulary choices in the text.

Are technical words used or more everyday terms?

Are there relatively few or many content words in the text?

Are there a lot of descriptive words in the text?

Do the choices of vocabulary carry strong feeling, emotion or judgement, or are they fairly neutral in this regard?

6   Consider the layout and script.

Is the layout an important clue to the meaning of the text?

Are some parts of the text emphasised in the layout?

A principled assessment checklist can be designed on the basis of our map of language (Figure 1.3 and 8.1). Teachers can use such a checklist to assess students' ability to work with whole texts at each level of language, that is, in terms of:

- use of the text in context
- structural patterns of the language of the text (text structure, texture and lexico-grammar)
- expression (for example, pronunciation or spelling and handwriting).

Here is an assessment checklist designed to assess texts written by beginning ESL students (Feez 1998: 131).

Assessment checklist for texts written by beginning ESL students

Purpose and staging	• Has the purpose been achieved, even partially? • Is the staging contributing to or detracting from the achievement of the purpose?

Text unity	• Is the text cohesive through the use of:
	  – lexical sets, both to do with the field and the writer's attitude
	  – conjunction
	  – reference
	  – distribution of information across paragraphs and clauses

Clause grammar	• Are noun groups, verb groups and prepositional phrases put together to construct effective single clause sentences?
	Consider:
	  – use of declarative, interrogative and imperative forms
	  – use of doing, thinking and speaking, feeling and perceiving, being and having processes (verb groups) and accompanying participants (noun groups) and circumstances (prepositional phrases)
	  – use of theme/first position in the clause to establish what the message is concerned with and placement of the new information at the end of the clause

Groups/words	• Consider the learner's control of the following: – verb groups (verb forms, tense, voice, modals, number, agreement) – noun groups (plurals, articles, numeratives, describers, qualifiers) – prepositional phrases (use of prepositions with noun groups) – vocabulary sets related to field (specific/general, concrete/technical/abstract, nominalisations, describing words and phrases) and attitude (intensified words and phrases, expressions of modality, describing words and phrases)
Graphology	• Consider the learner's control of: – spelling – punctuation – layout – script

Using an assessment checklist of this kind, teachers are able to identify both the strengths and weaknesses of a student's use of a particular type of text. This enables them to finetune their response to student need as language use develops through the course. It also enables the teacher to report in some detail what the student knows and can do with language at the end of a course.

If you want to find more about how functional grammar has been applied to language assessment, read Derewianka (1992), Feez (1998), Macken and Slade (1993) and Rothery (1992).

Teaching about text in and beyond the English-speaking world

In Chapter 9 we included a brief note about the difference between register variation and dialect variation (page 215). We noted that register variation is motivated by *use*, in contrast to dialect variation which refers to the different speech habits of *users*.

In this book we have been concentrating on register variation. In other words, we have been concentrating on the way language varies according to the functions, or uses, we have for it. We have seen how the variety of language we use is shaped by what people are doing (field), who is taking part (tenor) and the role language is playing (mode). In our discussion of functional grammar and language education we have discussed how an understanding of the way language varies according to use might be translated into planning and implementing language teaching programs. When teachers plan a language teaching program, they also have to think about dialect variation. In this section we would like to introduce some of the issues associated with dialect variation which may impact on the design of language teaching programs.

Halliday (1985: 44) describes a dialect as the variety of language you speak habitually because of the social group you belong to. For example, a particular dialect will be associated with people who come from a certain geographical region, people who belong to a particular social class or people of a particular age group. The dialect teachers use as the basis for a language teaching program, therefore, aligns students with a particular social group.

In the field of English language teaching, dialect variation is most often thought of in geographic and regional terms. Students of English are often conscious that they are learning Australian English, British English, American English, Canadian English or New Zealand English. They may even be conscious of dialect variations within these very broad categories, for example, the English spoken in Scotland, Ireland or the Southern states of the USA. They may be less conscious, however, of the social class or age group associated with the dialect of English they are learning.

Quite often communities assign different values to different dialects. Some dialects are considered more mainstream, more 'standard' or more prestigious than others. These values change over time and are often related to the socioeconomic status of the social groups associated with the dialect. Sometimes dialect variation can cause communication difficulties for those who speak more mainstream dialects of the language and this may also cause the dialect to be considered 'non-standard'. There are also associations between certain dialects and certain registers; for example, some students have to learn a new dialect of their first language in order to manage the registers of formal education in that language.

Language teachers often find themselves at the centre of debates around language standards. Often the debate can be quite confusing, even misleading, especially when those involved in the debate are unable to separate their prejudices against particular dialects from their concerns about language functionality.

British colonialism of earlier centuries and the spread of global communication in this century have resulted in the English language playing an important role in international communication. Recognisable dialects of English have emerged in regions where English is one of several mainstream languages, for example, the English spoken in India, Nigeria, Singapore and Hong Kong. At the end of the twentieth century we are reaching a time when people who speak English as a first language will be outnumbered by those who speak English as a second or foreign language. For this reason, no doubt, new dialects of English are emerging in many parts of the world. English is also the common language of international aviation, of much academic and business communication, a large part of the entertainment industry and, so far, it is the most common language used in electronic communication. These uses have resulted in certain combinations of dialect and register variation of English having a global impact.

The changing demographic of English language use around the world demands that language teachers think carefully about the registers and dialects of English they teach. The varieties they teach, as we have already noted, will reflect the learning needs and goals of students. It is also important, however, to consider the social impact their teaching might have on different communities of language users. For example, teachers need to consider whether their work is privileging some varieties of English over others, and why. They also need to consider the impact of their work on communities who speak languages other than English.

If you want to find out more about English as a world language, read Crystal (1987), Graddol (1997) and Kachru and Nelson (1996).

To sum up

At the end of previous chapters and in this chapter we have discussed some of the ways functional grammar can be used by language teachers to improve language teaching and learning. The ideas presented in this book, however, are only a starting point. Language educators are constantly debating, developing and expanding the ways functional grammar is applied to teaching. It can be quite challenging to keep up with the debates and the developments – and certainly beyond the scope of this book. As you have discovered in your journey through the chapters in this book, functional grammar is a rich and detailed description of language and the way it is used. As you continue to explore functional grammar, you too will certainly think of new ways in which your increasing understanding of language can be applied to your own work and interests.

Exercises

1 Review the list of text-based syllabus elements:
   a. How do you incorporate each of these elements into your language teaching?
   b. How do you address each of these elements for different groups of students, eg beginners, intermediate, advanced?
   c. Are there any of these elements that you do not address explicitly in your language teaching?
   d. Do you think you address each of these elements in an effective way in your language teaching? How might you address each of these elements more effectively?

2 Review the four kinds of social interaction in the cycle of teaching and learning suggested in this chapter:
   a. Do you already use all these types of interaction in your classroom?
   b. How might you incorporate each of these types of classroom interaction into your language teaching?
   c. Do you think all of these interaction types are useful for all types of students and all macroskills (eg beginners, intermediate or advanced; listening and speaking; reading and writing)?
   d. Do you think there is a good balance of different types of interaction in your classroom? How might you improve that balance?

3 Review the steps for analysing a written text.
   Design a series of steps for analysing a spoken text.

4 Review the checklist for assessing beginning writing.
   Design a checklist for assessing another macroskill or level of language, eg speaking or academic writing.

5 Identify a good example of a type of text you would like your students to be able to use effectively. The text might be spoken or written. If you wish, you may choose one of the texts you have already worked with in earlier chapters:
   a. Describe the students and their language learning needs.
   b. Write a manageable set of language learning objectives relevant to these students.
   c. Analyse your chosen text to identify the elements of a course designed to achieve the language learning objectives. Identify elements at each level of the language map, that is, elements of context, elements of meaning and grammar, elements of expression. Modify the language learning objectives if necessary.
   d. Select and sequence a series of language learning activities which will guide students towards achievement of the language learning objectives. Organise the activities in terms of context exploration, explicit instruction, guided practice and independent use.
   e. Prepare an assessment checklist which you can use to monitor student progress during the course and to assess student achievement at the end of the course.
   f. If possible, implement your program and evaluate its effectiveness.
   g. How would you modify your program to improve its effectiveness?

Further explorations

Those of us who teach grammar are often asked 'So what? Where can I go with all this academic knowledge of how my language works?' The answer is that what we have sought to teach is NOT merely an academic knowledge of language. We all live with our language every day, using it for both social and professional purposes. Human language is a powerful tool but also frequently a powerful weapon; we all use it to influence others, and in turn are often unknowingly influenced by other people's skilful handling of its functions. So there is a powerful pragmatic reason for knowing as much as we can about how our language system operates. The more we are able to articulate what is going on (linguistically) in a given situation, the more likely we are to notice when someone is using language to play power games with us, and the greater our chances of using language to suit our own ends.

There is also a sense in which the study of grammar needs no justification: it is the study of how a particular language works, the study of the organisation of what is perhaps the most characteristic and central part of human activity. Seen in that light, grammar – and the larger field of linguistics – are legitimate areas of enquiry and research, just as biology and psychology, for example also seek to understand specific patterns in the world and our functioning within it. Some people may even enjoy grammar or grammatical analysis as an end in itself – just as some people enjoy crossword puzzles or mathematical problems or studying maps, not for any particular goal but for the pleasure of the activity.

Many people, however, will think of grammar less as an end in itself than as a means to some other end. Some of the users of this book will be undertaking the task of grammar instruction in primary and secondary school systems; others will be teachers of English as a second or foreign language; yet others will be teaching beginner courses in functional grammar at university and college level.

The question of how grammar should be taught in schools and universities is not a simple one. On the one hand, just as we might expect good teachers of biology or psychology to inspire their students with some sense of excitement or wonder at the intricacies of plant life or the workings of human perception, so we might expect that good teachers of grammar might leave their students with some sense of amazement and delight at the systems and structures of language. On the other hand, just as the serious biologist or psychologist cannot make enthusiasm an excuse for neglect of analytical detail and scientific rigour, so also grammar (both in its teaching and in its application) demands more than vague generalisations and impressionistic judgements. If we are to use grammatical analysis, we have to take some trouble to ensure we have something to use. The challenge for teachers – and for books such as this one! – is to try to do justice both to the exciting riches of language and to an adequate set of tools to explain and unlock those riches.

We know that many of you are, or intend to be, teachers in school systems where grammar instruction has recently made a comeback, or has taken a functional turn away from the more traditional approaches of the past. When your students (or their parents) ask you, as inevitably they will, what is the use of learning functional grammar, you could point out that people with a good working knowledge of how their own language functions are well equipped to understand texts of all kinds. For instance:

- they have very specific ways of describing why a particular literary text works or doesn't work for them
- they are less likely to be hoodwinked by the way advertisers, politicians, journalists etc. manipulate the functions of language in order to manipulate their audience response
- they are less likely to feel dominated by the language behaviour of their doctors, bosses, parents, children, court officials or a whole host of other people who, consciously or not, are adept at establishing dominance through the language system.

Those of you who teach students who are learning a second or foreign language may also be asked what is the use of functional grammar. You could point out that the relationship between grammar and meaning and context is the key to mastering the target language accurately and fluently. A knowledge of the structures of the target language (accuracy) needs to combine with knowledge of how and when to link these structures together into real world texts that work within the target language's cultural contexts (fluency). Knowledge of grammar from a functional perspective will help second language learners to identify *what* people in a culture talk about – and *how* they talk about it – in their various contexts.

For those of you who may be inspired to take your grammar study even further, there are many exciting possibilities in linguistic research and application. Professional linguists in Australia and other parts of the world are using grammatical analysis to explore many areas of human discourse. For instance, there is important linguistic and stylistic research going on in:

- language in the classroom
- language in the courtroom
- language in conflict resolution situations of several kinds
- language in hierarchical relationships like mother/child, doctor/patient, nurse/doctor
- analysis of 'disordered' language
- the application of functional grammar to the analysis of literary texts, including work on children's literature
- analysis of student writing and the problems of student writers at various levels of education: primary, secondary, tertiary.

Functional linguists are also applying the theory in a wider context: to intonation patterns as resources of spoken language; to systems in art, music, theology and theatre; to the description of other languages; and to translation studies.

But if that all sounds very serious, grammatical analysis is also creative and enjoyable. We hope that many of our readers will develop the same sense of fun we have in using our grammatical tools to analyse the discourse patterns of ourselves, our families, close friends and colleagues, newspaper columnists, advertisements etc. Whenever a group of linguists gather together socially, someone is sure to throw in a comment like 'Just listen to that modality!' or 'Watch your interpersonals!' or even 'What gives with all the agentless passives?' This, of course, is a bunch of professionals having fun with shop talk, but we would hope that our readers might have gained some insights along the way about the many possibilities for a practical application, either social or professional, of grammatical analysis.

This book is the map and the guidebook for your journey towards linguistic understanding. Now it's over to you. Good luck in your own further explorations of your language and culture.

Appendix A

Summary of metalanguage for each analysis

type of analysis	metalanguage
constituency	nominal group (ng), verbal group (vg), adverbial group (adv g), conjunction group (conj g), preposition group (pg), prepositional phrase (pg)

experiential (transitivity)

choose Process: Participants follow	choose Circumstance:
material: Actor, Goal, Range, Beneficiary	Extent: time, place
behavioural: Behaver, Behaviour, Range	Location: time, place
mental: Senser, Phenomenon	Manner: means, quality, complement
verbal: Sayer, Verbiage, Receiver, Target	Angle
existential: Existent	Role:
relational attributive: Carrier, Attribute	Accompaniment:
relational identifying: Identified, Identifier; Token, Value	Cause:
	Contingency:
	Matter:

interpersonal include: mood and speech function

Mood Block					Residue		
Subject	Mood Adjunct	Comment Adjunct	Finite: time or modality	polarity	Predicator	Complement	Adjunct

textual

Theme			Rheme
textual	interpersonal	topical	

logical

relations between clauses in clause complex
relations between groups in group complex

cohesion

links between clauses and ties between items in clauses

appraisal

interpersonal appraisal motifs of attitude (judgement), engagement and graduation

Appendix B

Meaning patterns across a text

Above and below the clause

Logical meanings	patterns of taxis across a text (i) between clauses (ii) between groups and phrases

Summarising patterns in clauses

Experiential meanings	processs types across a text patterns of Circumstances across a text patterns of Participant across a text (i) large choices like what ng is Actor/Senser/Goal/Beneficiary (ii) smaller choices like whether ngs are proper or common; abstract or concrete; animal, vegetable or mineral; young or old, male or female, ng or embedded clause, and so on patterns of tense across a text patterns of pre- and postmodification patterns of groups/phrases simplex o complex
Interpersonal meanings	mood choice and speech function across a text patterns of Subject choice patterns of primary tense patterns of modality patterns of polarity
Textual meanings	patterns of thematic drift patterns of thematic progression

Summarising patterns that only emerge in the whole

Cohesion Appraisal Structure	the texture of a text – lexicogrammatical ties across the text attitudinal motifs across the text realisation of generic structure potential

Appendix C

Prepositional phrase (and adverbial group) help sheet

First identify the prepositional phrase based on this model:

preposition group +	nominal group:
on	the table
of	her father
to	my friend
at	all
as	a result

Questions 3, 4, 5 and 6 also apply to adverbial groups!

Now ask:

Q1   Is it a Participant in the process? eg **I posted the letter *to a friend*. He was bitten *by a snake*.**

Yes	GO TO	Participant	(see page 282)
No	ask the next question		

Q2   Is it telling me about the Thing in a nominal group immediately before it?

Yes	GO TO	Qualifier	(see page 282)
No	ask the next question Q3		

Q3   Does it make specific reference to the previous clause? eg **because of that**

Yes	GO TO	Conjunctive Adjunct	(see page 282)
NO	ask the next question Q4		

Q4   Does it make some comment on the experiential meanings of this clause?
eg **to my surprise**

Yes	GO TO	Comment Adjunct	(see page 282)
NO	ask the next question Q5		

Q5   Does it modify the polarity of the Mood Block in terms of probability, usuality, typicality, obviousness?

Yes	GO TO	Mood Adjunct	(see page 282)
NO	ask the next question Q6		

Q6   Is it telling me about the process in this clause?

Yes	GO TO	Circumstantial Adjunct	(see page 282)
NO	Start again with Q1		

Conjunctive Adjunct	Label it in interpersonal but leave out of Mood Block and Residue. **NB:** conjunctions are NOT Conjunctive Adjuncts Leave out of experiential meanings Treat as textual Theme if it precedes topical Theme
Circumstantial Adjunct	Label as Adjunct and include in Residue in interpersonal Label as Circumstance in experiential Treat as topical Theme if the first item in transitivity
Mood and Comment Adjunct	Label in interpersonal and include in Mood Block Leave out of experiential Treat as interpersonal Theme if it precedes topical Theme
Qualifier	Include in the nominal group. Continue the function label for the nominal group until the Qualification is ended!
Participant	Label with participant role in experiential, eg Actor, Receiver, Client, Recipient Treat as a prepositional phrase, ie, as Adjunct, in interpersonal Treat as topical Theme if first item in transitivity

Appendix D

Templates for summarising experiential meanings

NB: In each of these templates, the 'type' column may be used to differentiate independent and dependent clauses; the 'potential' column may be used for the person who is the addressee in imperative clauses or the implied Doer in non-finite clauses.

D 1: Material process clauses

Cl#	type	Actor	potential Actor	Goal	Range	Beneficiary	Circumstance type

D 2: Behavioural process clauses

Cl#	type	Behaver	Behaviour	Other Range	Circumstance type

D 3: Mental process clauses

Cl#	type	Senser	Phenomenon	embedded clause as Phenomenon	projected clause number	Circumstance type

D 4: Verbal process clauses

Cl#	type	Sayer	Verbiage or embedded clause	projected clause number ··········	Receiver	Target	Circumstance type

D 5: Existential process clauses

Cl#	type	Existent	Circumstance type

D 6: Relational attributive process clauses

Cl#	type	Carrier	Attribute	Circumstance type

D 7: Relational identifying process clauses

Cl#	type	Identified	Identifier	Token	Value	Circumstance type

Appendix E

Templates for summarising interpersonal meanings

E 1: Prose texts

Cl#	Type	Mood choice	Type of exchange	Subject	Tense Finite			Modal Finite			Md Adj		Com Adj	Gram Met	pol
					past	pres	fut	prob	oblig	abl	prob	usual			

E 2: Dialogic Clauses. Use a separate chart for each speaker

Speaker ....

Cl#	Mood Choice	Type of Exchange	Init	Con	Response		Subject	Tense Finite			Modal Finite			Md Adj	Com	Gram
					P	D N		past	pres	fut	prob	oblig	abl	prob	usual	Adj	Met	pol

It's a matter of personal choice whether to list all clauses consecutively and use colour to distinguish speakers, or to insert a column to identify each speaker (eg by initials), or, as here, to have a separate page for each speaker.

The init(iate), con(tinue), Response columns are just for dialogic texts and should show whether the speaker is initiating, continuing or responding. If responding, distinguish between P(referred), D(iscretionary), and N (dispreferred) responses.

Remember that there are more Mood Adjuncts than there are space for on these charts so you may have to adapt the columns for each text. Embedded clauses are not usually analysed for interpersonal meanings but you may want to analyse them if there is modality.

Appendix F

Template for summarising textual meanings of Theme

Cl#	type	textual Themes		interpersonal Themes				topical Themes	
		cont	conj'ion / Conj'ive Adjunct	Vocative	Finite	Mood Adjunct — Comment	Mood Adjunct — Modal	marked	unmarked

Appendix G

Template for exploring nominal group structures

NB: Although you may need to adapt this for different texts, you will find it provides a quick impression of the field of discourse.

Deictic 1	Deictic 2	Numerative	Epithet 1	Epithet 2	Classifier	Thing	Qualifier

Appendix H

*Sample text analysis: **News Story text*** (see also Chapter 9, page 233ff)

- division of text into clause complexes and clauses
- box diagram analyses for the three metafunctions of language
- charts of meanings showing the patterns of grammar in the text.

News story

(*The Australian*, April 15, 1999, Georgina Safe and Matt Price)

CITY BATTERED BY GIANT HAILSTONES

Hailstones the size of tennis balls smashed roofs, battered cars and injured people across Sydney in a freak storm last night.

Thirty motorists were stranded in the Royal National Park at Sutherland and cars taking shelter in the Sydney airport tunnel caused major traffic problems. Some 30 sets of traffic lights went out after the hailstorm hit at 8pm.

Roofs were torn off houses in Caringbah, in Sydney's south, roads were flooded in North Manly, and cars were 'floating away' in the eastern suburb of Edgecliff in the aftermath of the 20-minute pummelling, a police spokesperson said.

Ambulance crews were flat-out attending to people with head injuries and severe lacerations from huge chunks of ice, and a driver was taken to Royal Prince Alfred Hospital after blinding hail caused him to swerve off the road and into a power pole at Marrickville, in Sydney's inner west.

The storm caused a power failure in Collaroy and along Oxford St, in the eastern suburb of Paddington. Many motorists sought refuge by parking under eaves on the footpath. Chris Chambers suffered mild concussion when he was hit by a giant hailstone while walking 12m from his car into a Paddington hotel. The front and back windscreens on his $65,000 new model Alfa Romeo were smashed.

'It was just huge,' he said, blood pouring down his face as hotel staff provided medical treatment. Hundreds of people emptied restaurants and cafes to witness the hailstorm, many gathering giant samples from the streets and footpaths.

'It sounded like a plane was about to crash,' Robyn Bradfield said. 'Then stones the size of golf balls – no, cricket balls – started bouncing into the restaurant.'

Ms Bradfield's partner, a doctor, was busy treating the injured.

Weather Bureau spokesman Evan Bathe said the thunderstorm hit Nowra and Wollongong, on the NSW south coast, and was expected to drift out to sea, but came inland, hitting Bundeena. The storm then moved up to Sutherland Shire, in Sydney's south, wreaking extensive damage, and on through Sydney's inner west and across the eastern suburbs, before heading to the northern beaches.

Clause division of the text: News Story

NB 1: Where there is ellipsis and we need to retrieve part of the clause from a preceding one for a full analysis, the ellipsed constituents are set in block capitals after a ^.

NB 2: The verbal group in each clause has been underlined, including the verbal groups in embedded clauses.

CC A	cl.	1	City <u>battered</u> by giant hailstones
CC B	cl.	2	Hailstones the size of tennis balls <u>smashed</u> roofs,
	cl.	3	^THEY <u>battered</u> cars
	cl.	4	and ^THEY <u>injured</u> people across Sydney in a freak storm last night.*
CC C	cl.	5	Thirty motorists <u>were stranded</u> in the Royal National Park at Sutherland
	cl.	6	and cars [[<u>taking</u> shelter in the Sydney airport tunnel]] <u>caused</u> major traffic problems.****
CC D	cl.	7	Some 30 sets of traffic lights <u>went out</u>
	cl.	8	after the hailstorm HIT at 8pm.
CC E	cl.	9	Roofs <u>were torn</u> off houses in Caringbah, in Sydney's south,
	cl.	10	roads <u>were flooded</u> in North Manly,
	cl.	11	and cars <u>were</u> 'floating' away' in the eastern suburb of Edgecliff in the aftermath of the 20-minute pummelling,
	cl.	12	a police spokesperson <u>said</u>.
CC F	cl.	13	Ambulance crews <u>were</u> flat-out
	cl.	14	<u>attending</u> to people with head injuries and severe lacerations from huge chunks of ice,
	cl.	15	and a driver <u>was taken</u> to Royal Prince Alfred Hospital
	cl.	16	after blinding hail <u>caused</u> him <u>to swerve</u> off the road and into a power pole at Marrickville, in Sydney's inner west.**
CC G	cl.	17	The storm <u>caused</u> a power failure in Collaroy and along Oxford St, in the eastern suburb of Paddington.****
CC H	cl.	18	Many motorists <u>sought</u> refuge
	cl.	19	by <u>parking</u> under eaves on the footpath.****

CC I cl. 20 Chris Chambers <u>suffered</u> mild concussion****

cl. 21 when he <u>was hit</u> by a giant hailstone

cl. 22 while <u>walking</u> 12m from his car into a Paddington hotel.

CC J cl. 23 The front and back windscreens on his $65,000 new model Alfa Romeo <u>were smashed</u>.

CC K cl. 24 'It <u>was</u> just huge,'

cl. 25 he <u>said</u>,

cl. 26 blood <u>pouring</u> down his face

cl. 27 as hotel staff <u>provided</u> medical treatment.

CC L cl. 28 Hundreds of people <u>emptied</u> restaurants and cafes

cl. 29 <u>to witness</u> the hailstorm,

cl. 30 many <u>gathering</u> giant samples from the streets and footpaths.

CC M cl. 31 'It <u>sounded</u>

cl. 32 like a plane <u>was about to crash</u>,'

cl. 33 Robyn Bradfield <u>said</u>.

CC N cl. 34 'Then stones the size of golf balls – no, cricket balls – <u>started bouncing</u> into the restaurant.'

CC O cl. 35 Ms Bradfield's partner, a doctor, <u>was</u> busy

cl. 36 <u>treating</u> the injured.

CC P cl. 37 Weather Bureau spokesman Evan Bathe <u>said</u>

cl. 38 the thunderstorm <u>hit</u> Nowra and Wollongong, on the NSW south coast,

cl. 39 and ^IT <u>was expected to drift</u> out to sea, ***

cl. 40 but ^IT <u>came</u> inland,

cl. 41 <u>hitting</u> Bundeena.

CC Q cl. 42 The storm then <u>moved</u> up to Sutherland Shire, in Sydney's south, <xx> and on through Sydney's inner west and across the eastern suburbs,

cl. 43 <u>wreaking</u> extensive damage,

cl. 44 before <u>heading</u> to the northern beaches.

* Note that the verbs of clauses 2, 3 and 4 all have a common Subject (*hailstones the size of tennis balls*) and that the three Circumstances at the end of cl.4 (*across Sydney* | *in a freak storm* | *last night*) actually apply to all three clauses.

** We have treated *caused to swerve* as a complex verbal group with hypotaxis within the group (following Halliday 1994: 7). Here the Subject (the causer) is Actor of the first part of the verbal group but now glossed as Initiator, and the second participant (*him*) is Actor of the second part of the verbal group.

*** *expected to drift* can also be glossed as a complex verbal group, with hypotactic projection within the group (Halliday 1994: 287–91). The two verbs in the group have the same (ellipsed) Subject – the storm. But although the storm is the Actor of *drift*, it is not the Senser of *expected*, so this analysis does lose something of the underlying semantics of the clause. *Expected* is a passive voice mental process with the Senser not mentioned; *to drift* is a material process. The storm is part of the Phenomenon in the mental process and Actor of the (dominant) material process.

**** These clauses, variously analysed as material or mental, can also be analysed as relational attributive.

(Appendix H: continued)

Clause division of the text: News story (continued)

CC A cl. 1   City <u>battered</u> by giant hailstones

Minor clause; a nominal group with embedded clause Qualifier? or an ellipsed clause: *The city was/has been battered ...?*

CC B cl. 2
independent clause

	Hailstones the size of tennis balls	<u>smashed</u>		roofs,
experiential	Actor	Process: material		Goal
interpersonal declarative mood	Subject	Finite: past +	Predicator	Complement
	Mood Block		Residue	
textual	Theme	Rheme		

cl. 3
independent clause

	^THEY	<u>battered</u>		cars
experiential clause	Actor	Processs: material		Goal
interpersonal declarative mood	Subject	Finite: past +	Predicator	Complement
	Mood Block		Residue	
textual	Theme	Rheme		

Clause division of the text: News story (continued)

cl. 4
independent clause

	and	^THEY	injured	people	across Sydney	in a freak storm	last night.
experiential		Actor	Process: Material	Goal	Circ: Place	Circ: Manner	Circ: Time
interpersonal declarative mood		Subject	Finite: past + / Predicator	Complement	Adjunct	Adjunct	Adjunct
		Mood Block	Residue	Residue	Residue	Residue	Residue
textual	Textual	Topical					
	Theme	Theme	Rheme	Rheme	Rheme	Rheme	Rheme

CCC cl. 5
independent clause

	Thirty motorists	were	stranded	in the Royal National Park at Sutherland
experiential	Goal	Process: material		Circumstance: place*
interpersonal declarative mood	Subject	Finite: past +	Predicator	Adjunct
	Mood Block		Residue	Residue
textual	Theme	Rheme	Rheme	Rheme

NB: Unclear whether *at Sutherland* is a separate Circumstance of place here (with an adverbial function in the clause structure), or is a Qualifier of *Royal National Park* (adjectival in function – the analysis followed here).

Clause division of the text: News story (continued)

cl. 6

independent clause

and	cars [[taking shelter in the Sydney airport tunnel]]	caused	major traffic problems.
experiential	Actor	Process: material	Goal
interpersonal declarative mood	Subject	Finite: past +	Predicator	Complement
	Mood Block	Residue		
textual	Textual / Topical			
	Theme	Rheme		

Experiential: Actor | Process: material | Goal

Interpersonal declarative mood: Subject | Finite: past + Predicator | Complement; Mood Block | Residue

Textual: Textual · Topical (Theme) | Rheme

CCD   cl. 7

independent clause

Some 30 sets of traffic lights	went	out
Actor	Processs: material	
Subject	Finite: past +	Predicator	Adjunct
Mood Block	Residue	
Theme	Rheme	

independent clause

declarative mood: Subject | Finite: past + Predicator | Adjunct; Mood Block | Residue

textual: Theme | Rheme

Clause division of the text: News story (continued)

cl. 8
dependent clause

	after	the hailstorm	hit	at 8pm.
experiential		Actor	Process: material	Circumstance: time
interpersonal **declarative mood**		Subject	Finite: past + / Predicator	Adjunct
		Mood Block	Residue	
textual	Textual	Topical		
	Theme		Rheme	

CC E cl. 9
dependent clause (projected by cl. 12)

	Roofs	were	torn	off houses	in Caringbah, in Sydney's south
experiential	Goal	Process: material		Circumstance: place	Circumstance: place
interpersonal **declarative mood**	Subject	Finite: past +	Predicator	Adjunct	Adjunct
	Mood Block	Residue			
textual	Theme	Rheme			

Clause division of the text: News story (continued)

cl. 10
dependent clause
(projected by cl.12)

	roads	were	flooded	in North Manly,
experiential	Goal	Process: material		Circumstance: place
interpersonal declarative mood	Subject	Finite: past +	Predicator	Adjunct
	Mood Block		Residue	
textual	Theme		Rheme	

cl. 11
dependent clause
(projected by cl.12)

	and	cars	were	'floating	away'	in the eastern suburb of Edgecliff	in the aftermath of the 20-minute pummelling.
experiential		Actor	Process: material		Circ: place	Circ: place	Circ: cause + time?
interpersonal declarative mood		Subject	Finite: past +	Predicator	Adjunct	Adjunct	Adjunct
		Mood Block		Residue			
textual	Textual	Topical		Rheme			
	Theme						

Clause division of the text: News story ((continued)

cl. 12 — independent clause

a police spokesperson   *said.*

experiential	Sayer	Process: verbal
interpersonal **declarative mood**	Subject	Finite: past + / Predicator
	Mood Block	Residue
textual	Theme	Rheme

CC F   cl. 13 — independent clause

Ambulance crews   *were*   flat-out

experiential	Carrier	Process: relational (attributive)	Attribute
interpersonal **declarative mood**	Subject	Finite: past + / Predicator	Complement
	Mood Block	Residue	
textual	Theme	Rheme	

cl. 14 — dependent clause

attending   to   people [with head injuries and severe lacerations from huge chunks of ice]

experiential	Process: material	Goal	
interpersonal **non-finite clause;** **no Mood Block**	Predicator	Adjunct	Complement
	Residue		
textual	Rheme		

Clause division of the text: News story (continued)

cl. 15 — independent clause

	and	a driver	was	taken	to Royal Prince Alfred Hospital
experiential		Goal	Process: material		Circumstance: place
interpersonal declarative mood		Subject	Finite: past +	Predicator	Adjunct
		Mood Block	Mood Block	Residue	Residue
textual	Textual	Topical			
	Theme	Theme	Rheme	Rheme	Rheme

cl. 16 — dependent clause

	after	blinding hail	caused	him	to swerve	off the road and into a power pole at Marrickville, in Sydney's inner west.
experiential		Initiator	Process:	Actor	material	Circumstance complex: place 1 + place 2
interpersonal declarative mood		Subject	Finite: past + Pred-	Comp	-icator	Adjunct
		Mood Block	Mood Block	Residue	Residue	Residue
textual	Textual	Topical				
	Theme	Theme	Rheme	Rheme	Rheme	Rheme

Clause division of the text: News story (continued)

CC G cl. 17
independent clause

	The storm	caused	a power failure	in Collaroy and along Oxford St, in the eastern suburb of Paddington.
experiential	Actor	Process: material	Goal	Circumstance complex: place 1 + place 2
interpersonal declarative mood	Subject	Finite: past + / Predicator	Complement	Adjunct
	Mood Block	Residue		
textual	Theme	Rheme		

CC H cl. 18
independent clause

	Many motorists	sought	refuge
experiential	Actor	Process: material	Range
interpersonal declarative mood	Subject	Finite: past + / Predicator	Complement
	Mood Block	Residue	
textual	Theme	Rheme	

Clause division of the text: News story (continued)

cl. 19

dependent clause	by	parking	under eaves on the footpath.
experiential		Process: material	Circumstance
interpersonal non-finite clause: no Mood Block		Predicator	Adjunct
		Residue	
textual	Textual	Theme	Rheme

CCI   cl. 20

independent clause	Chris Chambers	suffered	mild concussion
experiential	Senser	Process: mental	Phenomenon
interpersonal declarative mood	Subject	Finite: past + Predicator	Complement
	Mood Block	Residue	
textual	Theme	Rheme	

Clause division of the text: News story (continued)

cl. 21

dependent clause

	when	he	was	hit	by a giant hailstone
experiential		Goal	Process: material		Actor/Agent
interpersonal **declarative mood**		Subject	Finite: past +	Predicator	Adjunct
			Mood Block		Residue
textual	Textual	Topical	Rheme		
	Theme				

cl. 22

dependent clause

	while	walking	12m from his car	into a Paddington hotel.
experiential		Process: material	Circumstance: place	Circumstance: place
interpersonal **non-finite clause:** **no Mood Block**		Predicator	Adjunct	Adjunct
		Residue		
textual	Textual	Rheme		
	Theme			

Clause division of the text: News story (continued)

CCJ cl. 23
independent clause

	The front and back windscreens on his $65,000 new model Alfa Romeo	were	smashed.
experiential	Goal	Process: material	
interpersonal declarative mood	Subject	Finite: past +	Predicator
	Mood Block		Residue
textual	Theme	Rheme	

CCK cl. 24
independent clause
(direct speech
projection from cl. 25)

	'It	was	just huge,'
experiential	Carrier	Process: relational (attributive)	Attribute
interpersonal declarative mood	Subject	Finite: past +	Predicator	Complement
	Mood Block		Residue	
textual	Theme	Rheme	

Clause division of the text: News story (continued)

cl. 25 independent clause

	he	said,
experiential	Sayer	Process: verbal
interpersonal declarative mood	Subject	Finite: past + / Predicator
	Mood Block	Residue
textual	Theme	Rheme

cl. 26 dependent clause

	blood	pouring	down his face
experiential	Actor	Process: material	Circumstance: place
interpersonal non-finite clause; a 'Subject' element but no Finite, so no Mood Block	'Subject'	Predicator	Adjunct
		Residue	
textual	Theme	Rheme	

Clause division of the text: News story (continued)

cl. 27

dependent clause	as	hotel staff	provided		medical treatment.
experiential		Actor	Process: material		Goal/Range?
interpersonal declarative mood		Subject	Finite: past +	Predicator	Complement
		Mood Block		Residue	
textual	Textual	Topical			
	Theme		Rheme		

CCL   cl. 28

independent clause	Hundreds of people	emptied		restaurants and cafes
experiential	Actor	Process: material		Goal
interpersonal declarative mood	Subject	Finite: past +	Predicator	Complement
	Mood Block		Residue	
textual	Theme	Rheme		

Clause division of the text: News story (continued)

cl. 29
dependent clause

	to witness	the hailstorm,
experiential	Process: mental	Phenomenon
interpersonal non-finite clause: no Mood Block	Predicator	Complement
	Residue	
textual	Rheme	

cl. 30
dependent clause

	many	gathering	giant samples	from the streets and footpaths.
experiential	Actor	Process: material	Goal	Circumstance: place
interpersonal non-finite clause: a 'Subject' element but no Finite, so no Mood block	'Subject'	Predicator	Complement	Adjunct
		Residue		
textual	Theme	Rheme		

Clause division of the text: News story (continued)

C 1   cl. 31
independent clause
(direct speech
projection from cl. 33)

	'It	sounded	
experiential	Phenomenon	Process: mental	
interpersonal **non-finite clause:** **no Mood Block**	Subject	Finite: past +	Predicator
	Mood Block	Residue	
textual	Theme	Rheme	

cl. 32
dependent clause

	like	a plane	was	about to crash,'
experiential		Actor	Process: material	
interpersonal **declarative mood**		Subject	Finite: past +	Predicator
		Mood Block		Residue
textual	Textual	Topical		Rheme
	Theme			Rheme

Clause division of the text: News story (continued)

cl. 33

independent clause	Robyn Bradfield	said.	
experiential	Sayer	Process: verbal	
interpersonal declarative mood	Subject	Finite: past +	Predicator
	Mood Block		Residue
textual	Theme	Rheme	

CCN cl. 34

independent clause	'Then	stones the size of golf balls – no, cricket balls –	started bouncing	into the restaurant.'
experiential		Actor	Process: material	Circumstance: place
interpersonal declarative mood		Subject	Finite: past +	Predicator	Complement
		Mood Block		Residue
textual	Textual	Topical	Rheme	
	Theme		Rheme	

Clause division of the text: News story (continued)

CCO cl. 35 independent clause

	Ms Bradfield's partner, a doctor,	was	busy
experiential	Carrier	Process: relational (attributive)	Attribute
interpersonal declarative mood	Subject	Finite: past + / Predicator	Complement
	Mood Block	Residue	
textual	Theme	Rheme	

cl. 36 dependent clause

	treating	the injured.
experiential	Process: material	Goal
interpersonal non-finite clause: no Mood Block	Predicator	Complement
	Residue	
textual	Rheme	

CCP cl. 37 independent clause

	Weather Bureau spokesman Evan Bathe	said
experiential	Sayer	Process: verbal
interpersonal declarative mood	Subject	Finite: past + / Predicator
	Mood Block	Residue
textual	Theme	Rheme

Clause division of the text: News story (continued)

cl. 38 dependent clause	the thunderstorm	hit		Nowra and Wollongong, on the NSW south coast,
experiential	Actor	Process: material		Goal
interpersonal declarative mood	Subject	Finite: past +	Predicator	Complement
	Mood Block		Residue	
textual	Theme	Rheme		

cl. 39 dependent clause	and	^IT	was	expected to drift	out to sea,
experiential		Actor*	Process: material		Circumstance: place
interpersonal declarative mood		Subject	Finite: past +	Predicator	Adjunct
		Mood Block		Residue	
textual	Textual	Topical	Rheme		
	Theme				

NB: see note to this clause on page 297.

Clause division of the text: News story (continued)

cl. 40

dependent clause

	but	^IT	came		inland,
experiential		Actor	Process: material		Circumstance: place
interpersonal declarative mood		Subject	Finite: past +	Predicator	Adjunct
		Mood Block			Residue
textual	Textual	Topical			
		Theme	Rheme		

cl. 41

dependent clause

	hitting	Bundeena.
experiential	Process: material	Goal
interpersonal non-finite clause: no Mood Block	Predicator	Complement
		Residue
textual	Rheme	

Clause division of the text: News story (continued)

CCQ cl. 42 — independent clause

Clause: The storm then **moved** up to Sutherland Shire, in Sydney's south, <xx> and on through Sydney's inner west and across the eastern suburbs,

	The storm	then	moved	up to Sutherland Shire, in Sydney's south, <xx> and on through Sydney's inner west and across the eastern suburbs,
experiential	Actor		Process: material	Circumstance complex: place 1 + place 2 + place 3
interpersonal declarative mood	Subject	Conj. Adj.	Finite: past + Predicator	Adjunct
	Mood Block		Residue	
textual	Theme		Rheme	

cl. 43 — dependent clause

Clause: wreaking extensive damage,

	wreaking	extensive damage,
experiential	Process: material	Goal/Range?
interpersonal non-finite clause: no Mood Block	Predicator	Complement
	Residue	
textual	Rheme	

Clause division of the text: News story (continued)

cl. 44			
dependent clause	before	heading	to the northern beaches.
experiential		Process: material	Circumstance: place
interpersonal non-finite clause: no Mood Block		Predicator	Adjunct
		Residue	
textual	Textual / Theme	Rheme	

A note on the Circumstances of this text:

Among the strong features of this text are the many Circumstances of place, hardly surprising given the item of news reported here. Some of these Circumstances presented interesting problems in the analysis:

Firstly, we have treated the multi-faceted Circumstantial elements of clauses 16, 17 and 42 as Circumstance complexes, rather than as separate Circumstances. Thus for clause 42 we interpret the message as: the storm moved to place 1, then place 2, then place 3, all three places combining into a one Circumstance to express the range of the storm's movement. Similar interpretations apply to clauses 16 and 17.

Secondly, we found a number of the clauses had Circumstantial elements of the type exemplified by the clause 9:

Roofs were torn off houses in Caringbah, in Sydney's south.

The comma here makes it unclear at first whether *in Sydney's south* is a separate Circumstance, or a Qualifier of Caringbah – which is the analysis we have chosen to follow. It can of course be moved to the front of the clause, which would support the alternative analysis, but which we believe would change the writer's intended meaning. It could also be interpreted as an ellipsed comment clause. The number of these elements in the texts suggests the writers' need to pin the storm's path down very precisely; the comma allows the introduction of two new pieces of information within the one Circumstance. In clause 38 the same feature is present in the Goal.

Experiential meanings:
material processes

(NB: **type** means **independent** or **dependent** clause; you may or may not want to use this information)

Cl#	type	Actor	potential Actor	Goal	Range	Recipient	Circumstance type
2	ind.	Hailstones the size of tennis balls		roofs			
3	ind.	THEY (hailstones)		cars			place; manner; time
4	ind.	THEY (hailstones)		people	extensive damage		place
5	ind.			thirty motorists			
6	ind.	cars[[taking … tunnel]]		major traffic problems			
7	ind.	some 30 sets of traffic lights					
8	dep.	The hailstorm					time
9	dep.			roofs			place; place
10	dep.			roads			place
11	dep.	cars					place; place; reason
14	dep.		(ambulance crews)	people			
15	incl.			a driver			place

Experiential meanings:
material processes (continued)

Cl#	type	Actor	potential Actor	Goal	Range	Recipient	Circumstance type
16	dep.	1. (initiator) blinding hail 2. him					(place 1 + place 2) (place 1 + place 2)
17	ind.	the storm		a power failure			
18	ind.	many motorists			refuge		
19	dep.		(many motorists)				place
21	dep.	a giant hailstone		he (Chris Chambers)			
22	dep.		(he)				place; place
23	ind.			the front and back wind-screens on his $65,000			
28	ind.	hundreds of people		restaurants and cafes			
30	dep.	many		giant samples			
32	dep.	a plane					place
34	ind.	stones the size of golf balls – no, cricket balls					
36	dep.		(the doctor)	the injured			place

Experiential meanings:
material processes (continued)

Cl#	type	Actor	potential Actor	Goal	Range	Recipient	Circumstance type
38	dep.	the thunderstorm		Nowra and Wollongong, on the NSW south coast			
39	dep.	IT (the storm)					place
40	dep.	IT (the storm)					place
41	dep.		(the storm)	Bundeena			
42	ind.	the storm					(place 1 + place 2 + place 3)
43	dep.		(the storm)	extensive damage ?	extensive damage?		
44	dep.		(the storm)				place

Experiential meanings:
mental processes

Cl#	type	Sensor	Phenomenon	Circumstance type
20	ind.	Chris Chambers	mild concussion	
31	ind.		it (the storm)	

Experiential meanings:
verbal processes

Cl#	type	Sayer	Verbiage	Receiver	Circumstance type
12	ind.	a police spokesperson			
25	ind.	he (Chris Chambers)			
33	ind.	Robyn Bradfield			
37	ind.	weather bureau spokesman Evan Bathe			

Experiential meanings:
relational attributive processes

Cl#	type	Carrier	Attribute	Circumstance type
13	ind.	ambulance crews	flat-out	
24	ind.	it (the storm)	just huge	
35	ind.	Ms Bradfield's partner, a doctor	busy	

Interpersonal meanings

Cl#	type	mood choice	Subject	Tense Finite			Modal Finite			Mood Adjunct	Comment Adjunct	polarity
				past	pres	fut	prob.	oblig.	ability			
1	minor	no mood										
2	ind.	declarative	hailstones the size of tennis balls	✓								positive
3	ind.	declarative	THEY (the hailstones)	✓								positive
4	ind.	declarative	THEY (the hailstones)	✓								positive
5	ind.	declarative	thirty motorists	✓								positive
6	ind.	declarative	cars [[taking … tunnel]]	✓								positive
7	ind.	declarative	some 30 sets of traffic lights	✓								positive
8	dep.	declarative	the hailstorm	✓								positive
9	dep.	declarative	roofs	✓								positive
10	dep.	declarative	roads	✓								positive
11	dep.	declarative	cars	✓								positive
12	ind.	declarative	a police spokesperson	✓								positive
13	ind.	declarative	ambulance crews	✓								positive

Interpersonal meanings (continued)

Cl#	type	mood choice	Subject	Tense Finite past	pres	fut	Modal Finite prob	oblig	ability	Mood Adjunct	Comment Adjunct	polarity
14	dep.	non-finite										
15	ind.	declarative	a driver	✓								positive
16	dep.	declarative	blinding hail	✓								positive
17	ind.	declarative	the storm	✓								positive
18	ind.	declarative	many motorists	✓								positive
19	dep.	non-finite										
20	ind.	declarative	Chris Chambers	✓								positive
21	dep.	declarative	he (Chris Chambers)	✓								positive
22	dep.	non-finite										
23	ind.	declarative	the front and back windscreens of his $65,000 Alfa Romeo	✓								positive
24	ind.	declarative	it (the storm)	✓								positive
25	ind	declarative	he (Chris Chambers)	✓								positive
26	dep.	non-finite	blood									

Interpersonal meanings (continued)

Cl#	type	mood choice	Subject	Tense Finite			Modal Finite			Mood Adjunct	Comment Adjunct	polarity
				past	pres	fut	prob.	oblig.	ability			
27	dep.	declarative	hotel staff	✓								positive
28	ind.	declarative	hundreds of people	✓								positive
29	dep.	non-finite										
30	dep.	non-finite	many (of the people)									
31	ind.	declarative	it (the storm)	✓								positive
32	dep.	declarative	a plane	✓								positive
33	ind.	declarative	Robyn Bradfield	✓								positive
34	ind.	declarative	stones the size of golf balls – no, cricket balls	✓								positive
35	ind.	declarative	Ms Bradfield's partner a doctor	✓								positive
36	dep.	non-finite										
37	ind.	declarative	weather bureau spokesman Evan Bathe	✓								positive
38	dep.	declarative	the thunderstorm	✓								positive

Interpersonal meanings (continued)

Cl#	type	mood choice	Subject	Tense Finite			Modal Finite			Mood Adjunct	Comment Adjunct	polarity
				past	pres	fut	prob.	oblig.	ability			
39	dep.	declarative	IT (the storm)	✓								positive
40	dep.	declarative	IT (the storm)	✓								positive
41	dep.	non-finite										
42	ind.	declarative	the storm	✓								positive
43	dep.	non-finite										
44	dep.	non-finite										

Appendix I

The structure of the Nursery Tale

By reflecting on the unfolding structure of nursery tales (following the work of Hasan in the early 1980s (see Hasan 1996), we can best illustrate the way in which one must argue, linguistically, for what counts as a text type. In essence, a text type (a register or genre) has to be established by shunting between three different kinds of linguistic statement, namely, statements of text structure, statements concerning the meaning involved in identifying these elements of text structure (ie semantic criteria), and statements elucidating the kinds of choices of words and grammar which are most likely 'on call', given the meanings being negotiated. In what follows, some of the details of Hasan's description are slightly modified, but the method is strictly maintained.

Typically, in Nursery tales, we find an opening stage in which the tale is oriented to time, place, and the persona. This opening, or Placement in text structure, has certain semantic requirements, or commonalities, across the genre. First of all, a character has to be singled out or 'particularised'. So too, the character's circumstances must involve 'distance in time' (nursery tales do not deal with our own domestic experiences, although they may do for animals for which 'domestic' then becomes a source of strangeness). Furthermore, the impact coming with the Initiating Event requires that the Placement set up a habit or pattern of events that is disrupted by a new, strange event. This intruding event carries the narrative on through the Sequent Event. This in turn can be repeated until resolved, or partially resolved, with the Final Event, along with the possibility of comments of what we learn (Moral) or simply that the cycle of narrative has closed (Coda).

For example, even in the direct wording which opens 'Henny Penny' (or 'Chicken Lickin' in America), 'One day while Henny Penny was strutting around the farmyard ...', the features discussed above are realised, albeit in a minimal or implicit fashion. In *One day*, we have the feature of temporal distance, in *Henny Penny* a persona is singled out or particularised, while the selection of *was strutting* implies typicality or habitude. Each of these features – Temporal Distance, Person Particularisation and Habitude – are crucial or nuclear meanings to Placement.

It is not the wording, however, but the semantic criteria which are crucial to the element Placement. This can be illustrated by moving to another tale in which the semantic features of Temporal Distance, Person Particularisation and Habitude are realised more explicitly and so in quite different wording. For example:

> Once, long ago, in Russia, there lived a little boy named .... Each morning he took his little boat out on the river ...

In this Placement, we can find the crucial meanings of Person Particulasization (realised by the grammatical feature of indefinite article, in *a little boy named* ...),

Temporal Distance (realised in *Once, long ago …*), and Habitude (typically realised in the choice of re-iterative tense or temporal circumstances as in *Each morning he took his little boat …*).

We can arrive at a description of the text structure, much in the same way as we work to build up a rigorous picture of grammatical structure, only here we are working on a different linguistic level.

Placement		Initiating Event		Sequent Event		Final Event		Moral		Coda
↓		↓		↓		↓		↓		↓
(P)		IE		SE		FE		M		C
(P)	∧	IE	∧	SE	∧	FE	∧	M	∧	(C)
[(P)	∧	IE]	∧	SE	∧	FE	∧	[(M)	•	(C)]

Text Structure
Generic 'Move' on text stratum: Placement

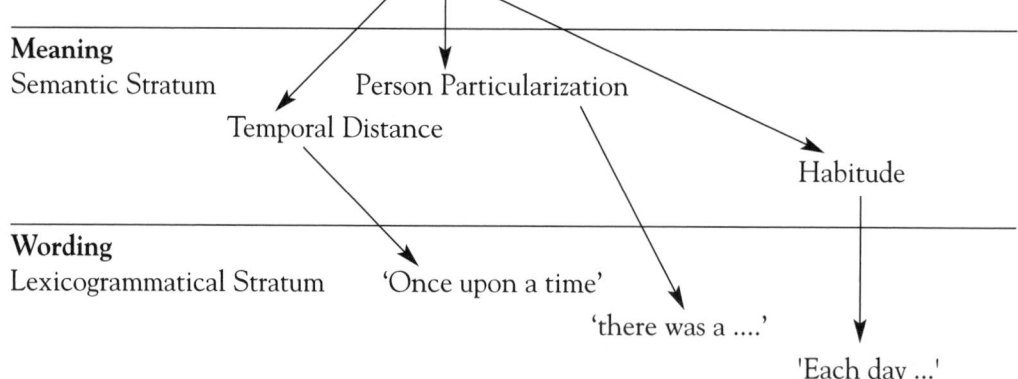

Meaning
Semantic Stratum   Person Particularization

Temporal Distance

Habitude

Wording
Lexicogrammatical Stratum   'Once upon a time'

'there was a ....'

'Each day ...'

Figure I.1

What this diagram (Figure I.1) says is that a nursery tale has a number of elements of text structure. Some elements are obligatory, while others are optional (optional elements are placed within curved brackets, ie (...). The sequence in which elements must or can occur needs also to be expressed. The symbol ∧ indicates elements in a fixed sequence. For example, the Final Event must follow the Sequent Event(s), which is indicated by placing the carat symbol – ∧ – between Sequent Event and Final Event. However, while the Moral and the Coda must come after the Final Event (as expressed in the description by Final Event ∧ [(Moral) • (Coda)]), in relation to each other, the Moral and Coda are not in a fixed order. In other words, the Moral can come before or after the Coda. This is indicated by the dot which is placed between Moral and Coda. Note that both Moral and Coda are optional, since they appear in the curved brackets. The square brackets [...] indicate that the symbol preceding the square brackets affects the contents of the brackets equally. In other words, the preceding carat symbol indicates that Final Event must come before both Moral and Coda. The final symbol to be explained is the curved arrow ↶ which appears above Sequent Event. This indicates recursion, that is, that this Event can occur more than once.

In describing the generic elements of a text, the nuclear or criterial meanings for each element need to be stated. This is because it is not any particular wording that defines the element. While the phrase *Once upon a time* may suggest to the reader that a nursery tale is coming, it is the semantic feature of Temporal Distance that is crucial, and not the wording, since the wording can be replaced by other wordings, so long as they realise the feature of Temporal Distance (ie *One day* ... or *Once, long ago* ...).

Figure I.1 also illustrates how the description of an element, in this case Placement, needs to be built up through the three kinds of linguistic statement.

- Proposed text structure
- Semantic consistencies
- Lexicogrammatical possibilities.

All text analysis demands the interrelation of these three kinds of statement. The statements need to be developed together, since each helps to clarify the others.

Answers to questions

Many of the exercises set in this book are really topics for class discussion, and it would be neither sensible nor in many cases possible for us to provide answers. Almost all the exercises for language teachers are designed so teachers can begin to apply what they have learnt about language to that particular teaching context. However, some of the exercise questions are of a more mechanical type and for those we offer our suggested answers.

We hope the answers will prove useful to students and teachers alike, and that you will enjoy the challenge of the more discursive exercises. For these latter exercises 'correctness' is often less of an issue than is interpretation (always provided the more mechanical, lexicogrammatical analyses are sound). In our experience, a well guided and motivated group of analysts might very well come up with several different but valid insights.

Chapter 1
All three questions are designed to encourage classroom discussion on the issues raised. You will be guided in these discussions by your teacher.

Chapter 2
1 &2   Questions 1 and 2 require you to do your own thinking and/or research which your teacher will then check.

3   a.   Pigs   might fly
(two constituents)

b.   crawling   cautiously   through the undergrowth
(three constituents)

c.   Do … want   you   some more coffee
(three constituents)

d.   Stop
(one constituent)
NOTE: in terms of the **rank scale** this sentence is a clause complex consisting of one clause, consisting of one group, consisting of one word, consisting of one morpheme

e.   protected   from the wind   on three sides
(three constituents)

f.   Next week   the committee   will announce   the winner of the competition
(four constituents)
NOTE: the prepositional phrase of the competition is part of the last constituent – it functions to define the winner

g.   The three wise men of Gotham   went   to sea   in a bowl
(four constituents)

Exercises for language teachers

2 | There | 's | this girl | in my class … ||| |
|---|---|---|---|
| word | word | group | phrase |
| | *event?* | *who?* | *where?* |

she	tried to do	a backward roll ||
word	group	group
who?	*event?*	*what?*

and	she	um like	her neck	clicked or something ||
word	word		group	group
	who?		*what?*	*event?*

and um	she	<u>was taken</u>	to hospital	in an ambulance ‖
word	word	group	phrase	phrase
	who?	*event?*	*where?*	*how?*

and	I	<u>had to write down</u>	[[<u>what happened</u>]] ‖
word	word	group	[[clause]]
	who?	*event?*	*what?*

because	I	<u>was</u>	in her group ‖‖
word	word	word	phrase
	who?	*event?*	*where?*

I	<u>'ve done</u>	that	before ‖
word	group	word	word
who?	*event?*	*what?*	*when?*

and	it	<u>doesn't hurt</u>	that much ‖‖
word	word	group	group
	what?	*event?*	*how?*

I	<u>think</u> ‖
word	group
who?	*event?*

she	<u>'s over-reacting</u>	just a bit ‖‖‖
word	group	group
who?	*event?*	*how?*

Chapter 3

1 There are obviously many correct answers to Question 1. The point of the exercise is to practise applying the correct functional labels to clauses of your own designing. As a guide for readers working independently, we provide the following short list of possible clauses for each of the three patterns.

a. | **Participant** | **Process** | **Circumstance** |
|---|---|---|
| The crowd | reacted | angrily |
| Four white geese | are swimming | in our dam |
| The four girls in the distance | are camping | near us |

b. | **Participant** | **Circumstance** | **Process** |
|---|---|---|
| The flood | gradually | subsided |
| The day when we had to leave | finally | arrived |

c. | **Circumstance** | **Participant** | **Process** |
|---|---|---|
| In the distance | dogs | were barking |
| Across the room | their eyes | met |
| Quietly | a new age of reason | seemed to be emerging |

2 a. | **Participant** | **Process** | **Participant** |
|---|---|---|
| Harry | loves | the bush |

b. | **Circumstance** | **Participant** | **Process** |
|---|---|---|
| In the aftermath of Christmas festivities | I | left |

c. | **Participant** | **Process** | **Participant** | **Circumstance** |
|---|---|---|---|
| Mr Bird | wiped | his tea wet lips | on the back of his hand |

d. | **Participant** | **Process** | **Circumstance** |
|---|---|---|
| The king | was walking | on the terrace |

3   a. | Deictic | Epithet | Thing | Qualifier |
|---|---|---|---|
| a | small | gnome | in the garden |

   b. | Numerative | Epithet | Classifier | Thing |
|---|---|---|---|
| Three | tall | gum | trees |

   c. | Epithet | Thing | Qualifier |
|---|---|---|
| clear | water | cascading over the rocks |

   d. | Deictic | Epithet | Classifier | Thing | Qualifier |
|---|---|---|---|---|
| that | big | guard | dog | that lives over there |

4   The teacher will need to check student responses to this question, but for the benefit of independent readers we offer the following short list of possibilities.

   a. | Deictic | Epithet | Epithet | Thing |
|---|---|---|---|
| Those | shiny | green | leaves |
| The | quaint | old | house |

   b. | Numerative | Thing | Qualifier |
|---|---|---|
| eleven | bottles | in the cellar |
| fifty | horses | galloping up the hill |

   c. | Epithet | Classifier | Thing | Qualifier |
|---|---|---|---|
| tall | pine | trees | growing in my garden |
| green | racing | cars | of many kinds |

5 | adverbial group | prepositional phrase |
|---|---|
| back | from the room |
| angrily | in silence |
| reassuringly | for a few seconds |
| calmly | to the secretary |

NOTE: *of the committee* is a prepositional phrase but it is part of the participant structure *the other members of the committee*, and so is not a Circumstance

6 | was driving | material | was | existential |
|---|---|---|---|
| noticed | mental | had been blackened | material |
| thought | mental | led | material/relational: attributive |
| must be | existential | had feared | mental |
| abandoned | material | would be | existential |
| headed | material | was | attributive |

Chapter 4

1 | | Mood tag | Subject | Finite |
|---|---|---|---|
| a. | aren't they | the gardens | are |
| b. | didn't he | Dr Foster | went (past tense) |
| c. | would it | the pig | would |
| d. | won't they | many people | will |
| e. | wasn't it | the truth of the matter | was |

2 | | Mood tag | Subject | Finite |
|---|---|---|---|
| a. | interrogative | you | will |
| b. | declarative | this | is |
| c. | interrogative | you | are |
| d. | imperative | no Subject | no Finite |
| e. | declarative | everybody | must |

NOTES:
a. The Finite precedes the Subject as is typical of the interrogative mood.

b. Subject followed by Finite – typical declarative pattern

c. Finite precedes Subject in WH- questions as is typical of interrogative mood

d. Simple (unmarked) imperative mood has no Subject or Finite

e. Modalised declarative where the pattern is Subject followed by Finite as usual for declarative mood.

3   There are several possible answers for each original clause here; we identify a few of the possibilities.

a. Join the dance.
   (imperative)
   You will join the dance.
   (declarative)

b. Is this a fine example of Goya's early style?
   (interrogative)

c. You are crying.
   (declarative)
   Cry!
   (imperative)

d. Could everybody stop that nonsense immediately?
   (interrogative)

e. Must everybody leave the theatre at once?
   (interrogative)
   Leave the theatre at once!
   (imperative)

4   You should be trying to bring to your work for this question all the concepts dealt with so far. Independent readers should read this chapter (4) and Chapters 1 and 3 again and then check your work for this question against the material provided in those chapters.

Chapter 5

1 & 2 Questions 1 and 2 are designed to foster class discussion of the various kinds of interpersonal meanings to be found in the respective texts. Discussion would need to focus very specifically on the language of the texts to answer the following key questions:
   - What kind of Mood structures are there?
   - Are there Modal Finites, Modal Adjuncts, Comment Adjuncts, Attitudinal Epithets or other specific expressions of the speakers' positions?

3   You should invent your own simple sentences for this exercise. We have used the first of the example sentences in the question to demonstrate how to do this exercise.

The house is empty

polarity:	The house is not empty.
modalisation:	The house is usually empty.
modulation:	The house ought to be empty.
Comment Adjunct:	Sadly, the house is empty.
Attitudinal Epithet	The tragic house is empty.

4 & 5 Questions 4 and 5 are intended for group discussion. The discussion should include among other things:
   - lexical items such as *strange, complex, inexplicable, powerful, barbarian*
   - adjustments like *awesomely, almost* and *quasi.*

You should also notice the dichotomies set up in the first clause by the complex nominal group *strange and complex.* The writer continues this by contrasting *love* and *hate, human* and non-human (*quasi-divine*), *barbarian* and (implicitly) civilised, and even by action on the stage (implicit) and action above the stage (explicit).

The writer's position is made to seem natural by consistent selection of positive declarative mood without modalisation, combined with emotive lexical choices.

Chapter 6

1   For the benefit of independent readers we offer some examples.
   - topical Theme: Circumstance (bold type)
     From time to time management would change the shifts without warning.
     By the end of the week the boats were ready for their crew.

   - topical Theme: Process (bold type)
     Enjoy your day at the races next week.
     Fill the tank slowly.

   - topical Theme: postmodified nominal group (bold type)
     That very ancient bicycle leaning against the wall is mine.
     The start of the race was delayed.

2

Theme			Rheme
textual	**interpersonal**	**topical**	
Because	obviously	from time to time	management ...
And	please	enjoy	your day ...
But	certainly	that very ancient bicycle	
		leaning against the wall	is ...

3

Theme			Rheme
textual	**interpersonal**	**topical**	
	Are	you	going to Scarborough
	Probably	we	're going tomorrow
		Remember	me to one who lives there
Because		she	was once a true love of mine

4   Again, this question is designed to encourage class discussion, but for the benefit of individual users of the book we have divided the text into clauses (numbered) and provided a Theme/Rheme analysis. To answer the rest of the question, students would be advised to look primarily at the Theme choices and Thematic progression patterning in the independent clauses (*).

```
         topical Theme                    Rheme
*1.  During this summer of 1846 <<2>> an anxiety of another kind was increasing
```

```
      textual Theme     topical Theme      Rheme
  2.  while             her literary hopes  were waning
```

```
      topical Theme           Rheme
*3.  Her father's eyesight    had become seriously impaired by the progress
                              of the cataract which was forming.
```

```
      topical Theme     Rheme
*4.  He                 was nearly blind
```

```
      topical Theme     Rheme
*5.  he                 could grope his way about
```

```
      textual Theme     topical Theme     Rheme
*6.  and               (he)               (could) recognise the figures of those he knew well
```
NOTE: the topical Theme is ellipsed in this clause and has to be retrieved from the previous clause.

	textual Theme	topical Theme	Rheme
7.	when	they	were placed against a strong light;

	textual theme	topical Theme	Rheme
*8.	but	he	could no longer see to read,

	textual Theme	topical Theme	Rheme
*9.	and thus	his eager appetite for knowledge and information of all kinds	was severely balked.

	topical Theme	Rheme
*10.	He	continued to preach.

Chapter 7

1 & 2 For Questions 1 and 2 there are obviously many possible clauses; we offer a few examples for students to test their own selections.

1   a. The teacher gathered up all the children [[whose work had not yet been assessed.]]
     b. The horse [[which can cope with a wet track]] will be a good one to ride tomorrow.
     c. There are many tourist attractions in the town [[where I live]].

2   a. **dependent, independent, independent**
     Although her voice was not what it had been, || the audience loved her || and showed it by a standing ovation at the end of the concert.

     b. **independent, dependent, dependent**
     My assignment is going to be late || because I only started it last night || and there are not many relevant references left in the library.

     c. **non-finite dependent, independent, dependent**
     Taking all the evidence into account || we would have to say || that we are not so far impressed.

3   Teachers will need to check student responses to Question 3, and to encourage class discussion of the issues involved in such an exercise.

4   Here we provide the relevant analysis for the first text (a). Students should then apply the principles to as many of the other sample texts as they need in order to feel confident about the concepts. Teachers might like to provide alternative texts here, depending on the types of texts the class is used to working with.

a.   *independent clauses*
- you will see a big service station on the right
- Just beyond it is an old factory [[that's now being converted into an old industrial museum]].
- you'll find a kind of open shed [[that looks like an aircraft hangar]]

NOTE that, because embedded clauses are part of the ranked clause in which they occur, you must include them in the three independent clauses here. Sentence two is a one-clause clause complex.

dependent clauses
- As you come into town
- If you drive around the back of the factory

embedded clauses
- that's now being converted into an old industrial museum
- that looks like an aircraft hangar

Chapters 8, 9 and 10

We make no attempt to offer answers to the exercises in these chapter. They are not the kinds of questions to which there are simple mechanical answers, or for which there is only one correct answer. Each question requires an in-depth understanding and application of the concepts and principles explained and explored in the book. Users of this text book should by now have the working knowledge necessary to tackle such exercises; and class teachers might very well want to design their own exercise material here, making connections with the kinds of texts and contexts relevant to their students' studies.

Bibliography

Bloor, T and M Bloor 1995. *The functional analysis of English: A Hallidayan approach.* London: Arnold

Bruner, J 1986. *Actual minds, possible worlds.* Cambridge, Mass.: Harvard University Press

Burns, A and H Joyce 1997. *Focus on speaking.* Sydney: NCELTR, Macquarie University

Celce-Murcia, M 1990. 'Discourse analysis and grammar instruction'. *Annual Review of Applied Linguistics*, 11, 135–151

Christie, F 1991. Preparing for literacy in the next century (1.1.5). In F Christie (ed). *Teaching critical social literacy: A project of national significance on the preservice preparation of teachers for teaching English literacy.* A report submitted to the Federal Minister for Employment, Education and Training, Canberra

Christie, F 1997. Curriculum macrogenres as forms of initiation into a culture. In F Christie and J R Martin (eds). *Genres in institutions: Social processes in the workplace and school.* Herndon, Va.: Cassell Academic

Christie, F and J R Martin 1997. *Genres in institutions: Social processes in the workplace and school.* Herndon, Va.: Cassell Academic

Clark, J and C Yallop 1995. *An introduction to phonetics and phonology: 2nd edition.* Oxford: Basil Blackwell

Cloran, C 1989. Learning through language: The social construction of gender. In R Hasan and J R Martin (eds). *Language development: Learning language, learning culture.* Norwood, N J: Ablex Publishing Corporation

Collins Cobuild English grammar 1990. London: Collins

Cope B and M Kalantzis (eds) 1993. *The powers of literacy: A genre approach to teaching writing.* London: Falmer Press

Cranny-Francis, A and J R Martin 1995. 'Writings/readings: How to know a genre'. *Interpretations: Journal of the English Teachers' Association of Western Australia*, 28, 3: 1–32

Crystal, D 1987. *The Cambridge encyclopedia of language.* Cambridge: Cambridge University Press

Derewianka, B 1990. *Exploring how texts work.* Newtown: Primary English Teaching Association

Derewianka, B 1992. Assessing oral language. In B Derewianka (ed). *Language assessment in primary classrooms.* Marrickville: Harcourt Brace & Company

Derewianka, B 1998. *A grammar companion for primary teachers.* Newtown: Primary English Teaching Association

de Silva Joyce, H and A Burns 1999. *Focus on grammar.* Sydney: NCELTR, Macquarie University

de Silva Joyce H and S Feez 2000. *Creative writing skills: Literary and media text types.* Sydney: Phoenix Education

Eggins, S 1994. *An introduction to systemic functional linguistics.* London: Pinter

Eggins, S and D Slade 1997. *Analysing casual conversation.* London: Cassell

Feez, S 1998. *Text-based syllabus design.* Sydney: NCELTR, Macquarie University

Feez, S and H Joyce 1998. *Writing skills: Narrative and non-fiction text types.* Sydney: Phoenix Education

Freebody, P 1997. 'Orienting to literacy lessons: Roles and resources in the primary classroom'. In *Meeting the challenge: NSW State Literacy Strategy.* Proceedings of *NSW Department of School Education Conference*

Fries, P 1992. 'The structuring of information in written English text'. *Language Sciences,* 14, 4: 461–488

Fromkin, V, R Rodman, P Collins and D Blair 1990. *An introduction to language: 2nd Australian edition.* Sydney: Holt, Rhinehart and Winston

Gibbons, P 1991. *Learning to learn in a second language.* Newtown: Primary English Teaching Association

Gibbons, P 1998. 'Classroom talk and the learning of new registers in a second language'. *Language and Education,* 12, 2: 99–118

Goffman, E 1975. *Frame analysis.* Harmondsworth: Penguin

Graddol, D 1997. *The future of English?: A guide to forecasting the popularity of the English language in the 21st century.* London: The British Council

Gray, B 1987. 'How natural is "natural" language teaching – employing wholistic methodology in the classroom'. *The Australian Journal of Early Childhood,* 12, 4: 3–19

Halliday, M A K 1975. *Learning how to mean: Explorations in the development of language.* London: Edward Arnold

Halliday, M A K 1976. *System and function in language.* London: Oxford University Press

Halliday, M A K 1978. *Language as a social semiotic.* London: Edward Arnold

Halliday, M A K 1980. Three aspects of children's language development: Learning language, learning through language, learning about language. In *Oral and written language development research: Impact on the schools.* Y M Goodman, M M Haussler and D S Strickland (eds). Proceedings from the 1979 and 1980 impact conferences sponsored by the International Reading Association and the National Council of Teachers of English. Newark, DE: International Reading Association

Halliday, M A K 1985. *Spoken and written language.* Geelong: Deakin University Press

Halliday, M A K 1992. October. 'Towards a language-based theory of learning'. Paper prepared for the Phonetic Society of Japan in the context of the *Symposium on Language Acquisition,* Tokyo

Halliday, M A K 1994. *An introduction to functional grammar: 2nd edition.* London: Edward Arnold

Halliday, M A K and R Hasan 1976. *Cohesion in English.* London: Edward Arnold

Halliday, M A K and R Hasan 1985. *Language, context and text: Aspects of language in a social semiotic perspective.* Geelong: Deakin University Press

Hammond, J 1990a. Is learning to read and write the same as learning to talk? In F Christie. *Literacy for a changing world.* Melbourne: ACER

Hammond, J 1990b. 'Teacher expertise and learner responsibility in literacy development'. *Prospect: A journal of Australian TESOL*, 5, 3: 39–51

Hammond, J, A Burns, H Joyce, D Brosnan and L Gerot 1992. *English for social purposes.* Sydney: NCELTR, Macquarie University

Hasan, R 1985. *Linguistics, language and verbal art.* Geelong: Deakin University Press

Hasan, R 1989. 'Semantic variation and sociolinguistics'. *Australian Journal of Linguistics*, 9, 2: 221–276

Hasan, R 1992. 'Questions as a mode of learning in everyday dialogue'. Thao Le and Mike McCausland (eds). In *Language education: Interaction and development. Proceedings of the international conference, Vietnam 1991.* Launceston: University of Tasmania

Hasan R 1995. On the social conditions for semiotic mediation: The genesis of mind in society. In A R Sadvnik (ed). *Knowledge and pedagogy: The sociology of Basil Bernstein.* Norwood, N J: Ablex Publishing Corporation

Hasan, R 1996a. What's going on: A dynamic view of context in language. In C Cloran, D Butt and G Williams. *Ways of saying: Ways of meaning.* London: Cassell

Hasan, R 1996b. The fairy tale as genre. In C Cloran, D Butt and G Williams (eds). *Ways of saying: Ways of meaning.* London: Cassell

Hasan, R 1996c. Literacy, everyday talk and society. In R Hasan and G Williams (eds). *Literacy in society.* London: Longman

Hasan, R 1996d. What kind of resource is language? In C Cloran, D Butt and G Williams (eds). *Ways of saying; ways of meaning: Selected papers of Ruqaiya Hasan.* London: Cassell

Hasan, R and G Perrett 1994. Learning to function with the other tongue: A systemic functional perspective on second language teaching. In T Odlin (ed). *Perspectives on pedagogical grammar.* Cambridge: Cambridge University Press

Hood, S, N Solomon and A Burns 1996. *Focus on reading: New edition.* Sydney: NCELTR, Macquarie University

Hyon, S 1996. 'Genre in three traditions: Implications for ESL'. *TESOL Quarterly*, 30, 4: 693–722

Iedema, R and M Stenglin 2000. How to analyse visual images: A guide for TESOL teachers. In A Burns and S Coffin (eds). *Contexts, use and analysis of the English language: A global perspective.* Reader for Open University/Macquarie University Masters, TESOL Worldwide

Jones, J, S Gollin, H Drury and D Economou 1989. Systemic-functional linguistics and its application to the TESOL curriculum. In R Hasan and J R Martin (eds). *Language development: Learning language, learning culture – Meaning and choice in language*. Studies for Michael Halliday. Norwood, N J: Ablex Publishing Corporation

Kachru, B B and C I Nelson 1996. World Englishes. In S L McKay and N Hornberger (eds). *Sociolinguistics and language teaching*. Cambridge: Cambridge University Press

Kress, G and T van Leeuwen 1996. *Reading images: The grammar of visual design*. London: Routledge

Leech, G and J Svartvik 1975. *A communicative grammar of English*. London: Longman

Locke, G 1996. *Functional English grammar: An introduction for second language teachers*. Cambridge: Cambridge University Press

Lukin, A 1995. Functional grammar in the classroom. In A Burns and S Hood (eds). *Teachers' voices: Exploring course design in a changing curriculum*. Sydney: NCELTR, Macquarie University

Macken, M and D Slade 1993. Assessment: A foundation for effective learning in the school context. In B Cope and M Kalantzis (eds). *The powers of literacy: A genre approach to the teaching of writing*. London: Falmer Press

Macken-Horarik, M 1996. 'Construing the invisible: Specialised literacy practices in junior secondary English'. PhD thesis, University of Sydney

Macquarie dictionary: 3rd edition 1997. Sydney: Macquarie Library Pty Ltd

Martin, J R 1992. *English text: System and structure*. Amsterdam: Benjamins

Martin, J R 1993. 'Genre and literacy – modelling context in educational linguistics'. *Annual Review of Applied Linguistics*, 13, 141–172

Martin, J R 2000. Language, register and genre. In A Burns and C Coffin (eds). *Contexts, use and analysis of the English language: A global perspective*. Reader for Open University/Macquarie University Masters, TESOL Worldwide PUBLISHER

Martin, J R and C M I M Matthiessen 1991. 'Systemic typology and topology'. In F Christie (ed). *Social processes in Education: Proceedings of the First Australian Systemic Network Conference, Deakin University, January 1990*. Darwin: Centre for Studies in Language Education, Northern Territory University

Matthiessen, C M I M 1993. Register in the round: Diversity in a unified theory of register analysis. In M Ghadessy (ed). *Register analysis: Theory and practice*. London: Pinter

Matthiessen, C M I M 1996. Tense in English seen through systemic-functional theory. In M Berry, C Butler, R Fawcett and G Huang (eds). *Meaning and form: Systemic functional interpretations*. Norwood, N J: Ablex Publishing Corporation

Oldenburg, J 1987. 'From child tongue to mother tongue: A case study of language development in the first 2 1/2 years'. PhD thesis, University of Sydney

O'Toole, M 1989. Semiotic systems in painting and poetry. In M Falchikov, C Pike and R Russell (eds). *A festschrift for Dennis Ward*. Nottingham: Astra Press

Painter, C 1984. *Into the mother tongue: A case study in early language development.* London: Pinter

Painter, C 1985. *Learning the mother tongue.* Geelong: Deakin University Press

Painter, C 1996. The development of language as a resource for thinking: A linguistic view of learning. In R Hasan and G Williams (eds). *Literacy in society.* London: Longman

Rothery, J 1992. Assessing children's writing. In B Derewianka (ed). *Language assessment in primary classrooms.* Marrickville: Harcourt Brace

Rothery, J 1994. *Exploring literacy in school English.* Write it Right Project. Erskineville: Disadvantaged Schools Program, Metropolitan East Region, NSW Department of School Education

Rothery, J 1996. Making changes: Developing an educational linguistics. In R. Hasan and G Williams (eds). *Literacy in society.* London: Longman

Rutherford, W E 1987. *Second language grammar: Learning and teaching.* London: Longman

Safe, G and M Price 1999. 'City battered by giant hailstones'. *The Australian,* April 15: 5

Thompson, G 1996. *Introducing functional grammar.* London: Arnold

Unsworth, L (ed) 1993. *Literacy learning and teaching: Language as social practice in the primary school.* Melbourne: Macmillan Education Australia

Unsworth, L 1997. 'Subject-specific literacies, knowledge about language and the social construction of success in the middle years of schooling'. In *Meeting the challenge: NSW State Literacy Strategy. Proceedings of NSW Department of School Education Conference*

Ur, P 1996. *A course in language teaching: Practice and theory.* Cambridge: Cambridge University Press

Vygotsky, L 1978. *Mind in society: The development of higher psychological processes.* Cambridge: Cambridge University Press

White, P R 1998. An introductory overview of Appraisal Theory. [On-line 1999, November 22] Available: HYPERLINK http://www.grammatics.com/appraisal/

Williams, G 1994. 'Joint book-reading and literacy pedagogy: A socio-semantic examination'. Unpublished PhD thesis, Maccquarie University

Williams, G 1999a. Children's literature, children and the uses of language description. In L Unsworth (ed.). *Researching language in school communities.* London: Cassell

Williams, G 1999b. Grammar as a metasemiotic tool in child literacy development. In C Ward and W Renandya. *Language teaching: New insights for the language teacher.* RELC Anthology Series 40. Singapore: Regional Language Centre, SEAMEO

Zawadzki, H 1994. *In tempo: An English pronunciation course.* Sydney: NCELTR, Macquarie University

Index

Notes

Notes